QUE

Colonel Charles Stacey was ⬚⬚⬚⬚⬚⬚, Canada 1906, and was educated at th⬚ ⬚⬚⬚ities of Toronto Oxford and Princeton. For nine⬚⬚ years he was the official historian of the Canadian Army, and has written many books on Canadian military history. He is a member of the Canadian Historical Association and of the American Historical Association, and was awarded the Tyrrell Medal in Canadian History by the Royal Society of Canada. For the last thirteen years Colonel Stacey has taught history at the University of Toronto and is now a University Professor.

1⁵⁰₂

*Also available in this series*

BATTLES OF THE BOER WAR
BATTLES OF THE CRIMEAN WAR
*W. Baring Pemberton*

THE BATTLE FOR NORMANDY
*Eversley Belfield and H. Essame*

TOBRUK   *Michael Carver*

THE IRONCLADS OF CAMBRAI
*Bryan Cooper*

BATTLES OF THE INDIAN MUTINY
*Michael Edwardes*

THE SOMME
*Anthony Farrar-Hockley*

WELLINGTON'S PENINSULAR VICTORIES
*Michael Glover*

AGINCOURT
CORUNNA
*Christopher Hibbert*

THE SPANISH ARMADA   *Michael Lewis*

THE BATTLE FOR THE MEDITERRANEAN
THE BATTLE OF THE ATLANTIC
NARVIK
*Donald Macintyre*

CAEN – ANVIL OF VICTORY
*Alexander McKee*

WATERLOO   *John Naylor*

THE GOTHIC LINE   *Douglas Orgill*

ALAMEIN   *Lucas Phillips*

THE RUSSIAN CONVOYS   *B. B. Schofield*

MONS   *John Terraine*

BATTLE OF THE JAVA SEA   *David Thomas*

BATTLES OF THE '45   *Katherine Tomasson and Francis Buist*

ARNHEM   *R. E. Urquhart, CB, DSO*

TRAFALGAR   *Oliver Warner*

THE ROMAN CONQUEST OF BRITAIN
*Graham Webster and Donald R. Dudley*

BATTLES OF THE ENGLISH CIVIL WAR
*Austin Woolrych*

British Battles Series

# QUEBEC, 1759

## The Siege and the Battle

### C. P. STACEY

There would appear in this celebrated campaign
fully as much guid luck as guid guiding.
*Lord Selkirk's Diary, 1804*

UNABRIDGED

PAN BOOKS : LONDON

First published 1959 by the Macmillan Company of Canada Ltd
This edition published 1973 by Pan Books Ltd,
33 Tothill Street, London SW1

ISBN 0 330 23771 3

Printed and Bound in England by
Hazell Watson & Viney Ltd
Aylesbury, Bucks

# Contents

Introduction: Two Hundred Years of History    xv

1 Dramatis Personae    1

2 The Fortress    27

3 May and June: Contact    41

4 July: Montmorency    62

5 August: 'Skirmishing, Cruelty and Devastation'    84

6 The British Change Direction    98

7 The 13th of September: Approach    123

8 The 13th of September: Battle    141

9 The Fall of Canada    159

Postscript – Generalship at Quebec, 1759    170

Appendix – Wolfe's Correspondence with the
            Brigadiers    182

           Wolfe's Dispatch to Pitt    187

Abbreviations and Select Bibliography    195

References    197

Index    213

# List of Illustrations

(*between pages* 110 *and* 111)

Major-General James Wolfe (*McCord Museum, McGill University*)

Lieutenant-General the Marquis of Montcalm (*Public Archives of Canada*)

Quebec from Point Lévis (*Public Archives of Canada*)

The Western fortifications of Quebec (*Public Archives of Canada*)

The French fire-ships attack the British fleet (*Public Archives of Canada*)

The action at Montmorency (*Public Archives of Canada*)

Cap Rouge (*Public Archives of Canada*)

Ruins in the Upper Town of Quebec (*Public Archives of Canada*)

The landing at the Anse au Foulon (*Public Archives of Canada*)

The Anse au Foulon (Wolfe's Cove) in 1973 (*Canadian Army photo*)

Amherst's army running the St Lawrence rapids (*Public Archives of Canada*)

Patrick Mackellar's plan of Quebec, 1757 (*Public Archives of Canada*)

Part of Wolfe's last letter to his mother

# Maps

| | | |
|---|---|---|
| 1 | The St Lawrence theatre of operations, 1759 | ix |
| 2 | The river operations, June–September 1759 | x |
| 3 | The Quebec area, 1759 | xi |
| 4 | The Battle of Montmorency, July 31st, 1759 | xii |
| 5 | The Anse au Foulon, September 13th, 1759 | xiii |
| 6 | The Battle of the Plains, September 13th, 1759 | xiv |

# Author's Note to Second Printing

Since this book was published in 1959, a rather surprising amount of new contemporary evidence has come to light. I have discussed and summarized this in an article in the *Canadian Historical Review* for December, 1966. The new material includes an anonymous account possibly written by one of Wolfe's aides-de-camp, which among other matters indicates that the General's plan to attack the rear of the French at Beauport (page 99) was based on a reconnaissance of the route by Moses Hazen (a Ranger officer) and a French deserter. This document seems to me to support my suggestion that Howe's scaling of the Foulon cliff was an improvisation (page 131) and confirms Barré's story of Wolfe's issuing orders to stop the landing there after the 'first flight' was ashore (page 135). There are also two collections of letters, chiefly from Wolfe to Murray but including in addition a letter from Townshend describing the situation in London as he found it on his return there; the diary of an American Ranger; and the personal file of Captain Vergor, containing his account of events at the Anse au Foulon on September 13th, which has enabled me to correct on page 127 an incautious statement made in the first printing.

C.P.S.

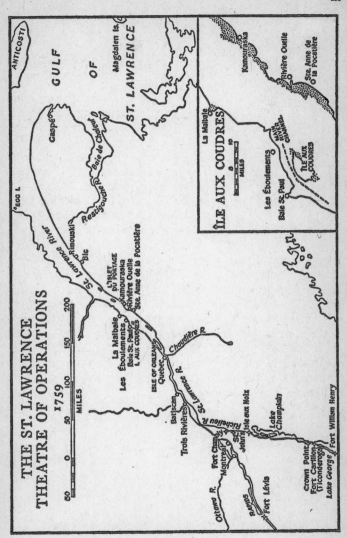

Map 1

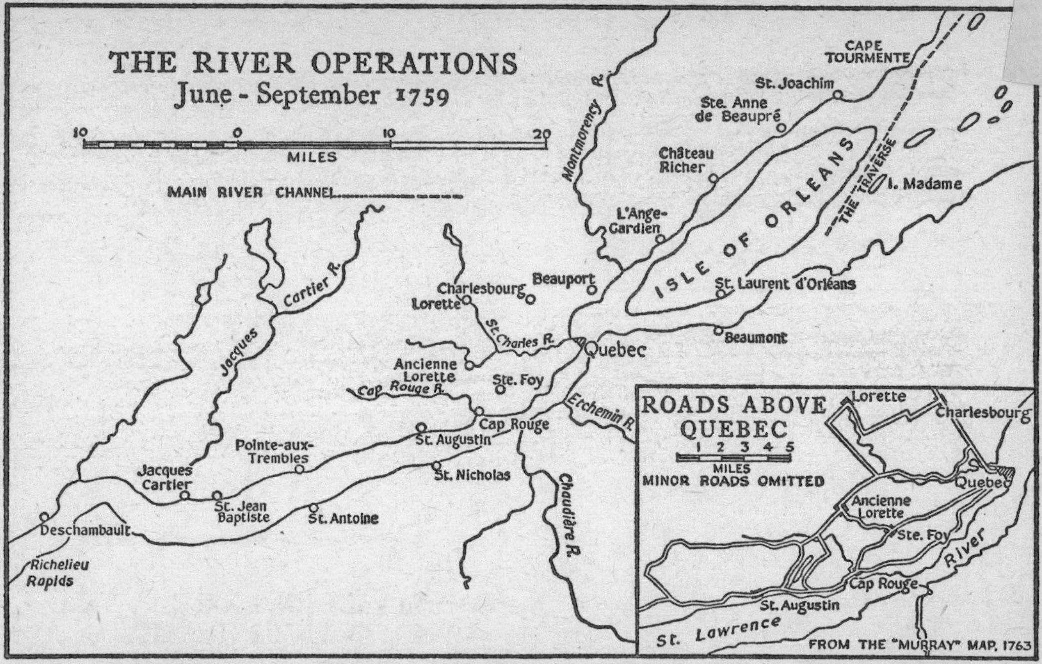

THE RIVER OPERATIONS
June - September 1759

MILES

MAIN RIVER CHANNEL

CAPE TOURMENTE

St. Joachim

Ste. Anne de Beaupré

Château Richer

L'Ange-Gardien

ISLE OF ORLEANS

St. Laurent d'Orléans

I. Madame

THE TRAVERSE

Montmorency R.

Beauport

Quebec

Charlesbourg

Lorette

St. Charles R.

Ste. Foy

Ancienne Lorette

Cap Rouge R.

Cap Rouge

Etchemin R.

Chaudière R.

Beaumont

St. Augustin

St. Nicholas

Cartier R.

Jacques Cartier R.

Pointe-aux-Trembles

St. Antoine

St. Jean Baptiste

Jacques Cartier

Deschambault

Richelieu Rapids

ROADS ABOVE QUEBEC

MILES
1 2 3 4 5

MINOR ROADS OMITTED

Charlesbourg

Quebec

Lorette

Ancienne Lorette

Ste. Foy

Cap Rouge

St. Augustin

St. Lawrence River

FROM THE "MURRAY" MAP, 1763

Map 2

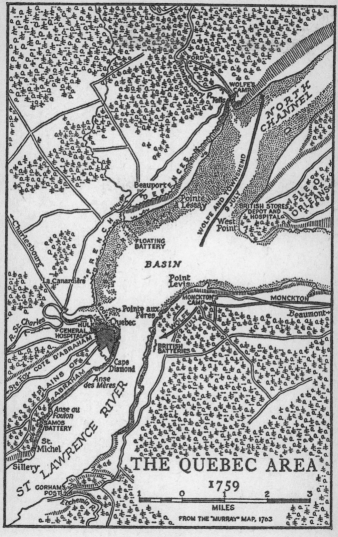

FORD

WOLFE 9 JULY

NORTH CHANNEL

Falls

DEFENCES

Beauport

Pointe Lesse

WOLFE AND TOWNSHEND 9 JULY

West Point

BRITISH STORES DEPOT AND HOSPITAL

ISLE OF ORLEANS

FLOATING BATTERY

FRENCH

BASIN

Charlesbourg

La Canardière

Point Levis

Pointe aux Pères

MONCKTON CAMP

MONCKTON

R. ST. CHARLES

HULL GENERAL HOSPITAL

Quebec

WOLFE 9 JULY

Beaumont

CÔTE D'ABRAHAM

BRITISH BATTERIES

Cape Diamond

Ste-Foy

PLAINS OF ABRAHAM

Anse des Mères

Anse au Foulon

SAMOS BATTERY

St. Michel

ST LAWRENCE RIVER

Sillery

GORHAM'S POST

Etchemin R.

## THE QUEBEC AREA

### 1759

1   0   1   2   3

MILES

FROM THE "MURRAY" MAP, 1763

Map 3

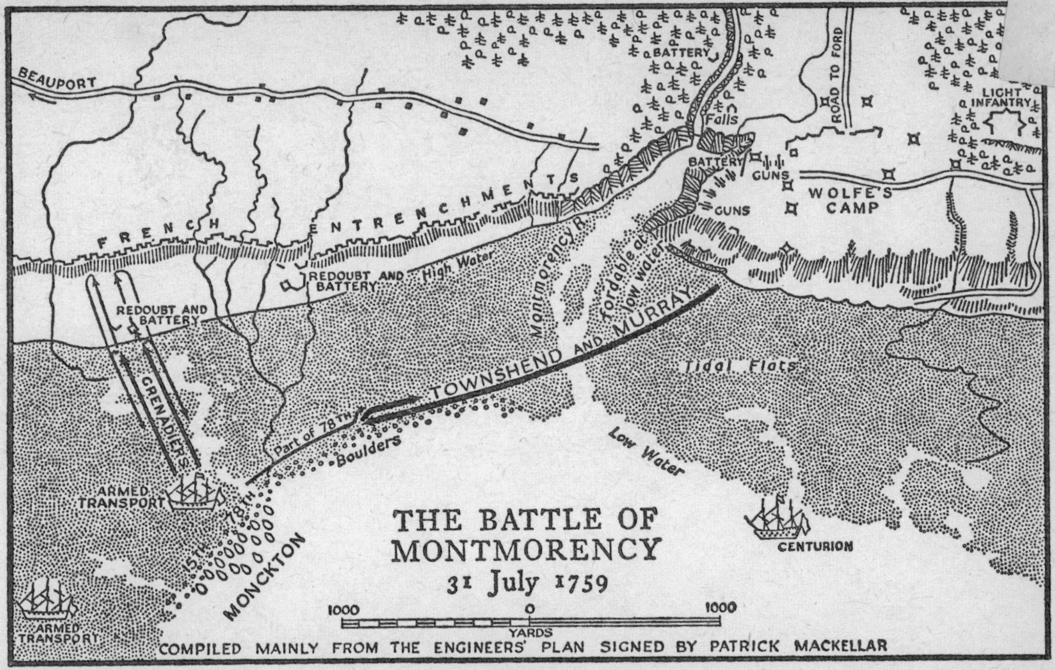
BEAUPORT
FRENCH ENTRENCHMENTS
BATTERY
Falls
LIGHT INFANTRY
ROAD TO FORD
BATTERY
GUNS
GUNS
WOLFE'S CAMP
REDOUBT AND BATTERY
High Water
REDOUBT AND BATTERY
Montmorency R.
fordable at low water
TOWNSHEND AND MURRAY
Tidal Flats
GRENADIERS
Part of 78TH
Boulders
Low Water
ARMED TRANSPORT
78TH
15TH
MONCKTON
CENTURION
ARMED TRANSPORT
THE BATTLE OF MONTMORENCY
31 July 1759
1000
0
1000
YARDS
COMPILED MAINLY FROM THE ENGINEERS' PLAN SIGNED BY PATRICK MACKELLAR

Map 4

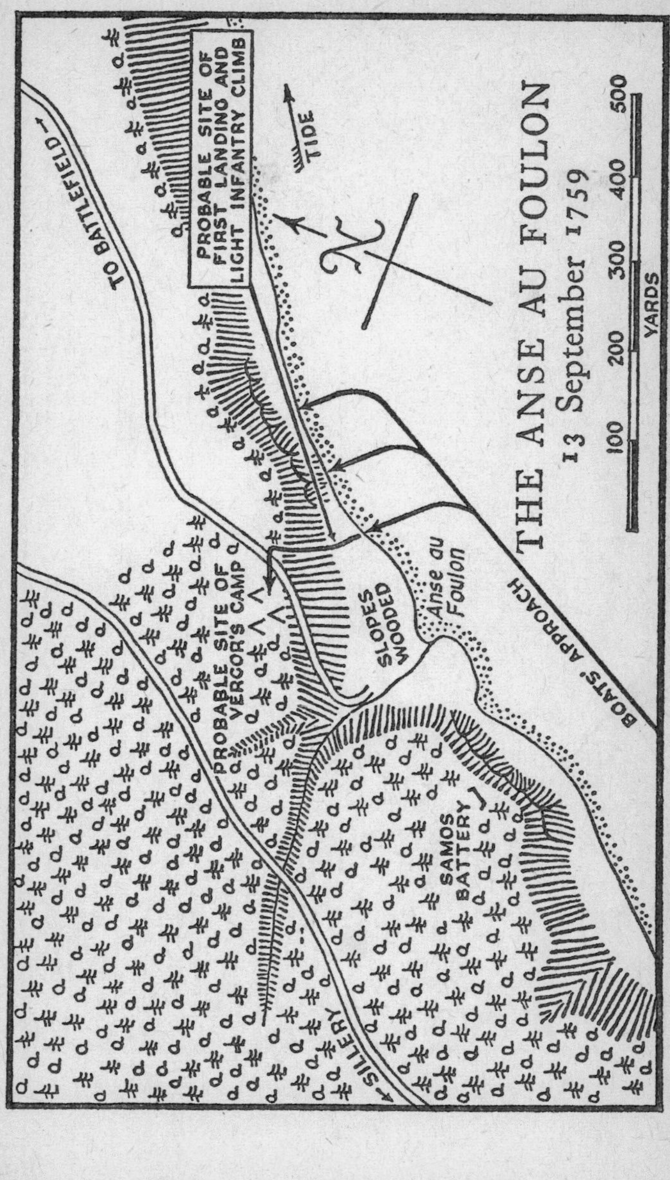

THE ANSE AU FOULON
13 September 1759

PROBABLE SITE OF FIRST LANDING AND LIGHT INFANTRY CLIMB

TIDE

TO BATTLEFIELD

PROBABLE SITE OF VERGOR'S CAMP

SLOPES WOODED

Anse au Foulon

SAMOS BATTERY

SILLERY

BOATS APPROACH

100 200 300 400 500

YARDS

Map 5

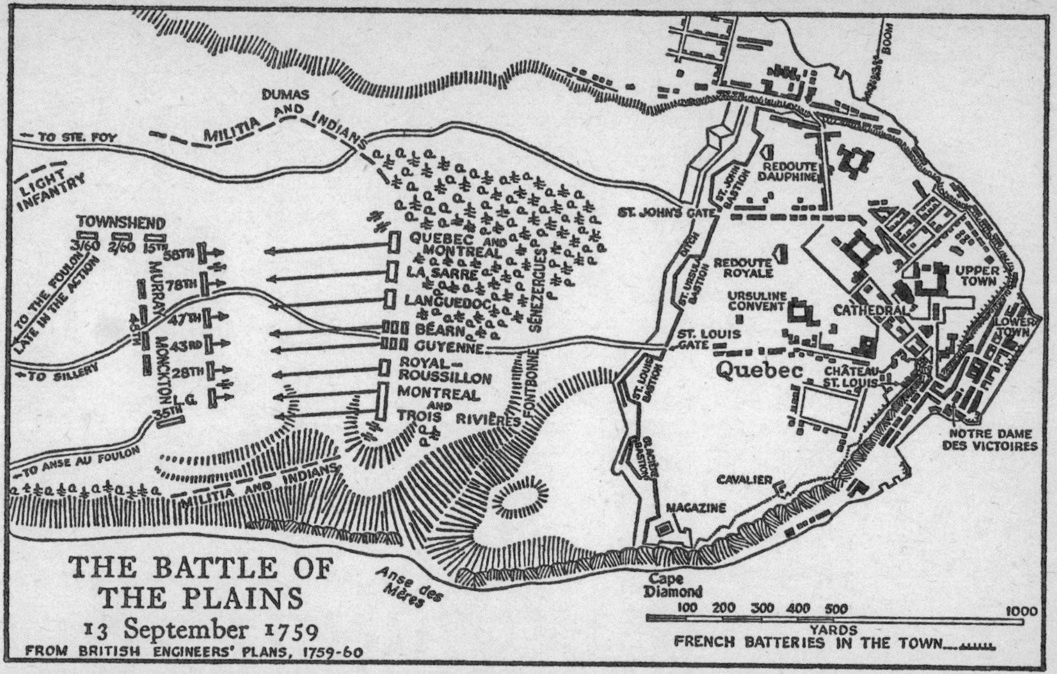
THE BATTLE OF
THE PLAINS
13 September 1759
FROM BRITISH ENGINEERS' PLANS, 1759-60
TO STE. FOY
LIGHT INFANTRY
DUMAS
MILITIA AND INDIANS
TOWNSHEND
3/60
2/60
15TH
58TH
MURRAY
78TH
48TH
47TH
43RD
MONCKTON
28TH
L.G.
35TH
TO THE FOULON LATE IN THE ACTION
TO SILLERY
TO ANSE AU FOULON
MILITIA AND INDIANS
QUEBEC AND MONTREAL
LA SARRE
LANGUEDOC
BÉARN
GUYENNE
ROYAL-ROUSSILLON
MONTREAL AND TROIS RIVIÈRES
SÉNEZERGUES
FONTBONNE
Anse des Mères
ST. JOHN'S GATE
ST. JOHN BASTION
DITCH
ST. URSULA BASTION
ST. LOUIS GATE
ST. LOUIS BASTION
GLACIÈRE BASTION
MAGAZINE
CAVALIER
REDOUTE DAUPHINE
REDOUTE ROYALE
URSULINE CONVENT
CATHEDRAL
UPPER TOWN
LOWER TOWN
Quebec
CHÂTEAU ST. LOUIS
NOTRE DAME DES VICTOIRES
BOOM
Cape Diamond
100 200 300 400 500 1000
YARDS
FRENCH BATTERIES IN THE TOWN

Map 6

# INTRODUCTION

# *Two Hundred Years of History*

---

'Very great rejoycings this night on the taking of Quebec.' So wrote 'Parson Woodforde' – not yet a parson, but merely a junior scholar of New College, Oxford – in his diary on the 18th of October, 1759. All across England the bonfires were burning, that evening 200 years ago.

The joy was all the greater because it was only two days [1] since people had read General Wolfe's pessimistic dispatch to his Government written on September 2nd – a communication which seemed designed to prepare England for the news of the failure of the campaign against Quebec. So the tidings of victory now burst upon the country with the utmost dramatic effect. And the story itself had all the appurtenances of high drama: the apparently impregnable fortress, the dark river, the midnight ascent of the frowning cliffs, the short fierce encounter on the Plains, the deaths of the two opposing commanders in the moment of victory and defeat. Horace Walpole, who had been as downcast as anybody at the earlier news, now wrote, 'What a scene! An army in the night dragging itself up a precipice by stumps of trees to assault a town and attack an enemy strongly entrenched and double in numbers!' It is not surprising that the episode has continued to catch men's imaginations for two centuries. The year 1959 sees the 200th anniversary of one of the most famous events in modern history.

The fall of Quebec was a towering landmark in the establishment of British Imperial power, and as such every British schoolboy knows about it. It was scarcely less important in the development of the United States, for the expulsion of France from North America relieved the British colonies from the need for their Mother Country's protection and opened the door to independence. And the events of 1759 mark the greatest turning-point in the history of Canada. It is not surprising that all through those 200 years people have gone on writing about these happenings at Quebec; or that a luxuriant crop of popular legends having no relation to historic truth has grown up around them.

It is perhaps rather more surprising that so much writing should have left so many questions essentially unsettled. The great Bostonian, Francis Parkman, published *Montcalm and Wolfe* in 1884. It was and is a magnificent book, which can still be read with the greatest profit; but more documents have come to light since Parkman's time, and other people besides those French Canadians who have been repelled by his robust anti-Catholicism or his strong conviction of the benefits brought to Canada by the British conquest would disagree with him on at least a few points. William Wood and Sir Arthur Doughty, two Canadian scholars who did much work in the field early in the present century, seem to have believed that they had attained finality, or something close to it; but it is now evident that they were mistaken. Wood, indeed, changed his mind late in life, and published an estimate of General Wolfe much less favourable than the one which he had advanced very forcibly some twenty years before.[2] He had apparently been influenced latterly by the views of eminent military leaders, almost all of whom, he had found, had serious reservations about Wolfe as a commander. Still more recently two distinguished McGill professors have presented diametrically opposite views of James Wolfe – one regarding him as a hero and a military genius, the other as a man of very ordinary attainments who owed his success to luck.[3] There has been equally violent disagreement on the characters and competence of the two chiefs of the losing side, Montcalm and Vaudreuil.

Historians of four nations have taken part in the debate. The French of France, the defeated party in the war, have naturally been least attracted to the subject; nevertheless, they have made important contributions, notably, Richard Waddington's massive work of scholarship *La Guerre de sept ans*. The British and the Americans have both done a great deal of writing; but in recent years, with certain exceptions – including the very distinguished one of Professor Lawrence Gipson – the field has been left largely to the Canadians, 'French' and 'English'. These two segments of the Canadian community have traditionally – and inevitably – viewed the affair in quite different lights. English-speaking Canada, in the nineteenth century, thought of it with cheerful simplicity as the real beginning of Canadian history.

> In days of yore from Britain's shore
> Wolfe the dauntless hero came,
> And planted firm Britannia's flag
> On Canada's fair domain.

French Canadians, on the other hand, saw the events of 1759–60 as the crisis of their national culture, and sometimes came close to taking the view that at that unhappy moment Canadian history came to a full stop. These attitudes are still not extinct, but happily they have weakened considerably on both sides of late.

The continuing controversies have turned largely on personalities. And it must be said that the leading figures have been magnified beyond their natural size by their connexion with the events of 1759. There were no giants among them; but the lurid light of a world crisis, reflected on the clouds of legend, has converted them into Brocken-spectres, figures far larger than they ever were in life. Inevitably, too, there has been reaction against this magnification, and some writers, seeking to cut these figures 'down to size', have made them smaller than they really were. The dauntless hero Wolfe has had many romantic adherents, and a smaller but very determined band of detractors. Montcalm has received similar adulation, not least from English-speaking writers. (No French Canadian seems to have got romantic about Wolfe, but it is evident that he gave them very little reason.) Some French Canadians have been doubtful about Montcalm, and some actually hostile to him. An even more extreme difference of opinion has centred upon the Marquis de Vaudreuil, who as a Canadian himself has been a focus of French-Canadian nationalism. Writers in English have in general made him a butt for their scorn, and often enough have overdone it, as we shall see. But French-Canadian historians from François-Xavier Garneau onwards have – again with certain exceptions – tended to err in the other direction, and a man of narrow views and modest abilities has received praise from them simply because of his Canadian birth and sympathies.

It is seldom realized outside French Canada how serious a breach of sentiment separated the French of France and the French of Canada in the eighteenth century. A degree of friction between British and Canadian soldiers has been a common-place phenomenon in more recent times, and it is perhaps not surprising that similar and sometimes stronger feeling existed between the French regulars and the colonial officers and men in the time of Montcalm and Vaudreuil. This is familiar to every student of the records of the period. It was stated in its most extreme form by Bougainville: 'What a country, my dear brother, and what patience is needed to bear the slights that people go out of their way to lay on us here. It seems as though we belonged to a different nation, even a hostile one.' [4] These ancient antagonisms are reflected in modern times in the very different interpretation of events presented by French and by French-Canadian historians. At this late date the connoisseur of scholarly invective can derive considerable amusement from René de Kerallain's commentary, published in *La Jeunesse de Bougainville* in 1896, on the works of that giant of the pro-Vaudreuil school, the Abbé H.-R. Casgrain – an investigator to whom, it must be said, students of the period owe much.

At the time of the British conquest, New France as a community was a century and a half old. The Canadians of 1759 were more distant in time from the founding of Quebec than we today are from the Battle of Waterloo. Their society was small (the last census under the French régime, that of 1754, showed a population of 55,009) and economically it was extremely weak and vulnerable: under war conditions it could not exist without importing large quantities of food annually from France. Yet they formed a proud and self-conscious community, with what must be called a definite national feeling; and the conflict between that feeling and the views and prejudices of the regular troops from metropolitan France was a serious complication in the French war effort in North America.

On the British side the parallel conflict between Briton and colonial was little in evidence at Quebec, for there were few British Americans there. But personal antipathies were almost as active as they were among the French. A very painful rift developed between Wolfe and at least two of his three able brigadiers; and the documents show that even the cooperation between Army and Navy was rather less free from friction than most histories represent. The Quebec campaign, in fact, is a fine example of how difficult it is for men, even men of one nation, to work smoothly together under the conditions created by war; we see the same clashes of personality, the same conflicts of ambition, the same inter-Service misunderstandings, which have been familiar in our own day. The weapons of war have changed beyond all recognition since the time of Wolfe and Montcalm; the men who wield them have changed, like the rest of mankind, remarkably little.

From time to time, we have said, new documents come to light. The last actual 'discovery' of fundamental importance was perhaps Wolfe's private journal. Only a part of this has survived, in three different versions, of which one is known to be a transcript by one of the General's aides-de-camp, Captain Thomas Bell. The journal has been known since 1910, when a great part of the Bell version was published by Beckles Willson.[5] That was nearly half a century ago; and it is a curious fact that books still continue to be published which take no account of it. Other material which has been available has been even less used. Wolfe's letters to Monckton have been in the Ottawa Archives since 1924, when Sir Leicester Harmsworth presented the inestimable Northcliffe Collection to the Dominion; but no historian seems to have utilized them. I have found them very valuable for the light they throw upon Wolfe's planning. I have also found that George Townshend's 'rough notes' (likewise in the Northcliffe Collection) are more enlightening than has usually been realized. Colonel Whitworth's recent life of Ligonier, calling attention to Wolfe's important letters to Amherst written in the winter of 1758–9 and the following spring, has enabled me to publish some passages from these letters never before in print. And I was surprised to discover that two paragraphs censored out of Wolfe's celebrated dispatch to Pitt when it was printed in 1759 have escaped the attention of almost all the historians and are missing from almost all the published versions of the dispatch.

Of the enormous body of writing on the Quebec campaign, much has been vitiated in greater or less degree by inadequate investigation of the sources, by personal or national prejudice, or by lack of military knowledge. Some distinguished writers have been guilty of surprising lapses. Thus, for instance, the late Sir Julian Corbett looked at the 'Proposals for the Expedition to Quebec' which Pitt sent to Amherst, saw the names of the three officers proposed for appointment as brigadiers – Monckton, Murray and Burton – and apparently took them for signatures to the document! The result was, first, that he asserted that in this 'curious paper' three colonels recommended to Pitt that Wolfe be appointed to command the expedition, and secondly, he missed the very interesting point that Burton was at first proposed as the third brigadier, but was subsequently replaced by Townshend.[6] Where so very many eminent predecessors have failed, I would certainly be unwise to claim to have attained to a definitive version of the events. But I have made a conscious effort to rise above prejudice and to put forward a new and independent interpretation based on a careful re-examination of the contemporary documents of both sides and on the 'military probabilities'.

I have had, for my sins, considerable experience in the interpretation of historical evidence on military operations, in connexion with a much more recent war. I have seen numerous examples of how memory can play tricks on an officer after some lapse of time, especially in cases where the officer's own interests or prejudices are engaged. The longer the lapse of time, the more probable are serious errors.

> Old men forget; yet all shall be forgot,
> But he'll remember with advantages
> What feats he did that day . . .

The 'advantages' are the trouble; also, men forget even before they are old. Many a man, in complete sincerity and honesty, has given versions of military events in which he took part that are completely at variance with the facts as reliably recorded in documents at the time. Undoubtedly this happened in 1759 just as it did in 1939–45, and I have kept this before me. I have also laid down for my own guidance a basic principle not always followed by earlier authors: to assume invariably that a contemporary document means precisely what it says, unless there is evidence to the contrary.

This book, a spare-time avocation of an author engaged in the larger task of producing the official history of the Canadian Army in the Second World War, could not have been written if I had not happened to be living within easy reach of the unequalled collection of original source material on the Seven Years' War in America possesed by the Public Archives of Canada. To Dr W. Kaye Lamb, the Dominion Archivist, I am grateful not only for the manner in which the great resources of the Archives were placed at my disposal, but also for personal interest in the project and a great deal of good counsel. The staff of the Archives has been vastly helpful; to Mr W. G. Ormsby of the Manuscript Division I am especially indebted for unlimited patience and for skilful help in the solution of a number of difficult problems; and Miss Juliette Bourque, the Librarian, has been equally generous. I owe much also to Mr C. H. Stewart and his staff in the Library of the Department of National Defence, Ottawa. Major C. C. J. Bond's admirable maps, the result of careful research in contemporary cartography, speak for themselves. For the help on special points I must thank the Dominion Observatory, Ottawa; Mr Charles-Marie Boissonnault of Quebec City; Mr C. M. Lapointe,

Librarian of the *Montreal Star*; and particularly Mr John Spurr, Librarian of the Royal Military College of Canada. Finally, I am most grateful to my good friend and wartime associate, WO II M. R. Lemay, who typed the book with the skill and accuracy for which he is well known.

# CHAPTER ONE

## *Dramatis Personae*

---

Colonel James Wolfe, Brigadier-General of His Britannic Majesty's Forces in North America and Major-General and Commander-in-Chief of a body of land forces 'to be employed on an Expedition against Quebec, by the way of the River St Lawrence', paced the quarter-deck of HMS *Neptune* as she stood out of Louisbourg harbour. Under his eager eye the great armament that carried his hopes and Britain's was getting under way. The day was the 4th of June, 1759.

The General was thirty-two, an age somewhat less youthful in his own day than it seems in ours. His conduct as a brigadier in Amherst's expedition against Louisbourg in 1758 had caught the eye of Mr Pitt, who like another British war leader nearly two centuries later made a practice of looking out for promising junior officers and promoting them over the heads of their elders. He now found himself entrusted with the most important and most difficult enterprise of the campaign of 1759.

William Pitt had been in power since June 1757, when he formed his coalition ministry with the Duke of Newcastle. He had gradually evolved a strategic 'system' whose one great object was the seizure of the French empire in America. All else was subordinated to that end; the British activities in Europe were mere containing operations, designed to divert France while the main campaign deprived her of Canada. But Pitt's plan for 1758 in America had not been entirely successful. Of three attacks, only two gained their objectives. Major-General Jeffrey Amherst took Louisbourg in Cape Breton

Island, but the Navy did not consider it practicable to push on to take Quebec as Pitt had hoped they might. Brigadier-General John Forbes, commanding in the southern colonies, moved against Fort Duquesne in the Ohio valley and duly captured it, while, as a bonus, Lt-Col John Bradstreet took Fort Frontenac (Kingston) and destroyed the ships that maintained French power on Lake Ontario. But the main operation, directed by the Lake Champlain route upon Montreal, and fumblingly commanded by General James Abercromby, met disaster on July 8th in front of Fort Carillon (Ticonderoga). The French regulars under the Marquis de Montcalm shot Abercromby's larger army to pieces when it made a frontal attack on their entrenchments.

Pitt's plan for 1759 was intended to finish the job. This time he proposed to strike at the heart of New France by both sea and land. Amherst was made Commander-in-Chief in America and ordered to advance on Montreal or Quebec by the Champlain line or down the St Lawrence from Lake Ontario. Pitt also asked for an attack on Fort Niagara, where the river of that name enters Lake Ontario; this mission fell to Brigadier-General John Prideaux. And Wolfe was given the honourable and formidable task of a direct sea-borne attack on the capital of New France by the St Lawrence.[1]

In making this appointment the great Secretary of State was in some degree gambling, for Wolfe had never been tested in a senior and independent command. He was the son of an un-distinguished and relatively impecunious lieutenant-general (who died in the spring of 1759 while James was preparing for his famous expedition). The youngster had received his first commission at the age of fourteen, and was in his first battle at Dettingen in 1743, when he was sixteen. He was a major when he served against Bonnie Prince Charlie at Falkirk and Culloden in 1745-6 and was wounded at Laffeldt in 1747. He became a lieutenant-colonel in 1750. And in 1757 he was ap-pointed Colonel of the newly-raised 67th Foot.

It is universally conceded that Wolfe was a first-class regi-mental commander, interested in his men's welfare and de-voted to their efficiency. He was a dedicated student of his profession to an extent most uncommon in that age. And not only did he think clearly about its problems, but he had the faculty of putting his thoughts on paper with unusual effectiveness. In 1757 he commanded his battalion of the 20th in the abortive expedition against Rochefort, the first of a series of pinprick enterprises against the French coast, which were the least effective part of the programme by which Pitt sought to 'contain' France in Europe while he deprived her of her colonies in America. The letter which Wolfe wrote afterwards to his friend and confidant Captain William Rickson [2] has become celebrated, and with reason; the soundness of many of its pungent comments on the nature of amphibious operations has been underlined by the experience of two more recent World Wars:

I have found out that an admiral should endeavour to run into an enemy's port immediately after he appears before it; that he should anchor the transport ships and frigates as close as can be to the land; that he should reconnoitre and observe it as quick as possible, and lose no time in getting the troops on shore; that previous directions should be given in respect to landing the troops, and a proper disposition made for the boats of all sorts, appointing leaders and fit persons for conducting the different divisions. On the other hand, experience shows me that, in an affair depending upon vigour and dispatch, the generals should settle their plan of operations, so that no time may be lost in idle debate and consultations when the sword should be drawn; that pushing on smartly is the road to success, and more particularly so in an affair of this nature; that nothing is to be reckoned an obstacle to your undertaking which is not found really so upon *tryal*; that in war something must be allowed to chance and fortune, seeing it is in its nature hazardous, and an option of difficulties; that the greatness of an object should come under consideration, opposed to the impediments that lie in the way; that the honour of one's country is to have some weight, and that, in particular circumstances and times the loss of 1,000 men is rather an advantage to a nation than otherwise, seeing that gallant attempts raise its reputation and make it respectable; whereas the contrary appearances sink the credit of a country, ruin the troops, and create infinite uneasiness and discontent at home.

Few officers, and probably fewer generals, are capable of producing a crackling paragraph of military commentary like this. (It is true that the easy reference to 'the loss of 1,000 men' jars on a modern ear, and Professor Adair may be right in seeing in this a glimpse of that unpleasant strain of ruthlessness which we shall discover in Wolfe's operations on the St Lawrence; though it is only fair to make allowances for the impatient colonel who had just returned from taking part in a mismanaged and unsuccessful enterprise.) Another example of Wolfe's writing, his dispatch to Pitt from before Quebec – a production greatly admired in its own day for lucidity and 'elegance' – forms an appendix to this book. It prompts the reflection that in Wolfe his country may have lost one of its greatest military historians.

Two more points about Wolfe, both well known, are worth recalling. As his letters amply show, he was ambitious and covetous of reputation. And his health was very bad. He wrote to Rickson on December 1st, 1758, 'I am in a very bad condition, both with the gravel & Rheumatism, but I had much rather die than decline any kind of service that offers.' He may well have come to the conclusion before sailing for Quebec that he could not expect to live much longer; and the illness he suffered during the siege would certainly have reinforced such a conclusion.

Louisbourg gave Wolfe his chance, and he improved it by personal gallantry and abounding energy. It was not altogether surprising therefore that he should receive a higher command in the next campaign. He came to the St Lawrence enterprise an officer of high and deserved reputation, who had had an unusual amount of operational experience for his years. But he had yet to prove his capacity for planning and coordinating an independent campaign.

We have his own account of his first discussion with the Commander-in-Chief, Lord Ligonier, concerning the Quebec expedition. This was after his return to England from Louisbourg. He wrote to General Amherst on December 29th, 1758, in a letter which none of his biographers is acquainted with: 'We had some discourse concerning the navigation of the River

S$^t$. Lawrence, & upon the project of beseiging Quebec, and I found it was a settled Plan to carry on two separate attacks, one, on the side of Lake George and one up the River, thus much passed at our first conversation with this addition, that I express'd my desire to go up the River, but to be excused taking the chief direction of such a weighty enterprise.' Whether this request was a mere conventional gesture of modesty, or whether Wolfe really mistrusted his own capacities for independent command, there is no way of telling. At any rate, he told Amherst, shortly afterwards 'M$^r$ Pitt ... named me to the King for the command in the River'. (Ligonier quite probably nominated him.) 'In short,' Wolfe went on, 'they have put this heavy task upon my Shoulders, and I find nothing encouraging in the undertaking, but the warmest & most earnest desire to discharge so great a trust to your satisfaction as my General, and to his Majesty and the Publick. I shall spare no pains, and shou'd be happy if the sacrifice of my own health & constitution, or even my Life, cou'd any how contribute to bring this bloody war, to an honourable & speedy conclusion.' [3]

He was given a splendid army. True, it was not large, and it was smaller than he was promised; the regiments he found in Nova Scotia were below establishment, and in the end the land force sent against Quebec amounted to only some 8,500 men instead of the 12,000 contemplated by Pitt. But its quality was excellent: ten regular British line battalions, plus a small provisional battalion formed from the grenadier companies of three battalions left in garrison at Louisbourg, and hence usually called the 'Louisbourg Grenadiers'; three companies of the Royal Regiment of Artillery with a powerful 'battering train'; and six companies of American Rangers, four of them newly raised. The army included hardly any Indians – there were a few in the Ranger companies – nor (until July, when 300 provincial pioneers joined it before Quebec) did it contain a single militiaman. (The Rangers were not militia provided by the colonial governments, but long-service units raised under the Crown. Wolfe, always lofty towards things American, called these Rangers 'the worst soldiers in the universe' before he had had a proper chance to get acquainted with them.[4]

They were not the best of their kind, and they were to be blamed for a certain number of 'atrocities' during the campaign; but they were hardly as bad as all that.) This was an army of skilled professional soldiers, and the infantry battalions were all serving in America before the campaign began; none was new to American conditions.

The army, moreover, was admirably officered. Wolfe's three brigadiers, Robert Monckton (the senior and second-in-command), James Murray and George Townshend, were all very competent soldiers, and Wolfe had apparently asked for the first two. All were somewhat older than Wolfe (in Monckton's case the difference was only a few months, in Murray's it was six years); Corbett's statement, 'With the exception of Wolfe and Townshend, all the general officers were under thirty', and his comment, 'It was a boys' campaign', are merely silly. Further, all three were the sons of peers; this may have made for a certain stiffness in relations with the upper-middle-class Commander-in-Chief. The two senior staff officers, Isaac Barré, Deputy Adjutant-General, and Guy Carleton, Deputy Quartermaster-General, were both able men and destined for distinction. So were a number of the battalion commanders, among them Lt-Col William Howe, whom Wolfe appointed to command the light infantry battalion which he formed from the light companies of the army. The General had written from Louisbourg the year before, 'If his Majesty had thought proper to let Carleton come with us as engineer and Delaune and 2 or 3 more for the light Foot, it would have cut the matter much shorter ...' Now Carleton was with him, and so was Captain William Delaune of Wolfe's own 67th Foot. It was to be Howe and Delaune who would lead the forlorn hope up the cliffs on the famous 13th of September. General Fuller's remark that Wolfe was supported by 'probably the finest body of English officers which has ever taken the field' is not much of an exaggeration.[5]

Wolfe's admirers have asserted that at Halifax and Louisbourg in the spring of 1759 he turned a motley collection of units into an army. But he reached Halifax only on April 30th and Louisbourg only on May 15th; and embarkation began at the beginning of June. It takes longer than this to make an army. Wolfe issued some excellent orders at Halifax, and he probably impressed his officers and men with the force of his personality before the force sailed. But the qualities that made his army formidable were in the regiments before they came under his command; they had been implanted there by years of training and experience. More than any individual, this efficient, smooth-functioning, hard-hitting army is the real hero of the Quebec campaign.

The army, and the fleet. For everything depended on the fleet. It was not merely that British control of the North Atlantic was the foundation of the whole war in America; it was not merely that the army could not reach its objective without the navy. As we shall see, the ships, their crews and their commanders played a vital part at Quebec in the tactics as well as the strategy of the campaign. And the fleet which Pitt had provided was a magnificent instrument, worthy of the occasion, as its performance proves. The reputation of Vice-Admiral Charles Saunders, who commanded it, has been overshadowed by that of his military colleague; he was an unassuming man – Horace Walpole said of him, 'No man said less, or deserved more' – but a very capable sea officer and a most admirable colleague. And whether or not one agrees with Wolfe's low opinion of Saunders' second-in-command, Rear-Admiral Philip Durell,[6] there is no doubt that the fleet contained more than its share of exceptionally able officers: men like Edward Hughes, who commanded the *Somerset*, John Jervis (later Lord St Vincent) who commanded the little *Porcupine*, and James Cook, master of the *Pembroke*.

In mere size the fleet was very formidable. It numbered 49 sail of the Royal Navy, of which 22 were ships of 50 guns or more. The largest was Saunders' flagship, the *Neptune*, of 90 guns, and there were two other three-deckers, the *Princess Amelia* and the *Royal William*. The fleet was larger than Sir Edward Hawke's which won the Battle of Quiberon Bay later in 1759, though inferior in gun-power; it is evident that the smaller ships of the line were considered most suitable for service up the St Lawrence. One of the two 50-gun ships, the

*Centurion*, had been Lord Anson's flagship in his voyage round the world in 1740–44; Saunders had served in her on that famous cruise. She and the other 50, the *Sutherland*, were to play special parts in the campaign. And no less than 119 transports, ordnance vessels and 'victuallers' sailed from Louisbourg with the fleet in June. Even this was not the whole story. The grand total of naval and merchant vessels employed in the St Lawrence campaign in 1759 may have been in the vicinity of 200 sail. This great fleet, with perhaps some 13,500 sailors and marines aboard, with its enormous number of guns and its stock of ammunition and stores, represented a tremendous reserve of power for Wolfe's army.[7]

Admiral Durell, who had wintered at Halifax, had been instructed by Pitt to push into the St Lawrence as early as possible in the spring to intercept any ships attempting to reach Quebec from France. Nevertheless, when Wolfe and Saunders reached Halifax (ice having kept them out of Louisbourg) they found Durell still there. A vessel he had sent to reconnoitre had reported heavy ice to the eastward, and merchant vessels had given him similar reports; and when he was at last ready to sail on April 28th, an accident to one of his ships delayed him. Wolfe now provided troops to accompany his force – Carleton with some 600 men of various regiments. Contrary winds prevented Durell from getting away from Halifax until May 5th, when he sailed with ten naval vessels and three transports. After much trouble with ice he finally reached Bic on May 21st. Two days before, he had heard from the master of a captured sloop that seventeen French ships had passed up towards Quebec on the 9th. Almost all the 'succours' from France – something over twenty sail – had got safely up the river, and Durell picked up only a couple of stragglers.[8] One cannot help feeling that, if the French could get through the ice, Durell should have been able to do the same. Had he succeeded in doing so, Wolfe would probably have been saved a siege and a battle, and might have survived to die undramatically in bed.

Pierre de Rigaud, Marquis de Vaudreuil, holder of the Grand Cross of the Royal and Military Order of St Louis, Governor and Lieutenant-General for King Louis XV throughout New France and the lands and countries of Louisiana, waited for the British in the city of Quebec. Quebec was more than his official station; it was his home, for he had been born there sixty years before. (Many respectable works of reference assert that he was born at Montreal in 1704; but the place was Quebec, and the date 1698.) [9] His father was then serving as commander of the troops in Canada. In 1703 the elder Vaudreuil became Governor General of New France. He held the appointment for twenty-two years and died in office, regretted and kindly remembered by the colony's people. The son began his career in the *troupes de la marine*, the regular military force permanently stationed in the colony and so called because it, and the French colonies generally, were administered by the Navy Department. This, combined with the fact that he held honorary naval rank – *capitaine de vaisseau* in his later years – is the origin of the oft-told story that he was a naval officer; but he never served at sea. He was appointed ensign at the early age of six, lieutenant at thirteen, captain at seventeen, major at twenty-seven. His father, reporting in his capacity as commander of the colonial forces, testified that he had no bad qualities.

In 1742 he was appointed Governor of Louisiana, and served there for the next eleven years. He seems to have done well in Louisiana, improving the colony's defences, dealing effectively with the Indian menace and leaving the country more prosperous and more civilized than he found it. He was and is remembered there as *Le Grand Marquis*. It was his ambition, however, to follow in his father's footsteps and govern his native land; and after a short interval of residence in France he achieved it. At the beginning of 1755 King Louis XV appointed him Governor General of New France. He arrived at Quebec that summer. Already the frontiers were aflame with the first skirmishes of the war that was to end in the extinction of the French empire in America.

Vaudreuil came late to the summit of his hopes. By the standards of his century he was already old – fifty-six when he was appointed Governor General, sixty when he faced the supreme crisis of 1759. An ageing man's tendency to be set in his ways had doubtless been intensified in his case by eleven years in supreme authority in a small and remote colony. He had given his best years to Louisiana, and his powers, whatever they had once been, were scarcely equal now to playing a role at the eye of the storm in a world crisis.

Canada, when he came back to her, had internal problems only less menacing than the threat of foreign conquest. Corruption, it could almost be said, had been erected into a system of government. Since 1748, François Bigot had been Intendant of New France. This official shared the civil authority with the Governor. He was responsible for finance and trade; and his authority extended into the military sphere, for it was his duty to see to supplying the forces. He had much the same responsibilities as a modern quartermaster-general. Bigot was undoubtedly an able administrator – he was perhaps the most capable man in New France in his day – but unfortunately he was also a rogue. He used his position and his capacities to feather his own nest, and he surrounded himself with associates of like mind. The best thing his biographer, Professor Frégault, can find to say for him is that he was a man of his times.[10] So he was; and yet there were honest men in France and in Canada in the eighteenth century. After the loss of New France, Bigot was called to account by the French Court; and in 1763 he was sentenced to exile, to the confiscation of his goods, to a fine of 1,000 *livres* and to restitution in the sum of a million and a half *livres*. (A *livre* of this period has been calculated as roughly equivalent to an American or Canadian dollar of our present day.)

In the latter part of Bigot's Canadian career, one member of his circle was engaged in corruption at his country's expense on an even greater scale. In 1756 Joseph Cadet obtained through Bigot a comprehensive nine-year contract to furnish all the food supplies and 'refreshments' needed for the King's service in the cities and garrisons of Canada. He thus became *munitionnaire général* and a tremendous monopolist.[11] The nature and scope of his operations can be deduced from the fact that in 1763 the judges in Paris condemned him to make good six million *livres*. These were only the greatest criminals. Montcalm reported that military officers, particularly in the more distant posts, had made enormous fortunes for themselves. He cited the case of Captain François Le Mercier, who, he said, had come to Canada twenty years before as a reinforcement private for the *troupes de la marine*. He had risen to command the artillery in the country, and when there were gun carriages or such things to be made, Le Mercier got the contracts 'under other names'. He was now worth six or seven hundred thousand *livres* – 'perhaps a million if this goes on'.[12] Here Montcalm may have exaggerated; but there is no doubt whatever that corrupt practices were very widespread, that largely as a result of this the expense of the colony to the Mother Country grew and grew, and that this situation contributed to produce defeatism and disgust at the Court of Versailles. Why go on pouring the resources of France into that bottomless pit called Canada?

Vaudreuil's attitude to all this was at best equivocal. He does not appear to have shared in the speculation. Quite possibly the old aristocrat was genuinely above such things. Although he saw the inside of the Bastille in 1762, nothing was proved against him. But unquestionably he shielded the peculators. His dispatches are full of praise of Bigot and Cadet. Versailles, which was more than suspicious of those characters, found these communications fulsome. When Vaudreuil went out of his way in a dispatch of May 28th, 1759, to emphasize Cadet's zeal and good will and how he had exhausted his fortune to keep his agreements with the King, somebody at the Court (probably Berryer, the Minister of Marine) minuted coldly in the margin, 'I don't like this jeremiad about the munitionnaire.'[13] It is impossible to believe that Vaudreuil did not know what was going on. Indeed, Mr Frégault (who is Vaudreuil's biographer as well as Bigot's, but unfortunately has not extended his detailed study of the Governor beyond the Louisianian phase) notes evidence that he deplored it in private. He suggests that the reason for his failure to denounce Bigot was the fact that in Louisiana his quarrels with two men holding the appointment of *commissaire-ordonnateur* (the official in that colony equivalent to the intendant at Quebec) had injured his career; he was determined not to let this happen again. This may be a sound interpretation, but if so it is very damaging to Vaudreuil.

He apparently did not impress his contemporaries as a man of commanding abilities. There is an interesting estimate of him by the well-informed author of the *Journal tenu à l'armée que commandoit feu M$^r$ de Montcalm, Lieutenant general*. Weight is lent to it by the fact that the anonymous writer is bitterly hostile to Vaudreuil's rival Montcalm. But he damns Vaudreuil with very faint praise indeed: 'Good sense, no insight, too much indulgence, an optimism about future events that often leads to precautions being taken too late, nobility and generosity of feeling, much affability – these are the principal traits which seem to me characteristic of M. le Marquis de Vaudreuil.'

The whole working life of this first native-born Governor General of Canada had been spent in French America. His opinions and prejudices were Canadian. And his prejudices were strong, as his reports on the operations of the war show. The colonial regulars, the Canadian militia, the Indians, are kept to the fore; the regulars from France are in the background – which they rarely were on the field of battle. Vaudreuil undoubtedly felt that his own military experience and his special knowledge of North American conditions entitled him to speak on such matters. Yet his military experience was actually very limited; he had never commanded or served with a large body of troops – the *troupes de la marine* had no permanent organization above the company – and he seems never to have been under fire. (He marched in an expedition against the Fox Indians in 1728, which produced no fighting and which gave Montcalm a chance to exercise his unfortunate talent for sarcasm thirty years later.) [14]

The self-portrait of Vaudreuil which he paints in his letters and dispatches is not attractive. One looks in vain for magnanimity. The dispatch written in October 1759, the month after the Battle of the Plains, in which he blames the disaster on Montcalm, pursuing the dead soldier beyond the grave, makes unpleasant and embarrassing reading even after two centuries. Vanity and pomposity were common failings in that age, but Vaudreuil in his writings manages to convey an impression of being vain and pompous beyond the average. He writes to the Court in May 1759, 'My firmness is generally applauded; it has entered all hearts and one and all say loudly, "Canada, our native land, will bury us in her ruins before we yield to the English." This is the course which I am firmly resolved upon and which I shall maintain inviolable.' In his plan of operations drawn up the month before he says of the two senior professional soldiers in Canada, 'M. le Marquis de Montcalm and the Chevalier de Lévis will be at Quebec; I shall always have much pleasure in informing them of all the movements I shall order, and similarly in making use of the reflections which the circumstances and the ground may suggest to them.' [15]

Vaudreuil was certainly a man of many faults. Nevertheless, his sins have been magnified beyond their true size by detractors always ready to believe the worst about him; of these the late Colonel William Wood, who often overdid the business of interpreting history in terms of heroes and villains, was one of the most active. As we shall see, the effect of Vaudreuil's interference with Montcalm has been somewhat exaggerated. Parkman's comment on the Governor General is still valid: he 'served the King and the colony in some respects with ability, always with an unflagging zeal; and he loved the land of his birth with a jealous devotion that goes far towards redeeming his miserable defects'.

At the moment when Vaudreuil became Governor General, the whole traditional pattern of North American warfare was being transformed; the system in which he had been trained was becoming a thing of the past. Both Britain and France had suddenly decided to send regular regiments from Europe to fight in America. The two battalions dispatched with Braddock in 1755 were the British Army's first essay in American warfare. The convoy that carried Vaudreuil to his post that same year brought to Canada the first battalions from France to serve in the country since the Carignan-Salières Regiment had been sent out to fight the Iroquois in the 1660s. It was the beginning of a military revolution. Montcalm described it, not inaccurately, four years later: [16]

> The nature of war in this colony has totally changed. Formerly the Canadians thought they were making war when they went on raids resembling hunting-parties – now we have formal operations; formerly the Indians were the basis of things, now they are only auxiliaries. We now need other views, other principles. I say this, but the old prejudices remain.

The old prejudices were particularly well established in the mind of the Governor General who continued to think of warfare in terms of the experience of his youth. He could not do without the regulars from France, the *troupes de terre* as they were called; but he thought he could do very nicely without regular generals to command them. When the first commander of these troops, Baron Dieskau, had the misfortune to get himself captured in his first operation, Vaudreuil told the Court that no replacement was necessary. Nevertheless, a replacement was sent. It was the Marquis de Montcalm.[17]

Louis-Joseph, Marquis de Montcalm-Gozon, seigneur de Saint-Véran, was born at his family's ancestral château of Candiac, in what is now the department of Gard in southern France, in 1712. Thus he was forty-seven in 1759 – fifteen years older than Wolfe, who used to call him 'the old fox', and thirteen years younger than Vaudreuil. Commissioned in the French Army at the age of twelve, he was an active soldier from fifteen. He saw his first war service in 1733 against the Austrians, and the following year took part in the siege of Philipsbourg. In 1742 he was wounded in the defence of Prague. Four years later, as a regimental commander, he fought in the disastrous battle of Piacenza. His regiment was wiped out, after he had twice rallied it; and he himself, disabled by five sabre-cuts, fell into Austrian hands. Paroled and later exchanged, he was promoted brigadier, and saw more service and received another wound before the War of the Austrian Succession drew to a close in 1748. Although he had never held high command, he was known as a brave and efficient officer; and in January 1756 he was appointed to command the *troupes de terre* in North America, with the rank of *maréchal de camp*, equivalent to major-general.[18]

The Canadian military system as it had now taken shape was highly complicated and involved baneful divisions of authority. Leaving the navy aside, there were three forces: the regular troops from France; the colonial regulars, the *troupes de la marine*, the traditional professional defenders of the country; and the citizen force, the militia. Every citizen was a militiaman; every parish had its company. From these companies the best or most available men could be drafted off for distant enterprises; and in great emergencies like that of 1759, as General Murray later put it, 'the whole were in arms for the defence of their country'. But the militia's training, inevitably, was rudimentary. More formidable were the colonial regulars: forty companies, with an official strength of sixty-five men each. These troops were closely identified with the country, the more so as most of their officers were Canadian-born. If only because of their lack of higher organization, their general efficiency was less than that of the battalions from France. They had proved their worth many times in the frontier fighting of the last two generations, but were less suited to the Europeanized warfare of the new era. As for the *troupes de terre*, there were eight battalions of them in Canada in 1759; the last two to arrive had been the 2nd and 3rd battalions of the Régiment de Berry, in 1757. Thereafter Canada got only drafts, though Louisbourg was reinforced just before Amherst's attack in 1758. These battalions were troops of the best European type, highly disciplined and highly drilled; capable of standing under fire and advancing under it; well able to meet their peers in the open field.[19]

In addition to these three forces, there were also *les sauvages*, the Indians. A great resource for the French in times past, they were now a wasting asset, more and more inclined to go missing as the balance of war turned against the lilies, more and more inclined to be difficult. They nevertheless played a considerable part in the campaign of Quebec.

The 'chain of command' was peculiar. The civil governor was also the commander-in-chief, and not in name only. Montcalm was not commander of all the forces of the colony; he commanded the *troupes de terre* alone, and was subject to the superior authority of Vaudreuil. The instructions which Montcalm received from the King in 1756 [20] were remarkably firm and explicit; in paragraph after paragraph they emphasized that he was under the Governor General's orders and must defer to him in everything. Thus Versailles sought diligently to avoid the evils of divided command. It did not succeed. The system could have worked only with a governor who was an experienced and respected senior soldier. Placing a regular general like Montcalm under the military direction of a man with the limited qualifications of Vaudreuil was indeed worse than placing him under a civilian. The colonial regulars and the militia were directly under Vaudreuil, who was also responsible for dealings with the Indians, a field in which, not without reason, he was held to be unusually competent.

The system broke down even sooner than might have been expected, thanks to the personal failings and total incompatibility of the two principals. Even while the French were winning victories it began to go to pieces. The great French triumph of 1756 was the capture of Chouaguen, called by the British Oswego. This is generally admitted to have been Vaudreuil's enterprise, and when it was over Montcalm's journal spoke warmly of the part in the victory played by the Canadians under Rigaud de Vaudreuil, the Governor's brother; their movement on August 13th was carried out, it said, 'in a brilliant and decisive manner'. (Montcalm was soon to stop saying kind words about 'Brother Rigaud' – this was his later name for him.) But the letters written by Montcalm and Vaudreuil after the action reflect growing jealousy between the French and Canadian forces. By 1757 the relationship between governor and general had seriously deteriorated. That summer Montcalm took Fort William Henry, at the head of Lake George (and failed to prevent the Indians from massacring British prisoners). In September Vaudreuil wrote to the Court recommending Montcalm's second-in-command, the Chevalier de

Lévis, for promotion. Characteristically, he said that Lévis had 'always held the most advanced posts, with M. de Rigaud de Vaudreuil, at the head of the Canadians and Indians', and went on to observe that he was sure that if Lévis had been commander-in-chief the success at William Henry would have been followed up; 'but, subordinated to M. le Marquis de Montcalm, he has not been able to follow the dictates of his own zeal'.[21]

Montcalm, conscious of the British superiority in force and the probable consequences of a disaster, pursued a cautious strategic policy, basically defensive and attempting offensive action only against limited objectives. Vaudreuil, in what tends to be the way of amateur strategists, demanded boldness. And in the summer of 1758 there was a violent explosion. On June 23rd, when Montcalm was just leaving Montreal for the Lake Champlain front, he received instructions from Vaudreuil which raised his southern blood to boiling point. He particularly resented a paragraph which began by telling him, in the event of the enemy attempting to besiege Carillon, 'to go to meet and fight them on their march or on the lake, or await them in an entrenched camp or other position as he may think best', and ended by cautioning him, in the event of his not being supported by a good number of Indians, 'not to expose himself to being compromised by a general and decisive affair'. He gave the Governor General an angry answer. Montcalm's great defensive victory over the British at Ticonderoga only a fortnight later did not improve matters; indeed, it made them worse.[22] As New France's supreme crisis approached, the governor and the general were at daggers drawn.

Just how bad the situation was, and something of the nature of Montcalm's own contribution to making it so, is to be read in his journal, which was normally kept for him by members of his staff. Until the summer of 1758, its references to Vaudreuil are generally restrained; they are in terms of respect suitable to comments on the King's representative and Montcalm's official superior. Then, on that June 23rd, comes this entry: 'This evening at ten o'clock the Marquis de Vaudreuil sent me his ridiculous, obscure and misleading orders.' From this time on the Governor is normally mentioned in terms of unmeasured scorn. Perhaps one example will be enough. It is of June 12th, 1759, at the moment when battle was about to be joined with the British before Quebec: [23]

> M. le Marquis de Vaudreuil, Governor General and in this capacity general of the army, made his first tour [of the new Beauport defences]; after all, youth must be instructed. As he had never seen either a camp or a work of defence, everything seemed to him as new as it was amusing. He asked singular questions. It was like a man born blind who has been given sight.

That Montcalm allowed a junior officer to set down things like this on his behalf indicates how imprudent and tactless he could be. The author of that *Journal tenu à l'armée* already quoted says, 'If he was only angry with someone, he never ceased tearing his reputation to pieces in indecent terms, even in front of his servants and, therefore, of the troops'; in this way, he claims, Montcalm undermined the confidence of the army, the people and the Indians in Vaudreuil. This seems only too probable, though one may assume that the writer considered any rude reference to Vaudreuil 'indecent'. In writing to his military subordinates Montcalm gives free rein to his feelings about the Governor General, frequently concluding, 'Burn my letter' – which they never did. (History seems to prove that the surest method of ensuring the permanent preservation of a piece of paper is to beg the recipient to destroy it.)

Montcalm's correspondence, it is true, tells us much else about him. In the letters to his officers he appears in an agreeable light: cheerfully pessimistic, flippant, affectionate, civilized. And those that went to the distant, much-loved home at Candiac to which he himself was never to return show us a deeply devoted son, husband and father. His last touching letter to his wife has often been quoted: 'I think I should have given up all my honours to be back with you, but the king must be obeyed; the moment when I shall see you again will be the finest of my life. Good-bye, my heart, I believe I love you more than ever.' [24] These aspects of the general's personality help to explain his appeal to posterity.

Montcalm will always be a gallant figure in Canadian history. He is and will be remembered in his shirt-sleeves in the thick of the fight that hot July day at Ticonderoga, and on his big black horse leading the doomed line in the Battle of the Plains. He was a brave, experienced and accomplished soldier. There is no reason to think him a military genius, and he made some bad mistakes. As for his relations with Vaudreuil, one cannot help feeling that a wiser and calmer man, one more richly endowed with the quasi-political talents which are so useful to any commander-in-chief, might have prevented the situation from developing as it did. Vaudreuil undoubtedly gave him much provocation, but provocations can sometimes be overlooked in the public interest. Lévis managed to keep on good terms with the Governor General – possibly at the cost of some dissimulation – and it would have been a good thing for the French empire in America if Montcalm could have done the same. The problem of dealing with small men in high office is a familiar one in political and military life; much can be done with tact, patience, circumspection and perhaps even a little flattery; but beyond a certain point these were not expedients which Montcalm was prepared to use.

Painful decisions faced the French Court at the end of the year 1758. Louisbourg was gone; Canada had been saved for the time being, but it was certain that the British would make a great effort against it in 1759. What strategic policy should France adopt to meet the crisis? The military problem was complicated by the distracted internal condition of the colony. Versailles knew the state of the relations between Vaudreuil and Montcalm. The Governor had reported, a bit obscurely, that he feared that the victory at Carillon would have 'pernicious consequences for the colony' and had recommended that Montcalm be recalled.[25] And the prevalence of corruption was well known.

Active help from the Mother Country being essential if the colony was to live, Montcalm took steps to explain its needs.

He proposed to send as emissaries his aide-de-camp Bougainville and the 'war commissary' Doreil. Vaudreuil agreed, wrote recommending them to the Court – and wrote more privately that they did not understand the colony and were 'creatures' of Montcalm. Bougainville carried, or composed, a series of detailed memoranda representing Montcalm's views. He seems to have reached Versailles on December 20th.[26]

Louis-Antoine de Bougainville was to play a considerable part in the Canadian drama of 1759. Though only twenty-nine, he had already given much evidence of versatility. He had combined diplomacy with a short army career, had written a treatise on integral calculus, and had been elected a fellow of the Royal Society of London. Later in life he was to win distinction as a navigator and a naval officer. His name was to be given to an island in the Solomon group and to a suitably brilliant tropical plant. He was an original member of the Institute of France, and died a senator under Napoleon.

Montcalm's requests as presented by Bougainville were relatively modest. Recognizing the great difficulty of sending really powerful reinforcements to Canada in the face of British naval superiority, he proposed that French strategy should be based on making a potent diversion against Virginia or the Carolinas. This would be less exposed to interception by British squadrons and would force the British to withdraw forces from their offensive against Canada; while the southern colonies had no strong defences, and it might be possible to organize revolt among the slave population. He recommended that direct aid to Canada should take the form of replacement drafts to fill the gaps in the ranks of the troops, plus certain specialists, especially artillerymen and engineers; ammunition in great quantity; a train of field artillery and a large supply of small arms; trade goods for the Indians; and, of course, assistance to the *munitionnaire* in providing the colony with the foodstuffs essential for continued defence.

In a separate memoir Montcalm put forward proposals for making more effective use of the Canadian militia in the increasingly Europeanized warfare which had lately been waged in America. He recommended a census of the whole force, dividing the men into three classes, good, medium and bad, and ordering that all the good men should serve throughout the next campaign. These would in turn be divided into three groups, one being incorporated into the regular battalions, one into the units of colonial regulars, while the third would serve separately as militia. Vaudreuil and his party regarded this as a plan to bring the militia directly under Montcalm's command, and this may well have been one of its objects; but there can be little doubt that it was mainly just what it purported to be – an attempt to use the manpower of the colony more effectively at a time when the defenders were certain to be outmatched both in numbers and in military quality. It was approved, but turned out to be an error of judgement. Incorporating the untrained men in the regular battalions merely reduced those units' effectiveness.

One peculiar scheme put forward by Montcalm, which indicates how little hope he had of successful defence of Canada, is his suggestion that, in case of capitulation becoming unavoidable, the regular troops, with the best of the colonial regulars and some Canadians, should withdraw down the Mississippi to Louisiana. The Court's decision on this, as reported by Bougainville, was 'regarded with surprise, not accepted'.[27]

It seems evident that Louis XV's Ministers had been grappling with these various problems before Bougainville arrived; for on December 28th, only about a week after he reached Versailles, and possibly before there had been serious discussions with him, two documents were ready to be placed before the King.[28] One dealt with the general strategic situation of Canada, on the basis of a dispatch from Vaudreuil, dated November 3rd, which urged large efforts to save the country. To do what he asked, it pointed out, would mean using all the French naval forces, either directly or in a diversion against the British colonies; but the state of the navy forbade such a venture, which moreover would leave the coasts of France unprotected. It seemed best therefore, the memorandum went on, to instruct Vaudreuil simply to stand on the defensive and do his utmost to hold at least part of the country until new orders could be sent to him in 1760. Direct help to Canada would consist merely of four royal ships carrying what munitions and trade goods they could, while encouragement would be given to the *munitionnaire* and private traders to send forward provisions; this would limit the Government's immediate expense to the cost of the four vessels and their cargoes. The King approved the paper the same day.

The other paper dealt with the disastrous disagreements between Vaudreuil and Montcalm. It pointed out that Montcalm was now to be made a lieutenant-general (in recognition of his victory at Carillon) and remarked, 'He could scarcely serve in this new rank under the orders of the Marquis de Vaudreuil, who is merely lieutenant-general as governor, a title which does not carry in the military mind the same degree of power as that of lieutenant-general of the armies.' A decision by the King was required; and it appeared necessary that he should 'be pleased to grant to the Marquis de Montcalm his recall, which he has requested . . . , his health and the debts he has contracted not allowing him to continue his service'. It was recommended that Lévis should succeed him.

This document is endorsed, 'On mature consideration this arrangement is not to be made, M. de Montcalm being necessary in present circumstances.'[29] Historians, including Chapais and Gipson, have assumed that this represents a change of mind on the part of Ministers after further thought and consultation with Bougainville. It seems much more likely, particularly in the light of the other memorandum of the same date, that it is in fact the Minister of Marine's record of an adverse decision by the King. Louis XV was not prepared to dismiss the victor of Carillon.

This was a natural decision, but probably an unwise one. The situation in New France called for drastic measures. Lévis was a skilful soldier, as his later record shows. He would quite probably have conducted the defence as well as Montcalm; and he was on good terms with Vaudreuil. To have accepted Berryer's recommendation might have involved some injustice to Montcalm, but it would have restored concord to the colony at a moment when concord was of vital importance.

The proper alternative to recalling Montcalm was to recall Vaudreuil. This was not done. Doubtless the Governor General's reputation for influence with the Canadians and the Indians was a factor. Doubtless also it was felt that such a change should not be made in the middle of a great crisis in the colony's affairs. The action the Court actually took was an ineffective half-measure. Vaudreuil was ordered to defer to Montcalm in military matters. The orders were almost as definite as the original ones given to Montcalm to defer to Vaudreuil. A dispatch addressed jointly to Vaudreuil and Bigot[30] said,

> His Majesty's intention is that M. le Marquis de Montcalm shall not only be consulted on all operations but also on all areas of administration relating to the defence and preservation of the colony; you will ask his advice, communicating to him the letters I write to you on all these subjects . . .

These instructions had so little visible effect upon the later actions of either Montcalm or Vaudreuil that one finds oneself wondering whether Vaudreuil ever showed this letter to Montcalm, as (elsewhere in it) he was specifically ordered to do. The Minister's letter to Montcalm on the subject merely said, 'I have written separately to M. de Vaudreuil recommending him to consult you on all operations and to act in concert with you . . .'[31]

The letter addressed personally to Vaudreuil on the subject must have made the Governor General deeply angry. After again telling him to consult Montcalm on 'all military enterprises' and related administrative matters, the Minister went on to say that while he did not prescribe to Vaudreuil where he should reside, 'you should not appear in the field except in so far as it may be a matter of an absolutely decisive action and of your being obliged to march the country's whole militia for the general defence of the Colony; in this case, you may do so after consulting M. de Montcalm as to the degree of necessity which there may be for you to show yourself. The affection the Canadians have for you and your name may raise their numbers and their courage when you are seen at their head on an occasion which may decide the Colony's fate; but except in such a case of necessity you should not quit the centre of the Colony, so that you may be in a position to watch over everything.' Vaudreuil must have particularly hated being told that in the event of his having to send all the able-bodied men to the front it would be a good idea for him to make an appearance in the countryside to inspire the old men and the women to get on with the work in the fields: 'such conduct on your part towards a people who have been so long attached to you cannot fail to produce a very good effect on their minds, and to procure for you special marks of His Majesty's satisfaction ...' [32]

The letter of these orders – which incidentally have been little noticed by English-speaking Canadian historians – was weakened by the fact that the paramount operations of the coming campaign were to take place at Quebec, which could certainly be said to be 'the centre of the Colony'. As for the spirit of them, there is little evidence that Vaudreuil made any attempt to live up to it. He can have been little reconciled to them by the fact that they were accompanied by the award to himself of the Grand Cross of the Order of St Louis. And one shudders to think of his reaction had he known that Bougainville explained to Montcalm how he had taken it upon himself to suggest that award as having been recommended by the general: 'that has gained credit for you; moderation, you know'. [33] One wonders, too, whether Montcalm was vastly pleased at being made responsible for decorating the Governor General. Bougainville himself did well out of his embassy. It brought him the rank of colonel, the Cross of St Louis, and the regard of the Court – including Madame de Pompadour, who, in his own phrase, 'was then Prime Minister'.

New France got less than Montcalm had asked for. Bougainville reported that the Pompadour favoured the diversion against the Carolinas, and that only lack of money prevented it; but the Court's decision was to attempt a more basic diversionary operation nearer home – directed against Britain herself. It would have been effective strategy had they had the naval strength and leadership to carry it out; but they did not. The programme announced to Vaudreuil and Montcalm was that approved by the King on December 28th. No attempt whatever was made to put a naval squadron into the St Lawrence – the ships that sailed thither, including the two royal frigates, were cargo carriers. The dispatch to Vaudreuil and Bigot [34] began with a grim reference to the enormous sums spent on the colony in recent years, and proceeded:

His Majesty would be equally disposed to send the same help to the colony now, but the continuation of the war in Europe, the too-great risks of the sea and the necessity of concentrating His Majesty's naval forces do not permit of dispersing those forces at the present moment and hazarding part of them in order to bring you assistance which might not reach you and which would be more usefully employed for the state and for the relief of Canada in nearer and more decisive expeditions.

The troops sent were limited to about 400 replacements, forty gunners and a few engineers and other specialists. The ships carried ammunition, artillery and trade goods – in precisely what quantities does not appear; and Cadet's vessels were freighted with food and drink. (*Eau-de-vie* was always a rather important munition of war in Canada.) The chiefs of the colony were told, in accordance with the royal decision, to do their best until more help could be sent, to limit themselves to a strict defensive, and to make it their principal object to keep control of at least a large enough portion of the country to provide a basis for recovering the whole of it when the time came to make peace.

The dispatches that told this story went to Canada with Bougainville on his return in the early spring of 1759. Discouraging they must have been to the leaders of the pinched and beleaguered community on the St Lawrence – and yet the discouragement was largely lost in the exultation of the safe arrival, contrary to so many probabilities, of the little fleet bringing the supplies that alone could carry the colony through another campaign. Admiral Durell's grip, as we have seen, had closed on the river just too late; nearly all the King's ships and Cadet's made safe harbour at Quebec.

The Court of Versailles has been accused of abandoning Canada. The accusation, it is evident, is not entirely without foundation; though the Court's difficulties were formidable, and the strategy which it adopted is militarily quite defensible. The worst charge against the Court, however, concerns the internal condition of the colony. It was well aware that New France was riddled with corruption; it knew that the Governor General and the commander of the troops were bitter enemies. It failed to do anything effective about either problem; in both respects Canada was in as bad a state as ever as her people faced the crisis that was sure to come in 1759.

# CHAPTER TWO

## *The Fortress*

The ancient fortress city of Quebec sits solidly upon its commanding rock on the north or left bank of the River St Lawrence, roughly 700 miles from the open Atlantic. Here the great river widens suddenly into what is really an estuary. The lowest point at which modern engineering science has found it possible to bridge the St Lawrence is a few miles above the city. At Quebec itself the stream at high-water mark is a scant 1,000 yards wide today; at Montmagny, some thirty-two miles below, the width is twelve miles.

The city occupies a point like the jutting prow of a ship, between the great River St Lawrence and its much smaller tributary the St Charles. Along these rivers, on either side of the point, is a narrow shelf of waterfront land; on this stands the Lower Town. Above it, along the whole circuit of both rivers, tower the rocky cliffs of the Upper Town. These, however, are much higher towards the St Lawrence than towards the St Charles; for the point is loftiest directly above the larger river, and all across the city and the land to the west of it the ground slopes steadily down towards the north-east. The Upper Town at the Château Frontenac hotel, site of the residence of the French governors, is about 200 feet above the St Lawrence. The highest point of the peninsula, however, lies farther west – the great long rocky hump of Cape Diamond, bearing the modern Citadel, which looks down upon the river from a precipice nearly 350 feet high at its loftiest point at the Cape Diamond or Prince of Wales Bastion.

It follows that the city is protected by a water barrier and cliffs (which for the greater part of the circuit are virtually unscalable) on all sides but one: the land front facing the open country – the Plains of Abraham – to the south-west. Whatever the natural strength of the other fronts, this one had to be protected by artificial fortifications, and the French, as we shall see, covered it with a continuous line of works, of a sort, before the seventeenth century was over. This line was subject to disadvantages arising from the manner in which the ground sloped towards the north, which meant not only that each successive bastion from south to north was lower than the one before it, but also that the northern face and flank of each was lower than the southern ones of the same bastion. This considerably interfered with the mutual supporting fire which the guns on the bastions could bring to bear. What is more, as harassed engineers often pointed out, the northern end of the line was actually commanded by the higher ground outside it to the south. At the same time, the whole line was 'enfiladed' – that is, exposed to flanking fire – from the ground on the other side of the St Charles. Luckily, however, this ground is not very high.

The exposed land front was protected from water-borne assault by the frowning cliffs which front the St Lawrence for miles above the city. These cliffs, 150 to 250 feet high, present at first glance an impassable barrier to landings from the river, and would seem to compel an attacker desiring to reach the city's south-west front to approach from the St Charles side, which is far more accessible. Formidable indeed they are; yet in 1759 the most famous episode in Quebec's history was to demonstrate that there was at least one point where an army, helped by luck and its enemy's inefficiency, could be moved without very serious difficulty from the river up to the Plains of Abraham within easy striking-distance of the town.

Immediately across the St Lawrence from Quebec are the heights of Point Lévis, less than a mile from the city. The French never fortified Point Lévis, and they paid dearly for the omission during Wolfe's siege.

More nonsense has been written about the fortifications of Quebec than on almost any other subject in modern history.

The late Sir Arthur Doughty, who as Archivist of the Dominion of Canada had an enormous number of plans of the fortress in his custody, but seems never to have looked at them with any care, was responsible for much of it; and none of his contemporaries appears to have challenged his authority. Sir Arthur originated, or at any rate popularized, an extraordinarily inaccurate account of the building of the great Citadel which has been repeated in a whole succession of books. He asserted that the Citadel was begun in 1823, that it cost $35 million, and that none of the fortifications existing early in the twentieth century antedated the construction of the Citadel. But records in the Archives in Ottawa over which Sir Arthur presided with such undoubted ability for many years establish that the Citadel was begun in 1820; that its first cost was about £236,500; and that large portions of the city's defences existing when Sir Arthur wrote, and still existing today (including the bastioned wall facing the Plains of Abraham) were built during the French régime. Indeed, within the King's Bastion of the modern Citadel there stands a 'cavalier' which was originally built by Count Frontenac in 1693. This small structure was sometimes called a citadel. However, when the term is used in contemporary documents in connexion with the operations of 1759 the reference is frequently to the demi-bastion at the extreme left of the town walls, immediately above the St Lawrence. This had been lightly closed in rear to form a 'polygon of masonry' which a contemptuous Briton called 'a sort of citadel',[1] and in this insignificant enclosure stood the main powder magazine (which houses the Citadel Museum today). Quebec never had a proper citadel until the present one was constructed by the British in 1820–31.[2] This has not prevented various historians, including some who ought to have known better, from writing as if the modern work had existed in 1759.

Although the history of the Quebec defences may be said to have begun with the building of Champlain's fortified *habitation* in 1608, the real process of fortifying the town com-

menced at the time of Sir William Phips' attack in 1690, when
Frontenac improvised a line of works covering its unprotected
southern and western front. This enclosed no part of the great
hump of Cape Diamond on which the Citadel now stands. That
was first fortified in 1693, when under Frontenac's direction
Josué du Boisberthelot de Beaucours (or Beaucourt) designed
a new system of defences running across the promontory – a
bastioned line of earthworks and wooden pickets supported
on the left by the 'cavalier' just mentioned.[3]

From this time onward a succession of engineers, each
noisily vilifying his predecessor, and each himself spending
great sums of public money to very little purpose, tinkered ineffectively with the problem of fortifying Quebec's land front.
Beaucours and Denis Levasseur de Néré were rivals for many
years. Just at the end of the seventeenth century Levasseur began building a new stone defence line for the city, commencing
work on the Cape Diamond hump on the left. Construction
was stopped with the task far from complete. In 1712 Beaucours was allowed to build two redoubts or bastioned towers,
the Redoute Royale and the Redoute Dauphine, to support
the right of the line of defence. At the same time his old *enceinte* of 1693 was repaired and in part at least faced with
stone. In 1720 Gaspard Chaussegros de Léry began work on
another and different project for a stone *enceinte* across the
promontory. Again the work was stopped when only nicely begun; nevertheless, a portion of the section that had been constructed (again on the Cape Diamond hump) remained in
existence and in part stands today, incorporated in the Citadel.[4]

Thus after half a century and enormous sums of money had
been devoted to the task of fortifying Quebec's western front,
the outbreak of the War of the Austrian Succession in 1740
found the city still almost open. The beginnings of a line of
stone defences stood on Cape Diamond; Beaucours' line of
1693 still mouldered some distance in rear; and the two had
been ineffectively connected at various times by entrenchments. In the autumn of 1744 Chaussegros de Léry, contemplating this hodgepodge, had to report to France that Quebec

was essentially unfortified and incapable of defence; in case of British attack, the defenders would have to pin their faith to preventing the enemy from landing in the vicinity of the city. Then, in 1745, the French received a severe shock: an expeditionary force of New England amateurs powerfully supported by the Royal Navy captured their great fortress of Louisbourg in Cape Breton Island. The Governor, Beauharnois, now took it on himself, without reference to Versailles, to authorize de Léry to resume the work that had been stopped a quarter of a century before; and he set about it with a will. By the summer of 1746 the greater part of the stone-bastioned wall, which still exists, had been completed from the left flank above the St Lawrence to the right flank overlooking the St Charles. But the Court, evidently frightened by the expense, then sent orders to halt the work. It was resumed a year later. By the end of the 1749 season the stone revetment of the walls was virtually complete and the earthen ramparts behind it were finished or nearly so.[5] For the first time Quebec was enclosed on the west by a single system of masonry defences.

Nevertheless, we find French officers on the eve of the British attack of 1759 complaining that the fortifications are useless, much as Chaussegros de Léry had done fifteen years before. At the end of 1758 Bougainville reported to the Minister of Marine in Paris, 'Quebec is without fortifications and is not capable of being fortified; if we cannot hold the approaches to it there is nothing for it but to lay down our arms'; and again, 'if the enemy once reaches the foot of its walls, we must capitulate'. Montcalm's own journal uses similar terms: the city's fortifications are 'so ridiculous and so bad that it would be taken as soon as besieged'. The general had the lowest possible view of the professional qualifications of Chaussegros de Léry, who had died in 1756 ('You need only look at his works') and suggested that he had 'robbed the King like the others'.[6]

Some writers have found it difficult to believe, after all the work that had been done, that these statements about the inadequacy of the defences could really be true; yet true they certainly were. We get a glimpse of the reasons in a report of the new King's Engineer for New France, Pontleroy, written in

October 1758. The Upper Town of Quebec, he says, 'in the
state it is today, is not capable of useful defence in case of
siege, having neither ditches, nor counterscarps nor covered
way', and being dominated by heights behind which the enemy
can make protected approaches.[7] A mere wall was of little use
without the exterior works designed to protect it from the
effects of direct artillery fire and the menace of capture by
escalade. A vital part of any contemporary fortification was a
deep wide ditch, usually dry, in front of the main work; its
almost perpendicular side closest to the enemy was called the
counterscarp. The walls were generally covered from direct
fire by exterior masonry works, 'counterguards' of various
types. Further protection was given by an earthen glacis sloping upwards as it approached the ditch, with a 'covered way'
cut into it along the edge of the ditch above the counterscarp.
These exterior works were almost entirely lacking at Quebec.
Lévis recorded at the time of his siege in 1760 that the ditch
was shallow, only some five or six feet deep in places, with
some of the earth carried to the counterscarp; and although de
Léry reported in 1749 that the counterscarps were made, and
a plan made by him in 1752 seems to suggest that the glacis
and covered way had been completed, British records of 1759
indicate clearly that these outer earthworks existed only on
the extreme right of the line, north of St John's Gate.[8]

A British engineer, Montresor, set down what amounts to a
serious indictment of de Léry's professional competence. Since
the ground was so rocky, he pointed out, a ditch could only be
made by blasting; and since the French had made the mistake
of building the wall before making the ditch, the latter could
never be made – because blasting to make it would bring the
wall down. The British fully agreed with Montcalm and Bougainville; their engineers' opinion on taking over Quebec was,
'the place Cannot for a Considerable Time be put in a Condition to Resist Cannon for above a few days'. Vaudreuil explained just a few weeks before the arrival of Wolfe's fleet at
Quebec that it was out of the question to get on with the exterior works of the fortress, for want of provisions; 4,000 men
would be required, and since flour was lacking they could be

fed only by killing the cattle which were being held as a last reserve in case all the convoys from France were intercepted.[9] So the city walls on the west remained fully exposed to enemy fire.

These defences had another serious weakness. Chaussegros de Léry had a theory about the armament of fortresses. The Public Archives of Canada possesses a great manuscript treatise on fortification which he wrote and illustrated, completing it in 1714, two years before he came to Canada. In this he suggests that the only effective means open to a besieged garrison to interfere with the siege works of the attackers is to make sorties with the object of destroying their batteries. He seems to have had no faith whatever in the use of the fortress artillery to reply to the fire of the enemy guns. His Quebec works were designed in accordance with this theory: he did not provide for mounting guns in the faces of his bastions, confronting the Plains of Abraham; with very few exceptions, all the embrasures were placed in the bastions' flanks, firing along the walls. One of the French diarists of the 1759 siege wrote that the western ramparts mounted fifty-two guns, from 2-pounders to 12-pounders, 'but none of them can fire towards the open country; they all fire in flank and in enfilade, so they are only useful in case of the enemy trying a scaling attack'. When the British found themselves in possession of Quebec, they lost no time in cutting embrasures in the bastion faces and mounting guns there – something the French had never done.[10]

All in all, the story of the city walls of Quebec is a truly extraordinary record of sustained inefficiency; and it tells a good deal about the administration of New France. The western defences, however, were not the only fundamental weakness of the fortress. Another was the failure to occupy the south bank of the river opposite the city.

Far back in 1702, Levasseur had planned two batteries here to command the nearby anchorages. They were to be on the shore, just above high-water mark, and would themselves have been dominated by the heights close above them on which the city of Lévis now stands.[11] It would seem that these batteries were never built; and it is the fact that the Quebec fortress was never extended to the south shore of the river until 1865, when three forts were built there in case General Grant should come that way. The result in 1759 was that the British were allowed to occupy the Lévis heights and establish batteries there which bombarded and largely destroyed the city and facilitated their ships' passage past Quebec into the upper river.

During the Anglo-French wars which began in 1689 Quebec was repeatedly threatened, and each successive period of alarm led to hasty measures of precaution and the making of plans for defence. But British forces actually attempted to launch attacks on the city only twice before 1759. These attacks had considerable influence on French thinking in the ultimate crisis.

In 1690 a New England force commanded by Sir William Phips appeared before Quebec and made an awkward effort to take it. Phips landed some 1,200 men on the Canardière, the section of the Beauport shore immediately east of the St Charles River. His plan was to cross the St Charles with the aid of the boats of his fleet and assail Quebec from the west in conjunction with an attack by the fleet on the St Lawrence side. But the New Englanders were inefficient; the various parts of their undisciplined force failed to cooperate with each other; and the plan collapsed, after an ineffective bombardment of the town by the ships, without any attempt being made to cross the St Charles.[12]

In 1711 there was an even worse fiasco. A British force larger and far more formidable than Phips' entered the St Lawrence under the command of Rear-Admiral Sir Hovenden Walker and Brigadier-General John Hill. But it never fired a shot against Quebec. It came to grief at Egg Island in the lower river, roughly 300 miles from the city. Several ships were wrecked, many men lost their lives, and the expedition was abandoned. Quebec rejoiced as she had rejoiced at the repulse of Phips; and the church of Notre Dame de la Victoire in the Lower Town, named in honour of the success of 1690, was re-christened Notre Dame des Victoires – Our Lady of the Victories.[13]

These events had their due effect, and from the French point of view it was not a good effect. The Phips episode probably tended to focus the attention of French defence planners on the Beauport shore, and so to lead them to neglect the possibility of attack above the city. The disaster to Walker must have contributed substantially to the complacent French reliance, so evident in 1759, upon the mere dangers of the St Lawrence navigation. In that 'wonderful year' of Britain's Royal Navy, those river perils were to prove a very inadequate safeguard for Quebec. The obstacles that ruined Walker presented no serious difficulty to men like Saunders and Cook. In the campaign that decided New France's fate, the French were to a considerable extent the dupes of their own past good fortunes.

Many features of the Quebec defence plan followed in 1759 had been worked out years before. Gaspard Chaussegros de Léry recorded that in the crisis of 1745 following the fall of Louisbourg he made a plan for Beauharnois which involved putting 4,000 men into Quebec as a garrison while at the same time forming on the city's outskirts a 'flying camp' of troops, militia and Indians to oppose landings. He calculated that some 10,000 men would be available for this camp. He also proposed to have several fire-ships in readiness for use against the enemy's squadron; he attached special importance to this weapon.[14]

It was in the autumn of 1757 that Montcalm seems to have first addressed himself seriously to planning the defence of Quebec. His journal describes in detail how with other officers, of whom Bougainville was one, he made in October a tour of the north shore of the St Lawrence as far east as Cape Tourmente, near the eastern point of the Isle of Orleans. He reconnoitred a lofty site on the Cape for a battery of four guns and two mortars which would command at short range the difficult river channel called the Traverse, which all ships approaching Quebec must pass. He concluded that no landing was possible between the Cape and Beauport; that the only course for the British was to bring their ships up the channel south of the Isle of Orleans, double the island's western point and come to anchor in the Beauport basin, within sight of Quebec but beyond range of its guns. In these circumstances he proposed building a number of redoubts along the Beauport shore between Pointe à Lessay and the St Charles River, and chose sites for most of them. (It is quite evident from the journal that he did not contemplate fortifying the coast between Pointe à Lessay and the Montmorency River.) He also favoured entrenching the west bank of the St Charles, from the vicinity of the General Hospital to the Lower Town, which would give the French a second line of defence if driven from the Beauport shore, and digging another trench line from the hospital to the slope of the Côte d'Abraham west of the city.

The engineer Pontleroy developed this theme in a memoir forwarded to Versailles a year later. He considered the Montmorency River with its steep wooded banks and few fords an excellent flank protection for the Beauport position. While recommending some defences to cover the main crossing below Montmorency Falls, he felt that no other works were necessary east of Pointe à Lessay. Like Montcalm he took the view that landings were possible only between Beauport and the St Charles. He recommended entrenching the west bank of the St Charles and constructing the line from the General Hospital to the Côte d'Abraham advocated by Montcalm; thus creating an entrenched camp which, well palisaded and garrisoned by all the regular troops and some Canadians, would cover the Lower Town, defend the passages of the St Charles and (with a good redoubt at the top of the Côte d'Abraham) give some protection to the Upper Town. He suggested bridging the St Charles and constructing defences on the east bank to cover the bridge and thereby facilitate retiring across it if the French were forced out of the Beauport position.[15] With some modification, apparently initiated by Lévis, this plan, originating with Montcalm and developed by Pontleroy, is the one actually followed. The single feature of it not carried out is the trench line from the General Hospital to the Côte d'Abraham and the entrenched camp whose western face it was to be.

On June 10th, 1759, when the leading British ships were almost within sight of Quebec, the Chevalier de Lévis signed a long and elaborate paper on the dispositions for the coming

clash.[16] He differed from Montcalm and Pontleroy chiefly in
his insistence upon the desirability of fortifying the whole
front from the St Charles to the Montmorency; it is evident
that he was the father of this idea. The Montcalm journal
notes on June 21st that Lévis is strengthening the left, nearest
the Montmorency, and has ordered the construction of
thirteen redans, two redoubts and two batteries in this area,
'although it is very strong by nature'. Events were to justify
his action. Lévis was an able soldier, as this memoir clearly
indicates; but it also indicates that like other French soldiers of
that time and place he had mentally 'made a picture' of future
happenings which was misleading. He wrote, 'There is no
reason to believe that the enemy is thinking of an attempt at
passing before the city and disembarking at the Anse des Mers.
As long as our frigates are in being there is no reason at all
to fear for that sector.' Since the French had only two naval
frigates, and two or three chartered by the *munitionnaire*
Cadet, it is evident that Lévis was thinking in terms of a British
boat enterprise; it did not occur to him that major units of the
fleet might be able to pass the city. This easy assumption is
the fatal weakness of Lévis' 'appreciation' and of the whole
French plan.

At the same time the controlling French authorities on both
sides of the Atlantic failed to take action that had been recommended to them to provide works below Quebec to delay the
British advance up the river. During his mission to France in
the winter of 1758–9 Bougainville put forward a programme
which in essence if not in all details certainly represented the
views of Montcalm. In addition to the 'redoubts and lines'
near Quebec, which he said had been recommended in a paper
sent to the Court at the end of 1757, he urged the construction
if resources permitted of batteries in the lower river at Gaspé
(to deprive the British of a base) and at Les Eboulements and
the nearby Ile aux Coudres to block their passage up. (At Ile
aux Coudres the main channel hugs the north shore, passing
north of the island.) In any case, he argued, the battery at Cape
Tourmente should be built, plus additional ones at the western
point of the Isle of Orleans and at Point Lévis on the south

shore. The lower batteries could be built by the forces sent from France in the spring; Vaudreuil should be ordered to build the ones close to Quebec.[17] But the Court refrained from issuing any such instructions; those sent to the Governor were in very general terms. Montcalm's journal records that the general had asked Vaudreuil to build the Beauport lines and the Cape Tourmente battery, and had 'redoubled his urgings' when the ice went out in the spring of 1759; but, says the diarist, 'unfortunately indolence triumphed again' and nothing was done. The Beauport defences were not actively begun until June; the battery at Cape Tourmente and those at the Isle of Orleans and Point Lévis were never built. The regrettable consequence of all this, from the French point of view, was that the British ships met no opposition of the slightest significance until they actually arrived before Quebec. Yet it was enormously important to the French to gain time; every week's delay imposed upon the British brought that much closer the autumn and the enforced departure of their fleet from the river.

The old French scheme of using fire-ships and fire-rafts continued to be an important part of the defence plan. Bougainville included it in his programme, and it was persisted in and actually carried out, though only to disappoint all its promoters' high hopes.

There had been much inefficiency and much dishonesty, and France — and New France — were to pay for these things now. It is possible that, even if all the engineers and contractors had been uniformly able and honest, and if all the soldiers' recommendations had been carried out, Quebec would still have fallen in 1759. As it was, the painful incompleteness of the defences made the loss of the fortress considerably more likely. Montcalm's position appeared strong, and strong in some respects it was; but as he sat down to play out the long summer's game against Wolfe he was grimly conscious of the weakness of the cards he held.

God seemed to be on William Pitt's side that season. Montcalm's journal in May and June dwells on the persistence of the north-east wind — the wind that is blowing the British ships up the river towards the ill-defended city. (The British logs do not give an impression of quite such overwhelmingly favourable conditions; but the fact is that the fleet never met really adverse ones.) While the French soldiers and militiamen dug at the Beauport entrenchments, and Vaudreuil's daily conferences wrangled, the great British armament glided majestically towards its goal.

> I see the lords of human kind pass by,
> Pride in their port, defiance in their eye.

So Oliver Goldsmith wrote, five years later. It might have been a reminiscence of the St Lawrence in June 1759. The inhabitants of the down-river seigneuries must have watched from their woody fastnesses with increasing awe as the imposing vessels multiplied and passed upwards. Durell's advanced guard of thirteen ships, daunting enough in itself, was soon dwarfed by the appearance of the tremendous main body. At Quebec Vaudreuil was in two minds whether or not to accept a recommendation of the Intendant to send the Three Rivers militia home in order to save food. He had about decided to let them go, Montcalm's journal indicates, when on June 21st a new report came up from the lower river: the British fleet had suddenly been augmented by no less than 132 sail. The militia stayed.

The British forces, strong, well found, efficient, were moving to a rendezvous with Britain's imperial destiny. It was four years now since Braddock's little army had been shot to ribbons on the banks of the Monongahela; and Anglo-Saxon countries have had a habit of becoming formidable by the fourth year of a war. Seldom if ever has Britain sent out a force more redoubtable than the crews and regiments, seasoned, experienced and confident, that were now closing upon Quebec. New France, with its defective fortifications, its painful shortage of provisions, its tragic internal divisions, jealousies and dishonesties, its scanty regular force, and the increasing isolation from the Mother Country imposed by British sea-power, was in deadly peril. But peril was nothing new to the Canadians. Canada was to be no easy conquest, for its people had the will to defend their country; and in the coming struggle the man-power of this remote and forlorn community was to be mobilized for action to an extent achieved by no twentieth-century totalitarian state. As Wolfe and Saunders sailed up the river the colony, grimly resolved, was making ready to battle for its life.

# CHAPTER THREE

## *May and June: Contact*

---

On May 10th, 1759, Colonel de Bougainville, returning from his eventful mission to France, arrived at Quebec. He found that Vaudreuil and Montcalm were at Montreal, and thither he hastened with his dispatches.

Among the papers which Montcalm received from France at this moment was, according to his journal, one warning him of a British expedition against Quebec. He at once informed Vaudreuil and sought his permission to go to Quebec immediately to see to its defences. Vaudreuil at first refused, but shortly he himself received a dispatch from the Court, presumably that dated February 16th, which told him that 'le Général Wolf' was being sent from England with 8,000 men and would pick up others at Halifax.[1] Vaudreuil was ordered to concert defence measures with Montcalm. The general was now permitted to go, and he lost no time. He left Montreal on May 21st, reached Quebec on the evening of the 22nd, and immediately fell to work.

The 23rd brought reports of British ships at St Barnabé, near Rimouski; they were, of course, Durell's. The news was confirmed at midnight by the flames of signal fires and by a courier from below. By that time Montcalm and, evidently, the Intendant had assembled the officers of the naval and merchant vessels at Quebec and arranged to put their crews to work; the next day 300 sailors were digging a trench-line along the right bank of the St Charles under the direction of an engineer who had come in from France only a couple of days

before. Orders went out in one direction to bring down to
Quebec the regular battalions which had spent the winter in
the districts of Montreal and Three Rivers where they could
most easily subsist, and in the other to the lower parishes to
hide their women, children and animals 'in the depths of the
woods'. The British officer prisoners were sent off to Three
Rivers. Arrangements were made to remove the navigation
marks of the Traverse channel, substitute false ones, and sink
a group of ships to block the channel.

On the 24th the Governor General arrived and confirmed
all the orders issued by Montcalm; according to the general, he
was astonished at how much had been accomplished in thirty-
six hours. He decided to hold a conference every evening to
issue orders for the following day. Preparations for defence
were continued. Five of the largest vessels in the harbour, along
with three smaller craft, were ordered converted into fire-
ships. A 'floating battery' was put in hand; gunboats were prepared; two hulks armed with guns were sunk in the mouth of
the St Charles. Additional waterside batteries, long talked of,
were now ordered built in the Lower Town. Steps were taken
to enclose the Upper Town on the river side – if only with
wooden pickets – and to obstruct the passages up from the
lower level. On May 27th, the regular troops began to arrive
from up the river, and were encamped west of the St Charles
to be close to the works there. The following day the decision
was taken to bridge that stream and fortify the bridgehead on
the northern bank. Three bridges, the records indicate, were
finally built; though a British survey made just after the fall
of the city implies that only the remains of one had been
found.[2]

A decision of June 1st was to have important effects upon
the strategy of the campaign. The provision ships were ordered
up-river to Batiscan, over fifty miles above Quebec, where they
would form a safe depot of food and munitions; some, including those carrying the prisoners, went still higher. Thus Quebec
became dependent upon a supply line from the west, the vital
stuff reaching the city either by river boat or overland in carts.
When the British naval activity made the river unsafe, the

latter method had to be used; but with almost all the country's able-bodied men with the army, it was extremely difficult to organize. The decision not to keep any considerable quantity of food in Quebec was based on the view that if the city were lost the army's food supply should not be lost with it. With the food at Batiscan, the army could retire westwards from Quebec and still be fed. The connexion between this idea and French confidence that the British fleet could not operate above the city is obvious. This exposed line of communication was to prove the fatal weakness of the French position.[3]

One measure, it was found, could not be taken. The Traverse could not be blocked; the channel simply turned out to be too wide. The French had held Quebec for a century and a half, and still knew remarkably little about the St Lawrence. The records are full of bitter comments on the incompetence of the French seafarers who had encouraged the authorities to rely on the difficulties of the river navigation to protect the capital. On June 25th, when the British ships were coming steadily through the Traverse, Montcalm noted acidly in a letter to Brigadier Bourlamaque that there was hope of having a good chart of the river 'next year': 'our best seamen or pilots seem to me to be either liars or ignoramuses'. When the year's fighting was over, and Quebec had fallen, Vaudreuil and Bigot reported much the same thing in less extreme terms.[4] It is quite evident that the scientific study of the river channel begins only with the arrival of the British fleet's hydrographers, of whom the famous James Cook was one, in this year 1759.

On June 4th, with the St Charles line now well under way, work began on the forward line along the Beauport shore. The grenadier companies of the five battalions of the *troupes de terre* at Quebec were encamped at Beauport under Bougainville to work on the entrenchments, and within a week several hundred Canadians were also digging there. By the 11th, Montcalm was fairly well pleased with the situation; he wrote to Bourlamaque, 'We now have three bridges across the River St Charles; on Wednesday we shall have three large redoubts and many small works completed between Beauport and the Canardière, defences at the head of our bridges, and entrenchments along the River St Charles.'[5] A great deal had been accomplished in a very short time.

The colony's small military resources had had to be divided. Following the tenor of the orders from France, which were in accordance with Montcalm's conception of giving ground in the less important sectors, whereas Vaudreuil had wished to hold all the territory of New France as long as possible, Bourlamaque, commanding on Lake Champlain, was told to give up Carillon when it was seriously threatened and make a stand farther north, at Isle aux Noix on the Richelieu. But troops had to be found for this delaying action designed to hold Amherst; and Bourlamaque was given three of the eight regular battalions, eight companies of the colonial regulars and some 1,200 militia, over 3,000 men in all.[6] Although Amherst's campaign was slow and ponderous, and gave little direct help to Wolfe, it was vital to his success all the same. Had Montcalm been able to concentrate his whole regular force at Quebec, things might have gone better with him. Nor was the Lake Champlain front the whole story; a detachment had to be found to garrison Fort Niagara, and another to take post at the head of the St Lawrence rapids to cover the approach to Montreal from the direction of Lake Ontario.

Nevertheless, the force assembled to defend Quebec was imposing at least in numbers. Although the plan to incorporate a proportion of militiamen into the units of French and colonial regulars was carried out, it is pretty evident that the other scheme, to call out only the most useful men of the militia companies, was not; almost every able-bodied man in Canada must have been under arms at Quebec when Wolfe arrived. Vaudreuil claimed that the works on the Beauport shore were 'occupied by more than 14,000 men'. Bigot, who was in a position to know, wrote, 'we had 13,000 men, and 1,000 to 1,200 Indians, without counting 2,000 men in garrison in the city'.[7] The *Journal tenu à l'armée* is categorical: the total strength of the army – which presumably means the field army at Beauport as distinct from the city garrison – was, it says, 13,718 combatants. A note appended to this statement, probably written by Vaudreuil, remarks that so large a force had not been expected, but Canadians as old as eighty and as young as twelve or thirteen came forward to offer themselves. Malartic of the Régiment de Béarn copied a return giving a total of 15,685 men, including nearly 1,500 sailors. The lowest figure is given by Montcalm in a letter to Lévis: 10,800 men. This evidently does not include the city garrison, the Indians, or the sailors, who together might amount to about 4,500 more. It seems hardly practicable to establish precisely how many militiamen were on active service in Canada in 1759; but the total on all the fronts cannot have been much less than 15,000. From a population of only some 60,000 this was an extraordinary mobilization. But the most formidable portion of Montcalm's force was the five battalions of French regulars, and these had been weakened by sending detachments to other fronts, including 'picquets' of all five battalions dispatched to Bourlamaque.[8]

What did Wolfe, sailing into the St Lawrence that June, know about the fortress that was his objective? His intelligence was much less full and accurate than has usually been stated.

His Chief Engineer, Major Patrick Mackellar of the Royal Engineers, had been captured at Oswego in 1756 and had been for some time a prisoner at Quebec. He had devoted much effort to collecting information about the defences, and on his release he submitted to the Office of Ordnance in London in July 1757 a report on the place accompanied by a detailed plan. These documents Wolfe had available to him, and so far as we know they were his best intelligence on the fortifications. Doughty calls the report 'an admirable description of the city of Quebec'; and historians in general have accepted this.

The legend-makers have done better. They have even asserted that Wolfe had the Mackellar map in his hand when he got his death-wound. There is a story that Mackellar got his information from a traitorous Canadian, who was thus really responsible for the fall of Quebec; and the splendidly colourful detail is added that this Canadian's name is still safeguarded in a secret file locked in the vaults of the British War Office. Thus the descendants of the betrayer are protected from the obloquy which would presumably descend upon them if their ancestor's treachery were known in French Canada.[9]

The real facts are much less picturesque, as would have been apparent to either the historians or the romancers, if they had only taken the trouble to compare Mackellar's plan with the actual plans of the Quebec defences made by the French engineers before the capture of Quebec or by Mackellar himself and other British engineers afterwards. Mackellar made no special claims to accuracy for his account of the most important part of the defences, those facing the Plains of Abraham. 'The Defences to the Land,' he wrote, 'I can speak of only from the Plan and a Little imperfect Intelligence – The Plan appears to have been taken about the Year 1740, and I have not heard that there have been any Additions to the Fortifications since that Time.' Elsewhere he speaks of 'the Difficulty' the French made of the prisoners seeing the landward defences. These precautions worked. The plan which was the basis of Mackellar's had been published in 1744 in the *History of New France* by Father Charlevoix (Mackellar always calls him 'Charles Voix'). And, as has been noted above, a completely new system of fortifications on the land side of the city was undertaken in 1745. Nothing of the new line appears on Mackellar's map, which was thus fourteen years out of date in 1759. It still shows the untidy dog's-breakfast that had existed in 1744 – the unfinished stone works on Cape Diamond, the earthwork line of 1693, the 'Old Entrenchments' connecting them. It is interesting that even Beaucours' two redoubts of 1712 are missing from it.

Any Frenchman who gave Mackellar this sort of information would deserve, not his countrymen's abuse, but the Cross of St Louis. It was fortunate for Wolfe that the new defences were essentially ineffective and little more formidable than the old ones. Mackellar's general statement, though founded on totally inaccurate information, was still basically sound: 'An attack by Land is the Only Method that promises Success, against the High Town and in all Probability it Could hold out but a very few Days against a Sufficient Force properly Appointed.' When Wolfe found out about the real nature of the land defences does not seem to have been recorded; it is even possible that he never did find out, at least until the last morning of his life. A widely published contemporary map of the siege, Thomas Jefferys' crude but graphic *Authentic Plan of the River St. Laurence . . . with the Operations of the Siege of Quebec . . . down to the 5. Sep^r. 1759*, still shows the defences as known to Charlevoix in 1744 and Mackellar in 1757. (Versions of it are used to illustrate several quite recent books.)

Mackellar did his best, and used his eyes and ears to advantage so far as he was allowed; it was not his fault that he met no such traitorous Canadian as the man of the legend. He reported the French intention of using fire-rafts against an invading fleet; and he also stated that though the navigation of the St Lawrence was tricky, he was 'far from thinking it to be as Difficult, and Dangerous as the French would have the World believe'. His general account of the Quebec region was certainly valuable to Wolfe.

On the basis of such information as he had, Wolfe while still at Louisbourg was making such plans as he could. The letter which he wrote his uncle, Major Walter Wolfe, on May 19th [10] is very interesting. It seems to bear Mackellar's mark:

The town of Quebec is poorly fortified, but the ground round about it is rocky. To invest the place, and cut off all communication with the colony, it will be necessary to encamp with our right to the River St. Lawrence, and our left to the river St. Charles. From the river St. Charles to Beauport the communication must be kept open by strong entrenched posts and redoubts. The enemy can pass that river at low water; and it will be proper to establish ourselves with small entrenched posts from the point of Levi to La Chaudière. It is the business of our naval force to be masters of the river, both above and below the town. If I find that the enemy is strong, audacious, and well commanded, I shall proceed with the utmost caution and circumspection, giving Mr Amherst time to use his superiority. If they are timid, weak, and ignorant, we shall push them with more vivacity, that we may be able before the summer is gone to assist the Commander-in-Chief. I reckon we shall have a smart action at the passage of the river St. Charles, unless we can steal a detachment up the river St. Lawrence, and land them three, four, five miles, or more, above the town, and get time to entrench so strongly that they won't care to attack.

It has been suggested that this indicates that Wolfe already had in mind the final plan he carried out on the night before the Battle of the Plains. Of course, it indicates no such thing; it merely shows that he was considering a wide range of possible courses, of which a landing above Quebec was one. He would not have needed Mackellar's report to make it clear to him that the essential preliminary to capturing the city was attacking it on the weak landward face, the only one lacking natural defence; the problem was how to get there. It is pretty evident that at this time he inclined to the view that the line of attack most likely to succeed was that tried by Phips in 1690 – a landing on the Beauport shore and an advance across the St Charles. Wolfe had not yet had a chance to reconnoitre his objective, and he was wise not to 'make a picture' in his mind until he had done so. We shall see, however, that when he was before Quebec he continued to have extreme difficulty in deciding upon a line of action.

We learn more about Wolfe's ideas from a letter which he wrote to Amherst from mid-Atlantic on March 6th. After complaining of the smallness of his force, and suggesting that it would have been better to send Amherst up the St Lawrence with fifteen or sixteen battalions, he proceeds:

> If, by accident in the River, by the Enemy's resistance, by sickness, or slaughter in the Army, or, from any other cause, we find, that Quebec is not likely to fall into our hands (persevering however to the last moment), I propose to set the Town on fire with Shells, to destroy the Harvest, Houses, & Cattle both above & below, to send off as many Canadians as possible to Europe, & to leave famine and desolation behind me; belle resolution, & tres chrétienne! but we must teach these Scoundrels to make war in a more gentlemanlike manner.

These, we shall see, were not idle threats. Wolfe also suggests that, if Durell gets into the river before the enemy, it may be possible to assist Amherst 'by running up with Sloops &

Schooners as high as the Fort de Chambly' (on the Richelieu); 'here we shall find the very great use of a naval Force of this kind in the river St Lawrence cruising between Quebec & Montreal; and I have no doubt, but these small Vessels, will easily get by Quebec in the night'. Wolfe sees what an important influence a naval force in the river above Quebec can exert; but apparently he has not thought of the possibility of large vessels passing the city, nor does he speak here of a landing on the north shore.[11]

Down on the lower St Lawrence the French officers whom Vaudreuil had sent to watch for the British and direct the movements of the population were encountering trouble. We have the correspondence between the Governor General and Captain de Léry (a son of the Quebec engineer) who was dispatched early in May to take charge in the Kamouraska area of the south shore, from Rivière-Ouelle down to L'Islet du Portage. De Léry was ordered to send the old men, women, children and cattle from this region up to Point Lévis, opposite Quebec; all able-bodied men were to stay with him as militiamen. He was to report the movements of the British ships, oppose all attempts to land, and retire on Quebec with his men only as the fleet moved up.

The *habitants* made difficulties about carrying out this programme. They refused to believe that the English were really coming; they still had their oats to seed; they were unwilling to leave their homes. Some parishes were evacuated in the manner prescribed, but at the end of May Vaudreuil had to change his orders. He now authorized the people to hide themselves in the woods in their own districts. The English were already in the river, and it was too late to carry out the original plan.[12]

As we have said, there were no effective French measures of defence in the lower river. The militia limited themselves to coast-watching and passing information, and occasionally loosing off a few musket-shots when an isolated British boat's-crew offered a target. From the time when Admiral Durell's ships anchored off Barnaby Island on May 20th the British were in touch with the settled regions of Canada; but the first real contact between the opposing forces came only on or about

June 5th at Ile aux Coudres, and then it was more comic than serious. Durell's flagship, the imposing *Princess Amelia*, cast anchor on May 28th 'between the Island of Coudre, and the Main'. The island was found deserted, and next day the British landed troops on it.[13] When news of this reached Quebec, a large party of Canadians and Indians was sent off to try to take a prisoner, presumably for the sake of information. It was no very brilliant operation. The Indians, as so often, turned coy at the critical moment, and the party as a whole did nothing. But a few men of Ile aux Coudres who were members of it decided to have a go on their own; and they picked up three British midshipmen who were skylarking on the island with some of the horses that had been left on it. Two of them were riding on one horse when they were ambushed and dragged off as prisoners to Quebec. One of them is said to have been a grandson (another version says one was a son, one a nephew) of Durell.[14] The Admiral's journal says nothing about the affair; but it does tell us that on May 31st he had sent two midshipmen ashore 'to make Signals on seeing any Ships or Vessels coming up, or going down the River' – and that he issued instructions the following day forbidding soldiers and sailors to presume to 'harrass' the horses on the island. So the young gentlemen were disobeying orders when they met with their misfortune.

Durell, if he had been sluggish earlier, was active now. On June 3rd he ordered Captain William Gordon of HMS *Devonshire*, 66, to take under command the *Centurion, Pembroke* and *Squirrel* and the three transports, 'and proceed with them as far up the River as the Isle of Orleans, and as much higher as he will find it practicable', to destroy the 'fire stages' (rafts) which had been reported, and collect information. Colonel Carleton went with him. Unfavourable winds prevented Gordon from getting away from Coudres until the 8th; but that afternoon he was at the foot of the famous Traverse channel, in sight of the dark commanding height of Cape Tourmente, on which the battery recommended by Montcalm had never been built. Early the following morning the *Devonshire* signalled 'for all boats man'd and arm'd in order to go and sound the channell of the Traverse'. The work continued on the 10th; and on the 11th the *Pembroke*'s Mr Cook 'returned satisfied with being acquainted with ye Channel'. So simple had it been! – and now the way to Quebec lay open. On the 14th Gordon's division sailed up through the Traverse and came to anchor in the far end of it, between Isle Madame and the Isle of Orleans. He had already asked Durell for small vessels to assist his operations; now he told him that he did not think his little military force sufficient to land on Orleans, where it might be struck by greatly superior forces from Quebec.[15]

The 17th of June saw the first real encounter. That well-heeled and ingenious gunner, Le Mercier, had suggested to Vaudreuil that he be allowed to take cannon over to the Isle of Orleans to harass the British ships; and the Governor General agreed (incidentally without consulting Montcalm). Le Mercier's idea was to use red-hot shot; but apparently this was abandoned when it came to light that there was no artilleryman in the colony who knew how to heat shot! On the 17th, as Le Mercier's guns were moving down the island, Gordon ordered boats manned and armed to try to cut out a small French vessel (actually a fire-ship) which had been observed near St Joachim in the channel north of Orleans. But the Indians on the island swarmed out in their canoes; Le Mercier opened fire on the boats – possibly only with musketry; HMS *Porcupine*, which had been ordered to cover them, could not do so for want of wind; and the French captured the *Squirrel*'s cutter with her crew of eight men. It was first blood to the French, and they got quite a bit of information from the *Squirrels*.[16]

Although Montcalm had been very sarcastic about Le Mercier's plan, it did the British some little harm. On the morning of the 18th the *Centurion* observed a battery 'errecting' on shore, and she and other ships opened fire on it; her log remarks a bit ruefully, 'rec$^d$ sev$^l$ shot from d$^o$ which cutt away a bobbstay and the clue of our maintops$^l$'. There was further mutual cannonading next day, and the *Pembroke*'s log seems to indicate that the French fire forced her and the *Centurion* to change position; after which Le Mercier evidently withdrew. No casualties are recorded on either side.[17]

A brief pause ensued. Captain Gordon made no further advance pending the arrival of reinforcements. The French pushed the work of entrenching the Beauport shore as rapidly as bad weather would let them; and on June 21st, as we have already seen, they heard of the arrival of the main force of British ships in the river. If there had been any doubt in their minds of the seriousness of the crisis confronting them, it was now removed.

. Wolfe himself was now approaching his objective. On June 19th the *Neptune* anchored off Bic. The frigate *Richmond*, one of Durell's ships, joined her there and reported on events up the river. Wolfe transferred to the *Richmond* and on the 23rd she was at Coudres. The General went aboard the *Princess Amelia* and asked Admiral Durell to push two more ships with troops up to the Isle of Orleans; Durell immediately ordered the *Alcide* and *Sutherland* thither. Within a few hours the *Richmond* was off again up the river, Durell having ordered her captain 'to proceed with General Wolf up the Traverse, and land him when he shall think proper'. Behind the clipped phrases of the naval records one senses the impatience of the young General to be at grips with his adversary. On this same day the first division of transports arrived at Coudres. On the 25th Admiral Saunders reached Coudres in the *Hind*, shifted his flag to the *Stirling Castle*, 64, and passed up the river.[18]

The great armament, assisted by sounding boats, passed the Traverse with as little trouble as Gordon's ships. The most famous account of the operation is that of Captain John Knox of the 43rd Foot, who tells how Thomas Killick, master of the *Goodwill* transport, refused the services of a captured French pilot and took his ship through himself, making disrespectful ejaculations concerning the alleged dangers of the St Lawrence navigation: 'D— me, if there are not a thousand places in the Thames fifty times more hazardous than this; I am ashamed that Englishmen should make such a rout about it.' On the morning of June 27th, thirty-eight transports were off St Laurent d'Orléans, on the south shore of the big island and six miles from its western end; and there Wolfe proceeded to land himself and his army that day.[19]

Major Mackellar's report had recommended the Isle of Orleans as the best place for an initial landing; and Mackellar was at Wolfe's elbow immediately after the landing as, accompanied by an escort of Light Infantry, he pushed through the woods to the West Point of Orleans. (We owe our knowledge of this excursion to Captains Knox and Bell; Wolfe's own journal – which perhaps, like other journals, was not always written up promptly – does not mention it.) The General's eagerness to see and reconnoitre the famous fortress he had crossed the ocean to assail may be imagined. As they came out on the point, they saw less than four miles away, across the waters of the Basin of Quebec, the city on its legendary rock. They saw more. Much closer to them was the Beauport shore; and there, from the St Charles to the Montmorency, along the whole six-mile front, were camps and batteries and redoubts. During the past few days the French regular battalions had begun to occupy the Beauport positions; and Montcalm himself, with the balance of the force, would be there on the morrow.[20] Now for the first time Wolfe was able to see the full proportions of his problem. Montcalm had anticipated him. The shoreline which he had hoped to seize and fortify had been seized and fortified by his enemy. His ardour had received its first check. He would have to think again.

The French had made no attempt to oppose the landing on the Isle of Orleans, and indeed at once withdrew such forces as they still had there. But it seemed to them that the time had now come to use their fire-ships against the British vessels in the channel south of the Isle; and on the night of the 28th the whole flotilla of seven – the eighth had burned prematurely three weeks before, nearly causing a disaster in the harbour – ran down the river. The operation was a spectacular fiasco. The French evidence as to precisely what happened is contradictory; but it appears that the ships were fired too soon. The most westerly British ships hastily weighed (the *Centurion* had to cut her cable) and ran for it, firing guns to warn the shipping below; and the boats of the fleet rowed out, grappled the burning menaces and coolly towed them clear. The useless enterprise, the author of the *Journal tenu à l'armée* tartly recorded,

had cost the French King a million *livres*. The sight and sound
of the blazing ships coming down the channel with their
shotted guns exploding had frightened some of Wolfe's outposts on the island and caused a general alarm; this was all
Louis XV got for his million.[21]

In his letter to his uncle Wolfe had forecast establishing himself on the south shore from Point Lévis westwards. This was
the first positive action he took after the landing on the Isle of
Orleans; and although he wrote in his journal under the date
June 27th, 'determind to land at Levy & below the Falls of
Montmorency', it was taken on the recommendation of Admiral Saunders, who sent Captain Wheelock to Wolfe with the
suggestion on June 29th. Saunders presumably feared the possibility of the French placing a battery on Point Lévis and making the Basin impossible as an anchorage. Wolfe now acted
speedily; some light troops landed in the Beaumont area the
same night, followed next morning by Monckton's brigade of
four battalions. There was some opposition from the Canadian
militia under our friend Captain de Léry, who in accordance
with his orders had moved up the river as the fleet advanced
and was now the senior officer in this sector. Some Indians
crossed from the north shore to help him.[22]

This operation might have produced a serious engagement.
As we have seen, Montcalm, speaking with the lips of Bougainville, had recommended fortifying Point Lévis, but nothing had
been done. Now, on June 30th, he rode in to Quebec and urged
Vaudreuil to send a strong detachment over to the Point before
the British could establish themselves there. According to one
of the French diarists, the author of the *Journal du Siège de
Quebec*, who was usually well informed about events in official
circles in the city, the Governor favoured the plan, because
Point Lévis was a woodland region where his beloved Canadians and Indians could use their bush-fighting tactics to
advantage. But a peculiar event prevented action. A prisoner
had been taken in the Lévis fighting; and he declared that the
landing there was a mere feint, that the British were going to
deliver their real attack that night, against the positions between Beauport and the St Charles. The projected operation

against Point Lévis was cancelled; Montcalm came galloping back to the camp, and dispositions were made to meet the attack. Vaudreuil and Bigot, who had apparently intended to take up residence in the camp that day anyway, duly appeared and, according to Montcalm's acidulous diarist, 'stayed in their quarters ready to mount their horses and escape'. All night the French stood to their arms, but no attack came. At dawn the troops were dismissed, only to be aroused again by a false alarm which caused the Canadians on the right of the line to deliver a tremendous musketry fire at nothing at all, which aroused both the city and the British camp on the island.[23]

On July 1st the whole thing, it seems, happened over again. Again the plan was made to send troops to Point Lévis; but the *Journal du Siège* says that Vaudreuil took it into his head to return to Quebec and interrogate the prisoner again; and the man declared that the attack must have been postponed, but would certainly be made that night. So the French operation was cancelled a second time, and a second time the troops spent the night manning their entrenchments awaiting an assault which did not take place. By this time Monckton's brigade, after considerable skirmishing with the Canadians and Indians, had moved west and was approaching the heights opposite the city; and Carleton had occupied the West Point of Orleans on the 29th and begun fortifying it.[24] Saunders' ships could now lie in the Basin with less apprehension of coming under bombardment from the land.

Montcalm apparently still desired to undertake an enterprise against the British on the south shore. His diarist (probably at this point Lieut Marcel, his ADC) wrote as follows on July 2nd: 'After dinner M. le Marquis de Montcalm called me into his office, where he dictated to me a memoir concerning the Point Lévis expedition. He gave it immediately to M. le Marquis de Vaudreuil. This proposal, presented in all its details and from all points of view, was not accepted.' The memoir has not survived, and this is all we know about the incident. It is at least interesting as suggesting that the Court's instructions to Vaudreuil to defer to Montcalm in operational matters had not had much effect. The next day, according to the same source, Montcalm, who apparently had never become fully reconciled to Lévis' leftward extension of his Beauport line, proposed to strip the left of troops, leaving the tents standing, form a reserve, 'and thereby shorten our enormously extended line of defence'. Again 'the generalissimo's irresolution', says Marcel, prevented action; and since Wolfe landed close to the French left at Montmorency Falls only some four days later, it cannot be said that this was unfortunate for the French.

Wolfe on his side was struggling with his problem as actively as his wretched health would let him. (On July 2nd he wrote in his diary, 'Bladder painful. A good deal racked — Studied Plans'.) On the 1st he had visited Monckton and evidently been displeased both with his dispositions and with the fact that the French gunboats were firing on his positions without being effectively interfered with by the navy. On this 2nd, we learn from Captain Bell, Wolfe himself went again to Point Lévis and marched west with a detachment until directly opposite Quebec. He reconnoitred the city from across the river, and himself wrote that the place was 'weak to excess in the Lower Town & an appearance of great Want. — Easy bombardment of the Place from P$^t$. aux Peres.' On the spot he ordered the construction of batteries.[25]

On July 3rd Wolfe consulted with Saunders. From the naval point of view a vital feature of the situation was the 'Beauport Bank', a wide expanse of shallows in front of the French positions which made it impossible for the fleet to close in to bombardment range. Wolfe's journal sums up the discussions:

> Our notions agreeing to get ashore if possible above the Town we determind to attempt it. Troops & Ships prepard accordingly. Admiral was of opinion that none of the Ships c$^d$. be of the least use in an attempt on the Beauport side. Resolution to begin by a warm bombardment from P$^t$. aux Peres.

The following day the journal noted, 'B$^r$. Townshends Brigade orderd to be in readiness to land below the Falls of Montmorency to draw the Enemys attention that way & favour the projected attempt. . . . S$^t$ Leger, Goreham & 270 men detachd by B$^r$. Murray to reconnoitre the Chaudière, St Michel, Anse de Meres &c. – Sad attack of dysentery.'

A plan of sorts was taking shape. It involved a triple, indeed quadruple, division of Wolfe's relatively small force. The main effort was to be above the town (the Anse des Mères was only a few hundred yards above Cape Diamond, St Michel, some two and a half miles farther west). Batteries which, of necessity, needed a covering force, were being constructed on the Pointe aux Pères section of Point Lévis to bombard the city. The store depot and hospital which Wolfe had established on the Isle of Orleans also required protection. And one brigade – about one-third of the army's fighting strength – was to land below Montmorency Falls to attract the enemy's attention and prepare the way for the enterprise on the other flank. On July 5th Wolfe noted in his journal, 'B$^r$ Murray's Report. He is satisfied w$^{th}$ the practicability of the attempt at Michel.' It seems evident that St Michel (a short distance above the spot where the famous landing was made the night before the Battle of the Plains more than two months later) was the place where Wolfe proposed to land above the city. A letter written by Murray fifteen years later says that the intention at this time was to land 'by means of the Redans' – presumably *radeaux* or rafts.$^{26}$

This plan can be understood in terms of the letter to Major Wolfe written a month and a half before; it was the scheme of 'stealing a detachment' up above the town and entrenching. It must be said that it was a thoroughly bad plan, with its extreme dispersion of the British force and the very serious risk of defeat in detail which this entailed. (It is quite different from the plan finally adopted in September, when Wolfe landed virtually the whole disposable fighting strength of his army above the city.) And Wolfe entertained it only for a few days. His journal does not tell us when he abandoned it, but it had probably gone by the board by July 10th; for on that day – the day after Townshend's brigade landed below Montmorency Falls – Murray with two of his battalions joined Townshend there. It was Murray's brigade that would have had to carry out the St Michel landing. It is pretty evident that, for the moment at least, the Montmorency feint had now been converted in Wolfe's mind into the main operation.

Why was the St Michel scheme given up? Wolfe in his dispatch to Pitt gives two reasons which, however, probably refer mainly to the revised version of the plan later in the month. First, the French had reinforced the St Michel area; he saw, he says, 'that the enemy were jealous of the design, were preparing against it, and had actually brought artillery and a mortar (which, being so near to Quebec, they could increase as they pleased) to play on the shipping . . .' It was natural enough, with the English well established opposite the town, that the French should begin to worry about their weak up-river flank. Vaudreuil says he feared a landing in the area of the Anse des Mères, Foulon, St Michel and Sillery, and therefore on the 3rd set up a camp of Canadians and Indians there.[27] The *Journal du Siège* adds some details: 'To guard against this, 300 Canadians were sent to encamp at the Anse des Meres, with a quantity of Tents sufficient for a much larger body of Troops, in the hope of deceiving the English, and making them believe the detachment to be much more numerous than it was in reality.' This ruse may perhaps have worked.

The other objection mentioned by Wolfe is the fundamental one. 'But what I feared most was, that if we should have landed between the town and the river of Cap Rouge the body first landed could not be reinforced before they were attacked by the enemy's whole army.' It seems highly probable that Wolfe called the scheme off simply because on further reflection he decided that it was likely to prove disastrous.

He called it off even before it was really practicable to put it into action. He had agreed with the Admiral that a brisk bombardment from Pointe aux Pères was the first step, presumably to assist part of the fleet in passing the city; and the guns were not yet ready to open fire. Nor was the navy by any means in full control of the area of the Basin of Quebec. At this moment, indeed, Wolfe seems to have been thoroughly disgusted with his naval colleagues.

This campaign has traditionally been represented as the supreme example of harmony and effective cooperation between the Services. In the end the cooperation was very effective; but in the light of Wolfe's journal the traditional view needs some amendment. The journal contains a succession of querulous comments on the activities of the navy. Thus on June 19th in the river Wolfe complains of 'The Admiral running all the great Ships of War in amongst the Divisions of the Transports threatening some danger & a good deal of Disorder, as the Wind blew fresh.' On the 25th he tells of asking Captain Gordon for a 'Vanguard of Men of War to go before & secure the Transports', and of Gordon's decision to send the *Pembroke*, *Centurion* and *Porcupine*. He proceeds: 'Cap$^t$. M—ll's ideas on that subject nearly drove me into expressing my mind with some Freedom. Carleton's great good sense & management averted this.' 'Capt. M—ll' was Captain Mantell of the *Centurion*. There is something agreeable about Wolfe's frank avowal of being at fault here; but the passage does not suggest a good cooperator. Incidentally, Captain Bell made radical cuts in it when making his own transcription of the journal. On the 27th Wolfe speaks of the sudden fierce gale that came up after the landing on the Isle of Orleans and remarks, 'Multitude of Boats Lost & strange neglect of the Men of Wars crews'. (Montcalm's journal on this occasion was kinder to the Royal Navy: 'It is quite probable that in parallel circumstances a French fleet would have perished.')

Early in July Wolfe and his aide-de-camp are both criticizing the navy in their journals with considerable bitterness. Wolfe particularly complains of the ships' unwillingness to come to close quarters with the French batteries and gunboats. On the 6th he writes, 'Our Frigates & Bomb vessels moving from this Station – The Enemy permitted to insult us w$^{th}$. their paltry boats carrying Cannon in their prows—'; and again on the 8th, 'Disposition of the Frigates & Bomb Ketches – their prodigious distance from the Enemy – Amazing backwardness in these matters on the side of the Fleet . . .' (The General, to put it bluntly, is accusing the Royal Navy of being gun-shy.) Captain Bell makes similar remarks on the 6th and 7th, and on the 11th he writes, 'our fleet all retired within the P$^t$ of Orleans for fear of Bombs, the Passage from Montmorency to Levy for Boats

very dangerous, the floating Batteries still reigning triumph-
ant'. At this stage of affairs the French were getting large
dividends from their gunboats, which evidently were boldly
handled; the credit for this is doubtless due to Jean Vauquelin,
captain of one of the frigates, who had been appointed 'Commandant of the Road'. It is quite probable that the naval
situation influenced Wolfe's decision to cancel the St Michel
enterprise, which obviously would be risky as long as the fleet's
control of the waters about Quebec was so doubtful.

It is a pity that Admiral Saunders apparently kept no journal, and that his letters that have survived are few and uninformative; it would be interesting to have his side of the story.
But we have Admiral Durell's journal, and it helps considerably. We know from it that the squadron of Rear-Admiral
Charles Holmes, the admiral third in command, reached Ile
aux Coudres on June 27th; that next day Durell ordered
Holmes, in accordance with instructions from Saunders, to
take four ships up the river to join Saunders before Quebec;
and that Holmes unmoored on the 29th, but, evidently because
of contrary winds, could not get away until July 3rd. The journal also tells us that on July 9th Durell received orders from
Saunders, then off Point Lévis in the *Stirling Castle*, to come
up to Isle Madame himself with all his ships except two. He
too was evidently delayed by waiting for a wind, and did not
sail until the 17th. On July 20th he anchored between the Isle
of Orleans and Isle Madame – where his ships remained until
the campaign was over – and the same day sent up to Saunders
in four transports 100 men from the crew of each ship of the
line present, with firelocks, cutlasses and ammunition, and two
boats from each ship. The great *Neptune*, which had waited at
Coudres for a special pilot, arrived at Isle Madame on August
4th.[28] The picture one gets is that of a steady stream of the
elements of naval power moving up the river as the wind
serves, until in due time Saunders has so much strength in the
Quebec area that the French are no longer able to challenge
him.

It is evident that Saunders, as the situation became increasingly plain, was prepared to support Wolfe to the limit of his

strength, and did so. It may be that at certain points he could have acted somewhat more promptly, but there seems no sound basis for any important criticism of his action. Judging Wolfe by his own journal, it is clear that the impatient, sickly and captious young General was a difficult colleague, but Saunders shows no sign of having been influenced by such considerations. He had been sent to Canada to help the army take Quebec, and he carried out his mission.

# CHAPTER FOUR

## July: Montmorency

Somewhat after midnight on the night of July 8th/9th, Wolfe with the grenadiers of the army landed on the north shore of the St Lawrence about three-quarters of a mile below Montmorency Falls. Later that night Townshend's brigade joined him. There was no opposition.[1] On the 10th, as we have already seen, Murray with a great part of his brigade also moved to Montmorency. The main forces of the two opposing armies then faced each other at close range across the Montmorency River.

Wolfe had now adopted what may be called his third plan. The first was the basic scheme to land on the Beauport shore, which had been frustrated by the French getting there first; the second was the idea of landing a strong detachment to entrench above the town, which he abandoned from the fear of its being attacked by the French main force and perhaps also because of the naval situation. (These two had been foreshadowed in the letter to his uncle written in May.) The third may be called a variant of the first. Since the Beauport shore was inaccessible, Wolfe landed as close to it as possible. He now faced the task of evicting the French from the Beauport position to enable him to force the line of the St Charles and reach the weak side of Quebec.

For weeks to come he wrestled with this problem. What was the best approach to Montcalm's position? An attack across the Montmorency – a not inconsiderable obstacle – at one or more of the few points where it could be forded? A frontal waterborne assault from the Basin? Or a combination of the two? Concurrently he again considered from time to time an enterprise above the city (this becoming more and more practicable as the navy established firmer control) and a direct amphibious attack on the Lower Town of Quebec. It is not possible to reconstruct the course of his thinking with certainty. His journal is brief and tantalizing; and the authentic information found in other documents is fragmentary. The most helpful are the neglected letters of Wolfe to Monckton.[2] It is often necessary to fill the gaps in the records with conjectures.

Montcalm too had his problems. Should he attack Wolfe in his new Montmorency position, or should he stand strictly on the defensive and wait to be attacked? On July 9th he wrote Lévis a long letter which noted four possible courses of action.[3] If he and Lévis were in agreement, he said, he would be able to get Vaudreuil to concur. The four courses were, firstly, a limited offensive with the force at hand; secondly, to hold their ground, reinforce Lévis slightly and fight the British when they sought to advance across the Montmorency; thirdly, line the Montmorency with troops, leaving only 3,000 men between Beauport and the St Charles (which might, however, permit the British to re-embark and make a landing at that point); and, fourthly, reinforce the left strongly and secretly, make a night crossing of the three Montmorency fords and fall upon the enemy in a surprise attack at dawn. Apparently the decision was for the cautious policy. Vaudreuil, we read in the *Journal tenu à l'armée*, assembled a council of war the same day. Montcalm recommended standing on the defensive; the only voice raised for an attack on Wolfe's position was that of the Intendant Bigot, unless Montcalm's journal[4] is right in saying that Vaudreuil also favoured the bold course. Caution prevailed. Operations against the camp at Montmorency were limited to harassing attacks on the outposts by the Indians.

In the midst of his uncertainties and frustrations, there was one thing Wolfe could do to hit and hurt the French; he could press forward the project of bombarding Quebec from the heights of Lévis. And as the work on the batteries proceeded the people of the city very naturally took alarm. On July 11th the principal merchants and tradesmen presented a petition to Vaudreuil[5] offering to serve in an expedition to seize the batteries and destroy the British force on Point Lévis. Precisely what happened next is uncertain. Montcalm's journal tells us little, but Vaudreuil reported that after objecting strongly to the scheme in the first instance the general proceeded to organize a detachment of 1,600 men to carry it out.[6] The force was queerly composed: says the *Journal tenu à l'armée*, 'people of all sorts down to ordinary schoolboys offered their services in crowds'. The schoolboys presumably included the platoon of youngsters from the Jesuits' College whom some wag had labelled the Royal Syntax.[7] A group of volunteers from the French regular battalions and a body of Indians were included. The command was given to Jean-Daniel Dumas, *aide-major-général* (adjutant-general) of the colonial regulars, a celebrated forest fighter who had taken the leading part in the defeat of Braddock, and who had apparently asked to be allowed to have a go at the batteries. According to the parish priest of Quebec, Dumas, urged by the townsmen, obtained the consent of 'the generals' (Vaudreuil and Montcalm) to the enterprise after they had first rejected it.[8]

The force left Quebec on the night of July 11th/12th, but not until the following night was it able to cross the river, some distance above the city. This was Quebec's own particular attempt to strike a blow in her own defence against the enemy that threatened to destroy her, and 'the people all flocked to the heights to see the embarkation'.[9] In spite of this no information reached the British, and the force slipped across to the south shore in the darkness without being seen.

In a military sense the enterprise could hardly have been crazier. It was defended on the ground that the plan was to take up a wooded position commanding the battery and make it untenable by musketry fire, and that for this purpose the militia, all at least theoretically good shots, were well suited.[10] But the scheme involved a night move across broken country in the face of a formidable enemy, and the only people for such an operation were well-trained regulars or experienced bush fighters; schoolboys and tradesmen had no place in such a business, as soon appeared. As the amateur soldiers moved towards their objective they fell into disorder and panic, taking their own men for the British. 'Three times M. Dumas contrived to rally his people, and three times his soldiers, mutually mistaking one another for enemies, fired at their own men and went tumbling over one another down the hill to get back to the canoes.' [11] Only the Indians, who had formed the advanced guard, operated with any efficiency; and when they returned to report that the enemy was quiet and unsuspecting they found the situation among the palefaces beyond recovery. Early in the morning the whole force – with the exception of one or two men who had been killed by French bullets – was back on the north shore. The British knew nothing, or virtually nothing, of what had happened until five days later, when a deserter told the story and Wolfe set it down in his journal.

This bizarre and humiliating incident must have confirmed Montcalm's fear that a large part of his army was quite useless except for holding prepared positions; and he never attempted an offensive movement again until that last desperate morning on the Plains of Abraham. That he allowed Dumas' operation to take place at all, in the form in which it was tried, is a serious reflection on his generalship.

About nine o'clock on that same night of July 12th/13th, while Dumas' men were striving to make their way towards it, the battery that was their objective opened fire on Quebec. It consisted of six 32-pounder guns and five 13-inch mortars, and the French observed that the mortars' bombs were directed against the Upper Town, and particularly those parts where the buildings were largest and the houses most numerous, 'which shewed', says the *Journal du Siège de Québec*, 'that it was not so much their object to dismount the Batteries, as it was to frighten the people, and make them abandon the Town'. The diarist continues, 'The people all fled from their Homes and sought for refuge upon the Ramparts, on the side next to the Country. When day appeared, and the Gate was opened, Women & Children were seen flying in crowds along the fields;

and the damage done to the Town during the first night was very considerable.' He tells us that nearly 300 bombs were fired into the city between the time the battery opened and noon the next day, without a single person being wounded: 'a proof of the Houses in Quebec being deserted by the Inhabitants'. He also gives unconscious support to Wolfe's strictures upon the fleet by recording that a bomb vessel fired on the town ineffectively; the bombs fell short, and the craft did not dare 'to approach any nearer'.

A memorandum by the engineer Pontleroy dated January 16th, 1759, indicates that he calculated that bombardment from the Lévis heights could reach only the Lower Town.[12] The first night's firing proved how fatally mistaken this idea was. One of the buildings struck more than once was the Ursuline Convent, in the centre of the Upper Town. The poor nuns passed the night 'before the Blessed Sacrament, in such terrors as may be imagined';[13] and the next morning their Superior led them out to the safety of the General Hospital, on the St Charles, north-west of the city. A little group of volunteers remained behind to do what could be done to safeguard the convent buildings. No doubt they did the job which in London in 1941 was known as 'fire-watching'; and they evidently did it well, for the venerable convent, though sadly battered by shot and shell, was not burned, survived the siege, and stands today.

Wolfe continued to build up artillery strength on Point Lévis to smite the devoted town. Another battery of four sea mortars, brought ashore from the fleet (Wolfe wrote acidly to Monckton, 'they will be better upon the shoar than afloat – for the reasons that are very obvious'),[14] opened fire on July 20th, and new gun batteries on July 28th and August 28th. All told, twenty-nine pieces bombarded Quebec from this position.[15] They did enormous damage, chiefly through the use of 'carcasses' or incendiary projectiles. The first serious conflagration seems to have been on July 16th; then on the night of the 22nd/23rd 'all the centre' of the Upper Town was burned out, and Quebec lost its Cathedral. The worst fire of all was on the night of August 8th/9th in the Lower Town, when 152 houses were reduced to ashes and the Church of Notre Dame des Victoires was destroyed – a gloomy portent. 'In consequence of this last dreadful fire, and the two preceding ones in the Upper Town, above 180 houses had been burnt to the ground which was more than one half of the town, in the best quarter of it, and the finest Houses in Quebec.' [16]

To all this bombardment the French, though there were plenty of guns emplaced in Quebec, could make only a limited reply. The silence of the city batteries caused murmuring among the people, but there was too little powder in the magazines to permit of firing except when there was special reason for it.[17]

The bombardment of the city is an unpleasant part of the story of the campaign. Quebec was a fortified place, and it can scarcely be argued that bombarding it was a breach of the 'laws of war'; although it seems pretty evident that the fire was not directed exclusively, or even mainly, at 'military objectives'. Wolfe's motives in the matter are illuminated by his letter to Amherst written on March 6th. Two sound military reasons may have entered into his calculations. One was the desirability of mastering the fire of the town batteries in order to give Saunders' fleet more freedom of action and in particular to enable it to pass above the town; we have seen this referred to in the consultation with the Admiral on July 3rd. The other was concerned with preparing the way for a water-borne assault on the Lower Town, a possibility which was certainly seriously considered. But both these objects would have been best served by fire directed at the batteries. Wolfe had told Amherst that if he were frustrated before Quebec he would do as much damage to the city and the countryside as he could. Frustrated, so far, he certainly had been, and the city was now paying for the frustration; the countryside's turn would come. It seems likely that, as the French diarist suggested, his prime target was the people of Quebec. The twentieth century can scarcely afford to throw stones at him; for his policy may be said to prefigure, in little, the area bombing policy of the RAF Bomber Command, applied against German cities in 1941–5.

*

While the bombardment proceeded, Wolfe cudgelled his brains for a solution to his strategic problem. We must try to reconstruct the succession of expedients which he considered before attempting his attack on the Beauport lines on July 31st.

First of all, he assembled a powerful artillery on the dominant high ground in his Montmorency position. He was superior to the French in this arm, and wisely proposed to make the most of it. On July 12th he was writing to Monckton of his need for four 24-pounders 'immediately after the 12 Pounders are ashoar'. 'We shall establish,' he said, 'such a tremendous fire, that no human head can venture to peep up near it; by this little addition of trouble, I save men, & make things as I apprehend, safe, & secure.' (On the 18th Bell's journal lists fifty pieces of artillery that are ashore at Montmorency.) Wolfe asked for speed in the construction of rafts and floating batteries; 'our works here [at Montmorency] once finish'd, our Artillery ready, & the Radeaux &c made; Wind & Tide permitting we will attack them.' The General recorded in his journal on the 12th that the Admiral was displeased with him 'for speaking harshly' about irregularities committed by the seamen; so next day he visited Saunders 'to adjust matters with him & prepare to attack the French Army'. On July 15th and 16th he ordered the grenadiers of the army into the Isle of Orleans, 'where a Corps is to assemble for a particular Purpose'. On the 16th he had another conference with the Admiral 'concerning the projected Descent'.[18]

What was to be the nature of this descent, the means of implementing the Montmorency landing which we have termed Wolfe's third plan? Luckily a letter to Monckton at Point Lévis on the 16th provides the information:

> . . . If the Rafts are found to answer, they will carry your attack directly across the River, opposite to the right of the Enemy's encampment – But if the Rafts are defective, we must make the best shift we can, w$^h$. the long Boats of the Fleet. I only wait the naval preparations – every thing is ready on our side; and I flatter myself, that the prodigious fire from hence will make the enterprise easy. There is a woody Gully upon the Right of the French Camp; The Highland Reg$^t$. might penetrate there & to the left of

it & gain their Flank: the Redoubt must be vigorously attack'd, & kept, it is out of Musquet shot from their lines, & cou'd not either be supported by them, or retaken *when* in our possession. The Corps of Troops encamped above Beauport, will probably move towards the upper attack, or if they do not, the road is open to us, & we shall fall upon them behind . . .

Wolfe urged Monckton to reconnoitre with all possible care the ground on which he was to land.

It is evident that the Beauport lines were to be attacked at two widely separated points. Monckton's brigade from Lévis was to be ferried across and make a landing on the French right, between Beauport and the St Charles. On the French left the fire of Wolfe's great battery east of the Montmorency would prepare the way. Wolfe's eye had fallen on one of the French redoubts, the second from the Montmorency (the French defences are very clearly defined on the great map subsequently made by the British engineers under Major Mackellar's direction). This redoubt stood close to high-water mark at a considerable distance from the high ground in rear which the French had lined with their entrenchments. It is likely that Wolfe's plan at this moment was the same as that which he described at a later phase: to seize the redoubt in the hope that Montcalm would come out of the entrenchments and attack it, giving the British a chance to inflict heavy losses upon him in the open. Precisely how the attack here was to be conducted is not clear, but again it is likely that the plan was the same as that actually followed later, on July 31st: a landing in front of the redoubt supported by an advance of the British main body across the Montmorency from their camp by way of the ford below the falls. The landing at the redoubt may have been the 'particular Purpose' for which the grenadiers were concentrated in the Isle of Orleans. A different interpretation might be suggested by an undated note, evidently from Wolfe to Monckton, and probably of July 16th, which says, 'Your four companies of Grenadiers are gone into the Isle of Orleans, in readyness to embark, & join you upon the first order.' Perhaps, however, Monckton's grenadiers were intended to lead his attack on the French right, while the rest headed the assault on the redoubt.

By July 20th Wolfe had abandoned this plan, which he had been writing about so enthusiastically on the 16th. The reason was that the navy had now got ships past Quebec. In these circumstances a landing above the city was a more practicable proposition, and Wolfe immediately reverted to this idea. The original intention had been to have the ships pass the town on the night of July 16th/17th. Wolfe wrote in his journal under date of the 16th, 'The Wind fair, night seemingly favourable to their wish, but yet Capt Rous did not go there.' The log of Captain John Rous' ship, the *Sutherland*, 50, tells why: 'at ½ past 10 tho' we had a fine Wind the Pilot thought it not proper to weigh'. But on the night of the 18th/19th the *Sutherland*, accompanied by the frigates *Diana* and *Squirrel*, two armed sloops and two transports, had better luck. All except the *Diana*, as Wolfe wrote, 'passed the narrow passages between Quebeck & Levy without losing a man'. The city batteries fired furiously, but the *Sutherland*'s log records that their shot 'went over us, except one which struck our wall ab$^t$ a foot from the water'. The episode leaves one with a rather strong impression of the inefficiency of the French artillerists. The *Diana* had the bad luck to have one of the sloops foul her, and ran aground on the south shore opposite the town. The *Pembroke* and *Richmond* and numerous boats came to her aid, and she hove twenty-five of her guns overboard to lighten her, but she did not get off until the 20th. She was just out of range of the town batteries but was harassed for a time by five 'floating batteries'.[19]

Wolfe's attention was immediately diverted to the new opportunity. There is no letter to Monckton cancelling the Beauport attack, but the General, we know from Bell's journal, was at Point Lévis on the 19th, and he doubtless informed the brigadier verbally on this or an earlier occasion. On this day Wolfe wrote in his own journal, 'Reconnoitred the country immediately above Quebeck & found that if we had ventured the Stroke that was first intended we should probably ['infallibly' deleted] have succeeded.' This is clear evidence that the earlier St Michel enterprise had definitely been abandoned. It was now to be revived. On the 20th Wolfe went up to the Chaudière with a strong detachment and reconnoitred that area, and Sillery and Cap Rouge across the St Lawrence. Bell recorded, 'General chearful'. Historians, unacquainted with Wolfe's letters to Monckton, have not described this day's significant events. Early in the morning, evidently, Wolfe sent Monckton a detailed letter of instructions, written in such haste that he dated it *May* 20th by mistake:

> You will be pleas'd to embark, a part of your Brigade in 16, or more flat-bottomed Boats; & row along the South Shoar, until you perceive 3 Lanthorns, hanging a breast, upon that side of the Sutherland which is opposite to that shoar; I shall have these People ready to push ashoar, just as your Boats come up, to attack the Houses, & such Posts as the Enemy has thought proper to take. It is of consequence that we get to a rising ground over the Village; where the road leading to Quebec runs; & where we must begin an abbatis, with the utmost expedition; it is woody, & a little steep – for which reason – it may not be amiss to bring one or two Companies of light Infantry, with you – to attach themselves to this single point. Hatchets, bill-Hooks, & Axes, will be our principal instruments of defence, at first – till by Dint of Artillery, we can extend ourselves . . . the six field Peices, must be forwarded, by the Marines, or Sea-men, along the upper road, so as to be ready to fall down upon the shoar, when the Water rises again. If you cou'd be here, a little before the high Water, we should have time to fetch another load of Troops, before, the Tide ebbs . . .
>
> If we can take four or five good Posts; & keep 'em till our friends arrive, it may bring on a very decisive affair.

This may be called Wolfe's fourth plan; it was essentially a reversion to his second one. It is the old idea of seizing a lodgement above the town with a detachment and entrenching; 'till our friends arrive' presumably indicates that Wolfe intended to bring up troops from the camp at Montmorency. Saunders hastily sent boats there to bring howitzers and mortars, and announced that he would soon be sending for cannon. And nine companies of grenadiers from Montmorency were moved into the Isle of Orleans ready for action.[20] What was 'the Village'? It was almost certainly St Michel, which was close to Sillery, had been the objective of the earlier plan, and fits Wolfe's description. In his later letter to Pitt he says he 'thought once of attempting' a landing at 'St. Michael's'. He was likely thinking of his second scheme. The letter would probably have been more accurate if it had said that he thought *twice* of St Michel.

This fourth plan, developed in such hopeful detail on the 20th, was postponed the same day and later abandoned. At '1 o'Clock' (presumably PM) Wolfe wrote again to Monckton:

> Particular circumstances make it necessary to delay our attempt for a few days, & to keep it Secret. In the mean while we shall make all the diversion we possibly can. It will be in my power to receive, Dalling's light Infantry into the Squadron previous to our attack. You will countermand the embarkation & the march for a day or two ...

The 'particular circumstances' are a matter of conjecture, but they were probably action taken by the French, to whom the appearance of the *Sutherland* and her consorts above Quebec was a most alarming portent. As we have seen, they had complacently assumed that no major ship of war could pass the town. Montcalm's diarist now wrote, 'If the enemy takes the course of going up the river and is able to land at some point, he cuts off all communication with our food supplies and our munitions of war.' The British ships having anchored in the vicinity of the Anse des Mères, Dumas was sent there with 600 men plus some Indians; more (including a unit of 200 cavalrymen which Montcalm had organized in May) followed shortly; and Le Mercier hastened to the threatened point with two 18-pounders and a mortar. It was at this moment, apparently, that the 'Samos battery' was erected below Sillery. Le Mercier 'claimed', says the Montcalm diary, to have made it hot for one of the ships. So he had; the *Squirrel* set down in her log that in the early hours of the 20th 'the French began fireing from a gun and bomb battery w^ch they erected on the hill and haled us and stranded our main stay and wounded our main mast'. At eight o'clock the ship heaved her anchor 'and tow'd up the river'. All this probably explains Wolfe's change of mind; we have already seen his explanation offered to Pitt, that the French were ready for him and that he feared they would attack his detachment with their main army before he could support it. This may apply to this project, to the one earlier in July, or to both.

Wolfe seems to have been rather easily discouraged. There were other places besides St Michel where landing was possible above Quebec, and with the mobility conferred upon him by the fleet he could have gone in where Le Mercier's guns were *not*; indeed, he could well have taken a chance and defied them – as he ultimately did nearly two months later. Laden now with the responsibilities of high command, he seems to have forgotten the doctrine he had propounded after Rochefort, 'that nothing is to be reckoned an obstacle to your undertaking which is not found really so upon trial'. By rejecting the plan which he had embraced so enthusiastically only a few hours before, he certainly created a painful impression in the minds of his brigadiers. 'Indecision and hesitation,' Lord Montgomery has written, 'are fatal in any officer; in a C-in-C they are criminal.' When a general begins to display a semblance of these qualities, his subordinates' confidence in him rapidly wanes.

After changing his plan on the 20th, Wolfe sent a force under Carleton up the river, 'for intelligence' as he wrote in his journal (which incidentally mentions neither the plan nor the postponement). Carleton made a landing at Pointe-aux-Trembles, some twenty miles above Quebec, on the 21st, had a skirmish with some Indians, and dropped back down the river the same day with a large group of civilian prisoners. They included a number of women and a priest, who were sent over to Quebec under a flag of truce on the 22nd, the ladies full of praise for the treatment they had had. Some of them had dined with Wolfe, 'who jested a great deal about our generals' circumspection'. Another event of July 21st boded ill for the French in the long run. Rear-Admiral Holmes went up above

Quebec by land with an escort, and hoisted his flag in the *Sutherland*.[21]

Wolfe does not seem to have wholly abandoned the St Michel scheme for some days. On July 23rd, Wolfe's journal tells us, Admiral Saunders and the generals consulted: 'Resolution to attack the French Army. Debate about the method.' (One would give a good deal for a record of that debate.) As late as the 25th Wolfe was writing to Monckton, evidently from Montmorency, to send marines over to him the next morning to 'mask our real intentions' – possibly the plan to land above the city. 'This, & other Steps, I shall take, will sufficiently alarm them, on this side.' But the same evening his journal records that he ordered a 'Corps of Troops' to escort him 'to view the Ford of Montmorenci'. It seems likely that the St Michel plan had now been set aside. The General's restless mind had turned back to the French left flank.

On July 26th he made his reconnaissance up the Montmorency, to the ford some three miles above the camp, escorted by two battalions, one of which was Howe's Light Infantry, lately brought over from the Isle of Orleans. The movement brought on a fierce skirmish. Captain Bell wrote, 'Mem: I got my arm broke by the Rascals. We had about 45 killed & wounded.' The General told Monckton, 'They have a very practicable ford, a part of their Army entrenched, & encamped there.' His later dispatch to Pitt told a story of frustration: 'In reconnoitring the river Montmorenci, we found it fordable at a place about three miles up; but the opposite bank was entrenched, and so steep and so woody, that it was to no purpose to attempt a passage there.' Wherever Wolfe turned he seemed to meet a blank wall; and he had so far found it impossible to come to a firm decision and maintain it.

It is evident that still another possibility was being explored. In his dispatch to Pitt, but as usual giving no date, Wolfe describes how Saunders and himself 'examined the town, with the view of a general assault' (that is, upon the Lower Town); but after consulting Mackellar and noting the entrenchments barring the way from the Lower to the Upper Town, and the fact that 'the upper batteries cannot be affected by the ships, which must receive considerable damage from them, and from the mortars', he decided against 'an undertaking of so dangerous a nature and promising so little success'. Murray's letter written in 1774 suggests that the plan for this Lower Town attack was put forward by Captain Hugh Palliser of HMS *Shrewsbury*. It would seem that the decision against it was taken on July 28th, for on that day Wolfe wrote in his journal, 'Difficulties arising about our attack & assault on the Town'; and to Monckton, 'Our Allies of the Navy, have examin'd the Place (the Town) & think it formidably *entrenched within*.' One more expedient had been written off.

Before Wolfe got in his blow the French made their final major attempt to burn the British fleet. It was perhaps provoked by the danger to the fire-rafts at the Anse des Mères now that the British had ships above the town. At any rate, on the night of the 27th/28th the *cajeux* – a great mass of rafts and small craft chained together–came down the river. It is universally admitted that the officer in charge, M de Courval, did his work boldly and well, waiting until his great infernal machine was close to the ships before setting fire to it. Bougainville and some grenadiers had a part in the adventure. But it was all to no purpose. According to Montcalm's journal the French gunboats were to have supported the operation but failed to do so; and the boats of the British fleet again saved the ships from disaster by towing the monster aside. The *Stirling Castle*'s log noted, 'servd the boatmen for the above service ½ a pint of brandy each'. It must have been quite a big night on board.[22]

The summer was slipping away; it was a month and a day since the first landing on the Isle of Orleans; there had been only skirmishing between the contending forces, and although Quebec was sadly scarred by the bombardment it was as far from being taken as ever. What went on in Wolfe's mind we cannot know, but we may imagine that he now felt that it was vital to make a firm decision and strike a decisive blow. He resolved upon an enterprise against the Beauport lines, and reverted to an altered version of the plan described to Monckton on July 16th. This we may call his fifth plan. He announced it to Monckton on July 28th in a letter which begins with what seems almost a note of defiance: 'I am determin'd [decided] to attack the upper redoubt; Burton will have the direction of it.' The attack on the little work was to be made by only four companies, but all the grenadiers were to be embarked 'to be at hand in case of need'. An armed ship – subsequently changed to two – was to run aground close to the redoubt, with two of the companies on board. Wolfe prescribed the equipment required in detail, including '200 Spades, 200 Shovels, 50 Pick Axes, 20 felling Axes, & 100 Hatchets'. 'The first thing to be done,' he wrote, 'is to extend, & increase the work; that we may disappoint all the efforts, they can make to dislodge us . . . The Master of the Pembroke [James Cook] assures the Admiral that a Cat, can go within less than 100 yards of the Redoubt – if so, it will be a short affair. The business will be to keep it.'

The plan differed from that of the 16th in that now there is no mention of any attack on the French right. Nor as yet is any reference made to a move across the Montmorency. Only a small force, suitable to the size of the objective, was to be used in the first instance. The nature of the plan is further developed in another letter from Wolfe to Monckton, undated but probably written on July 29th:

> I take it to be better that the Marquis shou'd attack a firm Corps of our w$^h$. superiority of Numbers, than that we shoud attack his whole Army entrenched, w$^h$. what we can put on shoar at one landing – If the Marquis gives Burton and I, only two hours we shall knock his Batt$^{ns}$. about most furiously.

On the 29th Wolfe made a note similar to this in his journal. He also wrote: 'A Party sent to act upon a hazzardous & important Service – determin'd to execute that Design – if it appears upon examination to be practicable.' This project defies identification; but it evidently was not found 'practicable'.

The attack had been planned for July 30th; but a flat calm that day made naval movement impossible. The scale of the operation was growing. The General's journal noted, 'Probability of a general Engagement on attack from us – preparations for it.' He had already, in the letter probably written on the 29th, told Monckton to have his battalions, except one which was to make a demonstration above the town, ready to embark in the boats of the fleet 'if such a measure shoud become necessary'; and undoubtedly he warned Townshend and Murray at Montmorency to be prepared to march their troops across the ford below the Falls.

There is another note in the journal for the 30th – a disturbing one: 'Dislike of the Gen$^l$. Officers and others to this Business – but nothing better propos'd by them.' The last phrase suggests that the General himself was going into battle without much confidence in his own plan. What line the brigadiers' criticism took we are not told. Perhaps they had inquired what would happen if the British seized the redoubt and Montcalm then declined to oblige them by attacking it, but persisted in simply sitting tight in his entrenchments; it was certainly an embarrassing possibility. Wolfe in his dispatch to Pitt remarks that if this should happen he would at least have it in his power 'to examine their situation so as to be able to determine where best to attack them'.

July 31st dawned clear and extremely hot; there was breeze enough to enable the navy to act; and the operation was launched. The *Centurion* moved into the channel north of the Isle of Orleans, took up a station a little east of Montmorency Falls and began to cannonade the two most easterly French batteries – one alongside the objective redoubt, one closer to the Montmorency. The two 'cats' (armed transports) *Russell* and *Three Sisters* were duly run ashore near the redoubt; but Cook's calculations had evidently been at fault – presumably he had had to reconnoitre from a distance – and they did not get as close to it as Wolfe had hoped. The General himself, eager to be in the forefront and to get a really close look at the enemy's positions, boarded the *Russell*. It was a warm spot; the French batteries were firing hard; Wolfe later wrote to Saunders (by way of convincing him that his vessels' guns had not mastered the enemy's), 'I was no less than three times struck with the splinters in that ship and had my stick knocked out of my hand with a cannon-ball.' He was at his very best under fire, and this is the reason for his great reputation among the lower ranks of his army.

But what he saw from the shot-swept deck of the *Russell* destroyed the whole basis of his plan. The redoubt was much closer to the French entrenchments along the heights than it had appeared to be when viewed from the British camp, and it was clear to Wolfe that it was not tenable under their fire.[23] The idea of seizing it, strengthening it, and waiting for Montcalm to attack it was impracticable. What was he to do?

Wolfe must have been very loath to cancel the operation; any commander would have been, in the circumstances. The army, after the long time of waiting, was expecting a decisive battle. What would a cancellation do to its morale? Wolfe looked at the French entrenchments. The defenders were in motion, and they seemed to be disorganized. This decided him. He wrote later in his journal, 'Their confusion & disorder incline me to attack them.' Orders were sent to Townshend, commanding at Montmorency, and Monckton, commanding at Point Lévis, 'to prepare for Action'. Something of the General's thinking is indicated in his letter to Saunders:[24]

> You will please to consider the difference between landing at high water with four companies of Grenadiers to attack a redoubt under the protection of the artillery of a vessel, and landing part of an army to attack the enemy's entrenchments. For this last business, a junction of our corps was necessary; and to join, the water must fall a certain degree. I gave up the first point (that of the redoubt) upon finding my mistake as to the distance from the entrenchment, and determined upon the latter, (which I always had in view) upon observing the enemy's disorder, and remarking their situation much better than I ever could do before.

Thus the modest plan for seizing an isolated position and using it as a basis for a defensive battle was converted into a scheme for a full-dress assault upon the enemy's main defences – an assault in which the guns of the fleet could give no help. It was a bold if not a foolhardy decision, and such a fundamental

change in conception that we must call the new scheme Wolfe's
sixth plan.

The transports had run ashore about eleven o'clock. About
12.30, it seems, the boats with the landing force put off from
the Isle of Orleans and lay in the channel, under ineffective
French artillery fire, awaiting orders to attack. The afternoon
was well advanced before they were sent in; and then they
struck trouble in the form of an offshore 'ledge' or 'shoal' –
both words are Wolfe's – on which many of them grounded.
This was probably a barrier of boulders, running for about a
mile west of the outlet of the Montmorency, which appears on
the modern chart just above low-water mark. The landing was
suspended; an officer was sent to stop Townshend, whose force
was on the move; and Wolfe himself, on Saunders' suggestion,
went in with a naval officer in one of the fleet's flat-bottomed
boats (the contemporary equivalent of modern landing craft)
to find a suitable spot to go ashore. Much time had been lost,
and it was apparently about half past five when the boats,
under a sky now dark and lowering, made for the place which
Wolfe had selected.

The thirteen companies of grenadiers and 200 men of the
Royal Americans led the attack. It was the moment for which
the army had waited so long: the moment cheerfully foretold
by Sergeant Botwood of the grenadier company of the 47th in
his doggerel verses:

> When the Forty-seventh Regiment is dashing ashore,
> While bullets are whistling and cannons do roar,
> Says Montcalm: 'Those are Shirley's, – I know the lapels.'
> 'You lie,' says Ned Botwood, 'we belong to Lascelles'!
> Tho' our cloathing is changed, yet we scorn a powder-puff;
> So at you, ye bitches, here's give you Hot Stuff.'

This spirit now produced disaster. The grenadiers went up like
a sky-rocket. Whether, as Captain Knox and others aver, they
took leave of the control of their officers, or whether the
officers were in some degree at fault, seems impossible to say.
What appears to be the one surviving story by a grenadier
officer tells how they got out of the boats and formed 'as well

as we could' in waist-deep water; then, he says, 'The General ordered the Grenadiers March to beat, which animated our Men so much that we could scarce restrain them.' [25] Wolfe's own angry accounts indicate that the companies, instead of forming on the beach and waiting for Monckton's battalions to land and Townshend's to cross the ford and support them, made a wild dash for their enemy. (His journal speaks of 'their disorderly March and strange Behaviour'.) The French hastily decamped from the redoubt and the battery; and from the entrenchments on the heights a withering fire came down. According to Knox, the grenadiers now made attempts to rush the heights; the grenadier officer is content to say that the bank proved 'inaccessable'. But there is no doubt that the French fire quickly took a heavy toll.

At this moment, with Wolfe's plan gone awry and affairs at a crisis, Nature took a hand. The black sky burst suddenly in one of those violent summer storms familiar in the Laurentic Basin; Knox calls it 'the dreadfullest thunder-storm and fall of rain that can be conceived'. As the heavenly artillery flashed and roared, the weapons of puny man fell silent; both sides' powder was wet. According to more than one account,[26] the French troops were almost out of ammunition when this happened. In other circumstances, this would have been a moment of opportunity for the British, a chance to storm the heights with the bayonet while the French fire was blanketed; but the wet grassy slopes must have been beyond climbing, and a good part of the troops present were disorganized. Moreover, as Wolfe puts it, 'the tide began to make'; and there was danger of the retreat of Townshend's and Murray's brigades across the ford being cut off. The General decided to withdraw. Most of Monckton's men and what was left of the grenadiers were taken off by the waiting boats; and the two brigades from the Montmorency camp, which had never formed a junction with the landing force, withdrew across the ford in excellent order, as they had advanced. 'On the retreat,' wrote a naval officer who was watching, 'our Troops were very regular, and retired across the Falls and to the Boats with a sullen pride, and in good order.' Part of Fraser's Highlanders, who had landed with Monckton, were diverted to Montmorency, and covered the retreat across the river; Wolfe, characteristically, marching with them.[27]

Townshend's notes contribute a picturesque detail, which reminds us that the 78th were really less a British regiment than a war party of Clan Fraser. At the ford the Highland companies halted, he says, and 'would not retire with him until they knew their regiment had reimbarked'. One imagines the General and the brigadiers remonstrating with the obdurate Scots as the tide rose, and the Frasers refusing to cross until they were certain that their clansmen were not being abandoned on the hostile shore. Finally they were satisfied that the regiment was safely off, and consented to proceed. By that time 'ye tide of flood was so high that the Regiments could scarcely wade over ye ford'.[28]

The two 'cats' were damaged beyond salvaging; the crews were taken off and the vessels burned. Wolfe recorded in his journal a loss of 210 killed and 230 wounded – 'Many excellent Officers hurt in this foolish Business.' Ned Botwood, the bard of the 47th, would write no more verses; he was lying dead on the bloody Montmorency beach, with many another bold grenadier around him.[29]

Montcalm's army had won a second defensive victory, though a much less sweeping one than Ticonderoga; and the French breathed again. It had been the most anxious day of the summer. Montcalm (who, unfortunately for his reputation for prescience, had told Lévis six days before the attack that he was convinced the British would not attack his left) described it in a letter to Brigadier Bourlamaque at Lake Champlain. At noon, when he saw the troops at Point Lévis embarking, he had ordered the *générale* to be beaten; and the roll of the drums brought the French to their posts all along the six miles from the St Charles to the Montmorency. Montcalm's problem was to decide where the blow was going to fall; the redcoats lying in their boats under the hot sun off the point of Orleans might land anywhere on his front. As the British manoeuvre developed, he gradually reinforced the Chevalier de Lévis on the left with the regular battalions from the centre. For a time, the

units of Three Rivers and Quebec, composed of militia mingled
with colonial regulars, remained, as Montcalm said, 'floating
between Beauport and the River St. Charles'; then, about four
o'clock, when Townshend's troops were seen moving down on
to the beach, Montreuil, the Adjutant-General of the army,
ordered the Three Rivers men also to the left. Only the troops
of the Government of Quebec remained to watch the right.
There was a very adequate concentration of force to greet the
grenadiers' landing; though according to Malàrtic, *aide-major*
of the Béarn battalion, who was nearby, the only unit that was
close enough to fire on them (apart from the men in the redoubts) was that of the Government of Montreal. The Canadian
militia had been allowed to fight under conditions in which
they were very formidable. The French losses, some sixty men
killed and wounded, were entirely due to the cannonade from
Wolfe's great battery at Montmorency, for the British, as
many of their accounts emphasize, refrained from using their
small arms.

Through the heat of the day Montcalm seems to have disregarded Vaudreuil, who remained at his headquarters on the
right near the St Charles, taking no part in the action; he complained later that he had heard simultaneously of the British
landing and of the re-embarkation. He also asserted that the
repulse was due to the wise measures of Lévis and that Montcalm joined Lévis just after it had taken place. This last statement is confirmed by Lévis' own accounts, which indicate also
that Montcalm visited him at two o'clock, concerted arrangements with him and then went back westwards. Lévis certainly
gave a good account of himself; Malartic writes admiringly of
his unruffled demeanour as he issued his orders under the fire
of the British guns. Montcalm's own letter to Bourlamaque remarks that when the battle was over and the troops dismissed
he rode over to report to the Governor General, who seemed
well pleased.[30]

Pleased with the victory Vaudreuil assuredly was. His facile
optimism asserted itself, and he wrote to Bourlamaque that he
had no anxiety now for any front except that of the St Lawrence rapids, facing Lake Ontario. Montcalm's military know-

ledge and experience, reinforced perhaps by his natural pessimism, led him to write the same correspondent differently and more accurately. 'You see, monsieur, that our affair is undoubtedly only a small prelude to something more important, which we are now waiting for.' [31]

# CHAPTER FIVE

# August: 'Skirmishing, Cruelty and Devastation'

The repulse at Montmorency left Wolfe at a loss. The decision to attack there had come at the end of several weeks of indecision and mental struggle; and the attack had failed. For the moment, he was almost content to leave the initiative to the French. There is no counterpart in August – at least until nearly the end of the month – to the succession of abortive plans produced in July.

On August 1st Wolfe recorded in his journal that he had given orders for strengthening and fortifying the camp (meaning the camp at Montmorency) 'that we may receive no insult from an Enemy impatient to decide their fate by an Action'. The same day he wrote to Monckton, 'This check must not discourage us, the loss is not great.' He gave instructions for keeping the troops busy while preparing for 'another & I hope a better attempt'.[1]

In the meantime, he sought to make some use of the control of the St Lawrence above Quebec which had been established by the British naval forces. On August 3rd he ordered Brigadier Murray up the river 'to try at their Magazines their Shipping at the Trois Rivieres &c.', as well as 'to divide & distract them'. Another motive for this movement was his desire to 'open a communication' with Amherst (nothing was accomplished in this respect).[2] The movement of Murray's brigade initiated a phase of operations above the city which was to continue with little interruption until the final crisis of the campaign. The British, thanks to their command of the river, up and down which their vessels could drift with the tide, were able to threaten landings at a dozen different points. The only means the French had of countering the menace was following the ships with a force on shore, a very exhausting procedure, especially for an army possessing few mounted troops. On August 6th Montcalm reinforced the small force above the town to a strength of about 1,000 men, and placed Colonel de Bougainville in command of it.[3] It was the beginning of a difficult period in that brilliant young man's remarkable career.

Murray's early operations were not particularly successful. On August 9th he made two attempts at landing at Pointe-aux-Trembles, 'to favour the seamen in cutting off three floating batteries which lay on the north shore'. The first, made at low water, was frustrated by rocks; the second, at high water, was beaten off by the fire of Bougainville's force, which now had had time to assemble in strength. Murray is said to have had 140 men killed and wounded, including thirty seamen. On the 9th he wrote to Wolfe, 'The Ship Scheme wont do, I fear, we want water to carry us much higher.' Next day he landed his whole body of troops at St Antoine on the south shore, covered by the *Squirrel*'s fire and in the face of opposition from some Canadians and Indians. Since the inhabitants fired on Murray's detachments, he threatened to burn every house in the parish if this went on; and apparently the threat was effective.[4]

On the 18th, having gone up the river in boats by night, Murray made a more successful descent at Deschambault on the north shore. In a house here the spare equipment and baggage of the French regular battalions were stored; the house and contents were burned. Murray wrote, 'the rest of the day was employ'd in destroying all that could be of service to the Enemy, and in scirmishing with the french foot, Dragoons, and Indians, who never came near enough to hurt a man of my detachment tho they fired constantly upon Us for two or three hours. I impute this to the dread they had of the English Musket . . .' Another account says, 'though fired at all day, the difference of our arms kept the enemy at too great a distance to hurt us'. Bougainville's main force seems to have arrived only as the British were re-embarking.[5]

This raid greatly alarmed Montcalm, not because of the actual damage done but because of the threat to his communications. As soon as word of the landing reached him, he mounted 'and left immediately with the grenadiers to join M. de Bougainville'. En route he heard that the British had withdrawn, and accordingly returned to Beauport. His diarist commented on the enemy's destruction of the magazine:[6]

> It is fortunate for the country that he limited himself entirely to this operation instead of taking post and entrenching himself; it would not have been easy to dislodge him. We all feared this, and M. de Montcalm felt the importance of this position so strongly that he left here intending to attack it, strong or weak, entrenched or not. No more communication with our magazines, no or very little food here, the country open to the enemy; the colony was lost or next thing to it.

Vaudreuil, on the other hand – according to the same, undoubtedly prejudiced, source – had refused to worry and had regarded Montcalm's expedition as quite unnecessary.

By this time Wolfe was complaining bitterly of Murray's long delay up the river. The last entry in the portion of his journal that has survived (that for August 16th) says, 'No account from M[r]. Murray'; and in a letter on the 22nd he says that Murray, by staying above and detaining the boats, is putting 'an entire stop' to the operations. He had sent a midshipman with orders for Murray to return, but the messenger had been unable to reach the brigadier. In his dispatch to Pitt he says of Murray, 'Finding that their ships were not to be got at, and little prospect of bringing the enemy to battle he reported his situation to me. I ordered him to rejoin the army.' When this happened is not clear, but Murray returned to Point Lévis on August 25th.[7]

Murray brought news, obtained from prisoners, of a British success in the west. Fort Niagara had fallen, after a French relieving force had been defeated; Brigadier Prideaux had been killed during the siege, but Sir William Johnson had taken over and finished the job. This alarming information had reached the French in Quebec on August 9th, and had produced immediate changes in their dispositions. The 'Rapids' sector, facing Lake Ontario, now seemed imminently menaced. The same night the Chevalier de Lévis went posting off to take command there. On his heels went 800 men from Montcalm's army. The composition of this detachment was mixed, in accordance with the usual practice – partly French regulars, partly colonial regulars, mainly militia. Eight hundred men, Montcalm wrote grimly to Bourlamaque, was a great many 'from a little army, obliged to keep watch from Jacques Cartier to Montmorency Falls'. Reporting in the same letter Bougainville's repulse of the British at Pointe-aux-Trembles, he added, at least more than half in earnest, it would seem, 'I don't know which of us three will be the first defeated.' Montcalm himself now took post at the left of the Beauport position, where Lévis had stood guard.[8]

In sending Murray up the river, Wolfe had cherished the rather desperate hope that this further division of his force might encourage the French to come out of their inaccessible entrenchments and attack him. To Monckton at Point Lévis he wrote on August 5th, 'I have thought of your situation, when Murray is detached, & heartily wish you may be attacked – you have more than enough to beat the whole French army.'[9] But Montcalm had no intention of obliging him in this manner, and the possibility of it was further reduced by the diminution of Montcalm's own force.

Amherst had done less than Prideaux and Johnson to help Wolfe. Bourlamaque abandoned Ticonderoga to him, but that was really the limit of his success. He devoted himself to building a flotilla for Lake Champlain, and constructing an unnecessary fortress at Crown Point; he never came to grips with Isle aux Noix, to which the French had retired. And Wolfe got no solid news from him until early September, when some bold Rangers brought dispatches by the overland Kennebec route.

All was not well on the highest level of command in the British camp. For some weeks Wolfe's relations with his brigadiers, and particularly with Townshend, had been deteriorating.

Wolfe had not asked for Townshend, and he particularly wished, he told Lord Ligonier, the Commander-in-Chief, to be allowed to name his own subordinates. When Townshend was appointed to serve under him he wrote him a letter of welcome which, however, contained what Townshend probably considered a sting in the tail. Wolfe said that when Ligonier mentioned Townshend's name he had replied that 'such an example' in a person of Townshend's 'rank and character' could not fail to have the best effect upon the army; he continued, 'I took the freedom to add that what might be wanting in experience was amply made up, in an extent of capacity and activity of mind, that would find nothing difficult in our business'.[10] Townshend had had about as much military experience as Wolfe, though he had not served in America. It is interesting also that Townshend's appointment was not part of the original plan. Both versions of the 'Proposals for the Expedition to Quebec' among Pitt's papers show the three brigadiers as Monckton, Murray and Burton.[11] Horace Walpole wrote in a famous letter, 'The expedition, called to Quebec, departs on Tuesday next, under Wolfe, and George Townshend, who has thrust himself again into the service, and as far as wrongheadedness will go, [is] very proper for a hero.'[12] Perhaps the well-connected Townshend had literally thrust himself in, with the consequence that Ralph Burton, an officer for whom Wolfe had a special regard, remained merely lieutenant-colonel of the 48th. Here perhaps were the seeds of conflict. At any rate, conflict soon appeared.

There was clearly a crisis just before the occupation of the Montmorency position early in July. This entry suddenly confronts us in Wolfe's journal on the 7th: 'Some difference of opinion upon a point termd *slight* & *insignificant* & the Commander in Chief is threatened w[th] Parliamentary Inquiry into his Conduct for not consulting an inferior Officer & seeming to disregard his Sentiments!' What had happened? Wolfe tells us no more, and there seems to be no other evidence. Townshend's notes contain nothing for this day; but he was almost certainly the 'inferior Officer' concerned, for there is a fragment of journal by him covering the following day and several days thereafter, which reports a succession of passages at arms with Wolfe.[13]

After the landing below Montmorency Falls Townshend records that Wolfe criticized the manner in which he entrenched the position, saying he had 'made a fortress'. On July 13th Townshend, while engaged in improving his entrenchments to cover a new encampment necessitated by the threat of a newly-constructed French battery, heard that Wolfe was leaving Montmorency for Point Lévis without giving him any orders or any information as to his own intentions and movements. He pursued him to the waterside, and the brigadier's account of what followed testifies to the feeling between the two men:

> He received me in a very stately manner; not advancing five steps; I told him that if I had suspected his intention of going over I had waited on him for his Commands which I should be glad to receive & execute to his satisfaction. Sir says he very dryly The Adjutant General has my orders, permit me Sir to ask are ye Troops to encamp now on their new ground or not to do it until ye Enemies Battery begins to play.

This is one-sided, and we have no account from Wolfe of this affair or what preceded it. But it suggests that Wolfe, with all his great qualities, and they were considerable, lacked a sure touch in dealing with his subordinates. He was no magnetic Nelson, with a band of brothers round him.

As the days passed the situation grew worse instead of better. As we have seen, the brigadiers had disliked Wolfe's plan for the attack on July 31st, and its failure certainly did not improve matters. Even Guy Carleton, in whom Wolfe had had such special confidence, now fell out with him. Captain Bell wrote in his journal the day of the repulse, 'Colonel Carlton's abominable behaviour to ye General.' What Carleton had said or done we do not know. A letter[14] which one James Gibson, apparently a civilian, who was in the Montmorency camp, wrote to Governor Lawrence of Nova Scotia on August 10th, criticized Wolfe severely. He recalled the events of July 20th, when within five hours, he said, three different 'Orders of consequence' came from Wolfe, 'which were contradicted immediately after their reception; which indeed has been the constant Practice of the Gen. ever since we have been here to the no small amazement of everyone who has the liberty of thinking'. Gibson reported 'some Genl Officers' as making most adverse comments on the Montmorency attempt. 'One of them of Knowledge, Fortune and Interest I have heard has declar'd the attack *then* and *there*, was contrary to the advice and opinion of every officer; and when things are come to this, you'll judge what the event may be!' This officer was pretty obviously Townshend.

At the middle of August Wolfe, in trouble with Townshend (whose views were perhaps already shared by Murray), was faced with the possibility of a break with his second-in-command, Monckton. We do not possess all the facts, but we have a letter which the General wrote Monckton on August 15th making him 'hearty excuses' for any unintentional offence. It seems that Wolfe had weakened the garrisons of some of Monckton's posts, and thereby roused the brigadier's resentment. Wolfe now explained that Monckton had strengthened these posts to such an extent that there was no need of keeping such large garrisons in them. He wrote, 'I am too well convinc'd of your upright Sentiments, & zeal for publick service, not to set the highest value upon your friendship.' The following day Wolfe wrote again, making further protestations of the absence of any intention to give offence: 'I heartily beg your forgiveness'. What Monckton's response was does not appear. He was perhaps never as hostile to the General as the other two brigadiers were or became. On the other hand, this impression may be due to the fact that we have no journal of his and few letters. It is interesting that this day, August 16th, was the last for which Wolfe allowed his own journal to survive. Captain Bell wrote at the end of the copy he made of it that the portion destroyed 'contained a careful account of the officers' ignoble conduct towards him in case of a Parliamentary enquiry'. The atmosphere of these days of strain is reflected in Townshend's wickedly witty and very indecorous

caricatures of Wolfe, which survive to testify both to the
artist's cleverness and his feelings towards his General.[15]

About this time Wolfe's hand began to fall heavily upon the
unfortunate people of the St Lawrence parishes in the area
dominated by the British fleet.

It is a disagreeable story. To keep it in proper perspective
one must remember the conditions under which warfare in
America had been conducted for years – indeed, generations –
past. It had been a fierce and barbarous struggle; and though
the atrocities had not all been on one side the attacks delivered
upon the British colonial frontiers by war parties from Canada,
usually partly at least made up of Indians, had left a particularly deep mark. Midnight killings, burnings, scalpings had
been common form since Frontenac's time, and the British and
the British Americans undoubtedly considered that there was a
heavy balance of French 'war crimes' to liquidate and that
revenge and reprisals were in order. The Fort William Henry
massacre in 1757 had embittered the conflict still further.
Wolfe had written to Lord George Sackville in 1758, 'tho' I
am neither inhuman nor rapacious yet I own it would give me
pleasure to see the Canadian vermin sacked and pillaged and
justly repaid their unheard-of cruelty'.[16] He was now in a
position to give himself this satisfaction if he chose.

Immediately after his landing on the Isle of Orleans on June
27th, Wolfe had issued a manifesto to the Canadian population. It invited the *habitants* to return to their homes; promised that they would not be molested if they remained quiet;
but told them that if they took up arms against the British
they might expect to suffer 'everything most cruel that war
offers'. This 'placart', posted on the doors of various parish
churches, had little effect. Late in July, accordingly, Wolfe
issued another proclamation, referring to the 'barbarous'
attacks on his outposts by Canadians and Indians, and
threatening reprisals unless the people submitted by August
10th to the terms offered in his notice of June 27th.[17] These
threats were carried into effect, and Wolfe did not wait for
August 10th to make a beginning.

Among the early victims were the people of Baie St Paul,
down the river, where there had been considerable shooting at
British boats. On August 4th Wolfe wrote to Monckton, 'I propose to destroy the habitations & settlement in the Bay of S$^t$.
Paul; & will employ Goreham in that service w$^h$. 200 or 220
men.' Joseph Gorham was a Ranger captain. The American
Rangers, who had been actively employed in outpost fighting,
were to be Wolfe's chief instrument in this grim business, and
it was to keep them busy until the end of the campaign. On
August 6th Wolfe sent another letter to Monckton:

> If any more fire attempts are made, I shall burn all the Houses
> from the Village of S$^t$. Joachim to the Montmorency River — ex-
> cept exactly such as we have occasion for, & I would have you (if
> Goreham returns in time) enable him by reinforcements, to burn
> every House & Hutt, between the Chaudiere and the River Etche-
> mins; Churches must be spared. — I shall give notice to Vaudreuil
> obliquely, that such is my intention. The Houses Barns &c from
> your Camp down to the Church of Beau-mont may be consumed
> at the same time — such Houses only accepted, as you want. I
> hope they will attack you — because I'm sure you'll put an end to
> the War.[18]

Wolfe undoubtedly hoped that his policy of terror would goad
the French into coming out of their entrenchments and attacking him, for he avows this in a passage of his dispatch to Pitt
which the British authorities thought it well to censor out of
the dispatch as published. Monckton may have found the instructions obscure and asked for clarification, for on the back
of the letter is a faint pencil endorsement reading in part, 'Not
to burn till the time is Expired ...'

The *habitants* were in a miserable dilemma. By the law of
Canada, every man of military age was a militiaman, and as
such it was their bounden duty to harry the invader as ordered
by Vaudreuil. If they showed signs of cooperating with the
British, the French authorities had no compunction about using
the Indians to coerce them. There is a letter of Montcalm concerning a report that the people of l'Ange-Gardien and the
Beaupré shore may 'make a separate peace': 'A big detach-

ment of Indians and Canadians is needed to correct them.' [19]
On the other hand, the British were not prepared to treat the
*habitants*' resistance as legitimate warfare, insisting on nothing less than neutrality from them; and now they were about
to apply against them a degree of severity which in our own
day would be called Prussianism.

On August 9th the British troops at Point Lévis saw 'a great
smoke' down the river; Gorham was at work at Baie St Paul.
He posted on the door of the church (almost the only building
he left standing) another 'advertisement' of Wolfe's, announc-
ing that he could no longer refrain from rigorous measures;
he had ordered his officers to carry off cattle, destroy houses,
lay waste the country and make prisoners of the inhabitants.
On the 14th Wolfe wrote to Monckton, 'I hear Goreham has
been at Malbaye – & by the smoaks upon the South Shoar, it
is imagin'd that he has carried the terror of his Arms even to
that Coast.' He had. He had destroyed about forty houses and
barns at Malbaie (Murray Bay) and then crossed the river and
burned about fifty more at Ste Anne de la Pocatière.[20]

From this time the sky along the St Lawrence was seldom
free of the smoke of burning farm-houses. On the 15th Wolfe
wrote, 'All the Houses, & Barns between the Etchemin River
& la Chaudiere may be burn't whenever any opportunity offers.
It is to very little purpose to withhold the rod, seeing they are
incorrigible, they have had Indians upon the Isle of Orleans, &
have scalped four Sailors very lately.' On the 23rd the destruction of the villages on the north shore between Montmorency and St Joachim began. The French also mention
burning in the Isle of Orleans.[21] The biggest operation of all
was launched early in September, when Major George Scott
was sent down the river with a large detachment, composed of
Rangers, regulars and seamen from the ships of the line, for
the purpose of 'destroying the Buildings and Harvest of the
Enemy on the South Shore'. Wolfe had written on August 22nd,
'I intend to burn all the country from Camarasca to the Point
of Levy.' Scott sailed down to Kamouraska and marched back,
burning as he went. 'Upon the whole,' he reported with
apparent satisfaction, 'we marched fifty two Miles, and in that

distance, burnt nine hundred and ninty eight good Buildings, two Sloops, two Schooners, Ten Shalloops and several Batteaus and small Craft, took fifteen Prisoners (Six of them Women and five of them Children) kill'd 5 of the Enemy, had One Regular wounded, two of the Rangers kill'd and four more of them wounded.' [22]

Thus, by the time of the final crisis in mid-September the smiling parishes on both sides of the river below Quebec, and on the south shore for some distance above, had been turned into a desert. It was estimated — probably conservatively — that upwards of 1,400 fine farm-houses had been burned, and a New England newspaper reported cheerfully that it might take the country half a century to recover. [23]

This visitation had been accompanied by fierce guerrilla warfare between the destroyers and the inhabitants. The bitterest was on the north shore below Montmorency. Here the chief organizer of resistance to the British seems to have been a priest, René Portneuf, who is sometimes described as curé of St Joachim, but was called by Vaudreuil curé of Ste Anne de Beaupré, and appears to have had his headquarters there. He was at the head of a large armed party and kept up some correspondence with Vaudreuil. [24] Knox tells us how he sent an invitation to dinner to a British officer nearby, promising him safe conduct, and adding 'that, as the English Officer fought for his King and for glory, he hoped he himself would be excused in fighting for his poor parishioners, and defending his country'. His courage and courtesy were poorly rewarded. On August 23rd the British force in the area was reinforced to a strength of apparently some 300, under Captain Alexander Montgomery of the 43rd Regiment, with field artillery. It proceeded to attack the priest's position at Ste Anne. A gun drove his party out of the houses they were holding, and, says Knox, 'thirty of them, with their leader, were surrounded, killed, and scalped; the reason of their being treated with such cruelty proceeded from the wretched parishioners having disguised themselves like Indians: in this rencounter we had five men wounded'. (On July 27th Wolfe had issued his celebrated order, 'The Genl. stricktly forbids the inhuman practice of scalping, except when the enemy are Indians, or Canads. dressed like Indians.'[25] There were almost no Indians in Wolfe's army, but the Rangers were regular practitioners of scalping.)

Ensign Malcolm Fraser of the Highlanders, who was there, does not mention the priest, but he has something to say about 'the barbarous Captain Montgomery', who ordered the prisoners who were taken to be butchered in cold blood; among them were two whom Fraser had promised their lives. This regular officer was at least as savage as any Ranger. The decent Captain Knox, who would, one feels, have had a decided opinion of such proceedings, refrains from mentioning or commenting on his brother officer of the 43rd. Having destroyed Father Portneuf and his party, the detachment burned the houses of Ste Anne, and also reduced Château Richer to ashes before returning to Montmorency on September 1st.[26]

It may seem surprising that this policy of terror did not create a permanent and impassable gulf between the people of Quebec and the British nation and army. That it did not do so must be due to the fact that such happenings were recognized as natural accompaniments of war. The French of Canada well knew that their own Government had long been using a precisely similar policy against the frontier settlements of British America; and they would themselves doubtless have been glad to treat Boston, New York and Philadelphia and the lands about them just as the British were now treating Quebec and its dependent parishes, if they had had the chance. War in the eighteenth century was nasty business, just as it is in the twentieth; and no one knew it better than the people of Canada.

When all this has been said, however, Wolfe's policy of devastation remains unpleasant to contemplate, the more so as it is questionable whether it did anything to advance his campaign. It was a gruesome business for British soldiers to be engaged in, and most of them probably disliked it. Certainly George Townshend did (though he would doubtless have disliked any policy that was Wolfe's). Townshend did not write as well as the Commander-in-Chief, but he was capable of a pungent phrase, as a letter which he wrote to his wife, Lady Ferrers – a peeress in her own right – amply shows:[27]

The Captive Women & Children which I see every Day brought
in here, often tell me what I am & who belong to me, but above
all, the melancholly News I received the Day before yesterday
upon my arrival here from the cursed Camp of Montmorenci of
my poor Brother's death [in Amherst's army] has reproved me for
not consulting my own nature more, when I ask'd you to [let me]
return to the Army. It had then pleaded for you, when you did not
plead for yourself & I had not been now in a Sceene of Ambition,
Confusion, & Misery; and you oppress'd as I know you must be,
with Terrours & affliction . . . I never served so disagreable a Campaign as this. Our unequal Force has reduced our Operations to a
Sceene of Skirmishing, Cruelty & Devastation. It is War of the
worst Shape. A Sceene I ought not to be in, for the future believe
me my dear Charlotte I will seek the reverse of it.

Genl Wolf's Health is but very bad. His Generalship in my poor
opinion – is not a bit better, this only between us . . .

Wolfe's planning, we said, was suspended after the repulse
on July 31st. Towards the middle of August, however, there
are signs of renewed activity. On the 11th he wrote in his journal, 'Propose to undertake something of consequence in a few
days.' And on the 15th we read in the journal that seems to be
Townshend's 'Genl. Wolfe made known his intentions to
General Townshend of the way he designed to attack the
Enemy Next.' (And that is absolutely all we know about the
matter.) On the 19th Wolfe wrote to Monckton, 'I wish we had
Murray's Corps back, that we might be ready to decide it with
'em.' [28] He had evidently formed another plan, but what its
nature was will probably never be known. And before Murray
returned from the upper river Wolfe's miserable health had
grown worse.

On or about the 19th the General was forced to take to his
bed in the upper room of the house at Montmorency where he
had taken up his quarters. (He was nevertheless able to dictate
a letter to Monckton on the 22nd.)[29] The news of his illness
reached the army on the 22nd, but Knox tells us that the troops
had already suspected it, simply because of Wolfe's failure to
appear at the Point Lévis camp for several days. On the 24th
Knox visited the General's headquarters to receive his orders
for Monckton's brigade; but 'he was so ill above stairs as not

to be able to come to dinner'. The trouble, Wolfe himself told Pitt, was a fever. But on the 25th Knox recorded, 'His Excellency General Wolfe is on the recovery, to the inconceivable joy of the whole army.' It was not until the 31st, however, that he recorded the General's reappearance in the camp.

The British naval force in the river above Quebec was still comparatively weak – the *Sutherland*, the *Squirrel* and a few smaller vessels. Late in August the French were emboldened to plan a stroke against it. It was decided to re-arm and re-man the French frigates that had been sent up to Batiscan (their men and guns had been used in part to strengthen Quebec) and employ them in an attack upon the British detachment. On the 27th several hundred sailors were withdrawn from the city batteries and sent up the river in boats – not without attracting British notice and coming under fire. Immediately thereafter the British reinforced the upper squadron. This was not because they had fathomed the French design; it had been planned for some time. On the night of August 11th/12th the frigate *Lowestoft*, the sloop *Hunter* and four smaller vessels had tried to pass Quebec, but at the critical moment the wind dropped and only a schooner got by. Now, on the night of the 27th/28th, the other five ships tried again, utilizing a short period of north-east wind, and succeeded in spite of violent fire from the city batteries. The French immediately abandoned their plan, which, always doubtful, was now hopeless; their sailors were recalled. On the night of August 31st/September 1st five more vessels, including the frigate *Seahorse*, went above Quebec.[30] The British force there was now formidable.

The final crisis was now at hand in the relations of Wolfe and his brigadiers, in the development of the British strategic plan, and in the fortunes of New France.

# CHAPTER SIX

# The British Change Direction

By the 25th of August, we have seen, Wolfe was beginning to recover from his bout of fever. The immediate consequence was an active discussion of plans in the British camp, and from this in turn came a fundamental change in the British strategy.

It was now two months since the first landing on the Isle of Orleans. During this time Wolfe had never consulted his brigadiers about the operations; so Townshend told his wife,[1] and there is no reason to disbelieve him. But he consulted them now, because he was ill and the summer would soon be gone. The famous memorandum which the General addressed to Monckton, Townshend and Murray bears no date; but it was probably written on August 27th. Captain Bell's journal by this stage is getting very slight and uninformative; but at the end of his entry for August 27th and before the next one, which was made on the 31st, he entered the words, 'Consultation of the Brigadiers'. We know that the actual discussions between the brigadiers began on the 28th.

The memorandum begging the brigadiers 'to meet, & consult together for the publick utility & advantage, & to consider of the best method of attacking the Enemy' is printed in the back of this book, for it is a document worth examining.

It begins with a fundamental point, and one which indicates that Wolfe had been interrogating deserters to some purpose. (There was a constant two-way flow of deserters between the opposing camps. Most of them were foreigners. Thus Wolfe writes to Monckton early in August about information ob-

Major-General James Wolfe. Brigadier-General George Townshend disliked Wolfe intensely, but we owe to his skilful brush this most soldier-like portrait of the General. It was presumably drawn from life before Quebec in the summer of 1759

Lieutenant-General the Marquis of Montcalm, from the well-known
portrait in the possession of the Montcalm family

Quebec from Point Lévis. A general view, engraved from a drawing
by Richard Short

The Western fortifications of Quebec. Although painted in 1784, this
water colour by J. Peachey gives a generally accurate impression of
the works as they were in 1759–60

The French fire-ships attack the British fleet. This 'artist's conception' after a painting by Samuel Scott represents the attack on the night of June 28th/29th, 1759, with the British ships' boats saving the fleet by taking the blazing fire-ships in tow

The action at Montmorency, engraved from a drawing by Captain Hervey Smyth, one of Wolfe's aides-de-camp

Cap Rouge, engraved from a drawing by Captain Hervey Smyth, Wolfe's aide-de-camp. From this place the British boats and vessels dropped down the St Lawrence to land the army at the Anse au Foulon on the morning of September 13th, 1759

Ruins in the Upper Town of Quebec. Some of the damage done by Wolfe's batteries on Point Lévis

The landing at the Anse au Foulon, September 13th, 1759. This engraving after a drawing by Wolfe's aide-de-camp, Hervey Smyth, represents a succession of events which covered several hours as taking place simultaneously

The Anse au Foulon (Wolfe's Cove) in 1973

Amherst's army running the St Lawrence rapids, 1760. From a drawing by Captain-Lieutenant (later Lieutenant-General) Thomas Davies, RA, who was present. The lack of experienced boatmen caused over 80 soldiers to be drowned

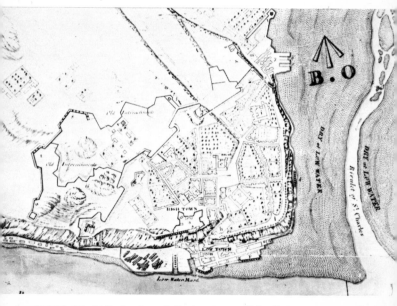

Patrick Mackellar's plan of Quebec, 1757. This plan was apparently the most up-to-date intelligence material on the city's defences available to Wolfe in 1759. Comparison with Map No 6 (see p xiv) demonstrates how wildly inaccurate it was

Dear Madam

My writing to you will convince you that no personal evils (poorer than disappointments) have fallen upon me. The enemy puts nothing to risk & I can in conscience put the whole army to risk. My antagonist has wisely shut himself up in inaccessible entrenchments, so that I cant get at him without spilling a torrent of blood, and that perhaps to little purpose. The Marquis de Montcalm is at the head of a great number of bad soldiers And I am at the head of a small number of good ones, that wish for nothing so much as to fight him — but the wary old fellow avoids an action doubtful of the behaviour of his army. People must be of the profession to understand the disadvantages & difficulties we labour under arising from the uncommon natural strength of the country. I approve entirely of my fathers disposition of his affairs tho perhaps it may interfere a little with my plan of quitting the service which I am determined to do the first opportunity. I mean so as not to be absolutely distressed in circumstances nor burdensome to you nor any body else

Part of Wolfe's last letter to his mother. This letter, now in the Public Archives of Canada, was presented to the Dominion by HM the Queen (now Queen Elizabeth the Queen Mother) in 1939. Note the reference to Wolfe's 'plan of quitting the service . . . the first opportunity . . . so as not to be absolutely distressed in circumstances'

tained from an Italian, while on the French side the great
source of intelligence was foreign deserters from the ranks of
the Royal Americans.) The point is this: the General 'does not
find they have any provisions in the Place'. This was the great
weakness of Montcalm's position, but strangely enough Wolfe
makes no reference to the possibility of interfering with the
movement of provisions into Quebec. His deduction is simply
that if the French army is defeated the town must surrender.
He is convinced that a direct water-borne attack on the Lower
Town would yield no good result. And how get at the army? It
is the old problem which he has been struggling with since
June, and he still seems no closer to a solution.

He lays before the brigadiers for their consideration three
possible courses of action. All of them involve attacks on the
Beauport lines, which seem to have had a certain fascination
for Wolfe. The first is an encircling night march by a large detachment, to cross the Montmorency by the uppermost ford
and take the French entrenchments at Beauport in the rear at
dawn, in conjunction with a frontal attack by the rest of the
army. Wolfe remarks that it is unlikely this movement could
be made without the French discovering it. The second is a
night attack by the troops at Montmorency, crossing the ford
below the Falls and marching across the French front to Beauport, where, 'trying different places', the force must attack the
line of entrenchments on the high ground. The 'upper redoubt'
– the famous little work captured on July 31st – is to be captured again; and Monckton's brigade from Point Lévis must be
ready to land when Townshend's men have gained the heights.
The third course is similar to the second. The main body of
the army is to attack (landing from boats) at Beauport, in conjunction with a movement across the Falls ford from the Montmorency camp an hour earlier. All the courses proposed, it will
be noted, and very notably the second and third, are merely
variations of the plan that had already failed so disastrously on
July 31st.

This is a curious document. A modern general who asked his
subordinates to make up his mind for him in this manner
would be accounted a very weak commander. But in 1759 the

idea of the council of war, though beginning to lose its force, was still current, and the procedure did not seem so strange to the men of those days. Wolfe's ultimate defence against criticism of the actual nature of his proposals, however, must rest upon the fact that he was a sick man.

The late Professor Waugh attempted to explain these proposals by the ingenious suggestion that Wolfe 'secretly favoured quite a different plan' but thought it useful to 'test the value' of the Beauport plans by taking the brigadiers' opinion of them; and that he may even have 'welcomed' their rejection of them. There is nothing whatever to support this, and indeed the idea is an absurdity. No general would imperil his reputation and expose himself to his subordinates' contempt by setting his name to military propositions which he knew or suspected to be unsound. In the absence of any evidence to the contrary we can only assume that Wolfe's memorandum meant just what it said, and that to him, at the time he wrote it, the courses suggested in it seemed to be the best possible.

The brigadiers had disliked Wolfe's plans for an attack at Beauport even before the action of July 31st. With that day's failure in their minds they were hardly likely to accept these proposals now. They consulted carefully together and produced on August 29th or 30th – the former date is on the signed copy in the Chatham papers, which may be the copy given to the General – a polite, crisp and effective reply to Wolfe which must be considered a very able military paper, and which was to have historic consequences. This too will be found at the back of this book.

The brigadiers point out the strength of the Beauport position – so 'evident from late Experience' – and the further obvious fact that, in the rather unlikely event of a successful attack on it, there is still the line of the St Charles to penetrate. The French, they suggest, can hold out there long enough to provision the city 'from the Ships, and Magazines above' and enable it, in turn, to hold out until the approach of winter forces Wolfe to withdraw. They therefore reject all three of the General's proposals, and advise him instead to 'bring the other Brigadiers'. No doubt there was a final discussion in Saunders' cabin that morning. Then 'at 12 they left ye Admiral & came down to ye Montmorenci Camp'. It is possible that they now presented the plan to Wolfe, though Townshend does not say so. In any case, there was a full-dress conference with the General the following day:

> The Admiral came on shore this morning when Genl. Wolfe & ye 3 Brigadiers had a consultation in consequence of it, – after ye former [approved?] ye Brigadiers orders were immediately given for all ye Artillery & Stores to be carried from ye Camp . . . all the Great Cannon & Stores were sent over to Point Levi that night . . .

In spite of this it was only on September 1st, it would seem, that Wolfe gave final orders for the withdrawal from Montmorency:

> The expedition up ye River under Genl Murray above ye Town & that on ye Beauport side having been unsuccessful Genl Townshend received orders from Gen. Wolfe to form a disposition of a retreat from Montmorenci . . .

One thing Townshend's account makes very evident. The brigadiers were in constant consultation with Saunders when making their plan, and the calculations in it concerning movements by water, embarkation and disembarkation are doubtless his. Naval officers are notoriously backward about giving advice on matters affecting land warfare; but this plan was as much a naval as an army one, and one cannot help wondering whether the silent, competent Vice-Admiral's association with it may not have been the factor that decided Wolfe to accept it.

The chronology of this episode is confused. It seems strange that the signed copy of the brigadiers' reply should be dated as early as August 29th, and a letter from Wolfe to Saunders, in which he announces his acceptance of the brigadiers' plan, as early as August 30th. Perhaps there is some error in the dating of these papers – or of Townshend's notes. But the point is not very material.

On September 2nd Wolfe dated his dispatch to Pitt, describing the brigadiers' plan. 'I have acquiesced in their proposal', he wrote, 'and we are preparing to put it into execution.' But his general tone was pessimistic: 'In this situation there is such a choice of difficulties, that I own myself at a loss how to determine.' This was also the tone of his last letter to his mother, written on August 31st, the day on which he had his consultation with the brigadiers and decided to accept their recommendation:

Dear Madam

My writing to you will convince you that no personal evils (worse than defeats & disappointments) have fallen upon me. The enemy puts nothing to risk, & I cant in conscience put the whole army to risk. My antagonist has wisely shut himself up in inaccessible entrenchments, so that I cant get at him without spilling a torrent of blood, and that perhaps to little purpose. The Marquiss de Montcalm is at the head of a great number of bad soldiers, And I am at the head of a small number of good ones, that wish for nothing so much as to fight him – but the wary old fellow avoids an action doubtful of the behaviour of his army. People must be of the profession to understand the disadvantages & difficulties we labour under arising from the uncommon natural strength of the country . . .[4]

The previous day Wolfe had written a letter to Admiral Saunders in reply to the Admiral's comments on a draft of his dispatch to Pitt, agreeing to remove certain remarks about the navy's part in the operation of July 31st which Saunders thought unjust.[5] This letter said, 'I am sensible of my own errors in the course of the campaign; see clearly wherein I have been deficient; and think a little more or less blame, to a man that must necessarily be ruined, of little or no consequence.' Later in it Wolfe wrote,

My ill state of health hinders me from executing my own plan; it is of too desperate a nature to order others to execute. The generals seem to think alike as to the operations; I, therefore, join with them, and perhaps we may find some opportunity to strike a blow.

This passage has been subjected to strained interpretations. Wolfe's admirers have said that it proves that the General already had in mind his final scheme; that 'my own plan' was an attack at the Anse au Foulon. There is no evidence at all to support this. It has been suggested that the 'desperate' plan was 'undoubtedly' a direct attack on the Lower Town.[6] But Wolfe's memorandum to the brigadiers had discarded this. There is a much more obvious interpretation. Only two or perhaps three days before Wolfe wrote this letter to Saunders, he had sent the brigadiers that memorandum suggesting three different versions of an attack on the Beauport lines; this they rejected (incidentally, after consulting Saunders) as being too dangerous as well as unrewarding. This in all probability was what Wolfe meant by 'my own plan'.

In a postscript the General added another note of depression. 'Beyond the month of September I conclude our operations cannot go. We can embark the superfluous artillery; and Barré has a list ready for you of quarters for the troops, supposing (as I have very little hope of) they do not quarter here.'

The decision to evacuate Montmorency having been taken, little time was lost in putting it into effect. On September 1st almost all the remaining guns were withdrawn from the position, and on the 2nd a considerable number of the troops were carried over to the Isle of Orleans. The final evacuation was to take place early on the 3rd. Wolfe, still hoping to draw the French into attacking him, laid a trap, designed to convince Montcalm that only a weak and vulnerable rearguard remained in the camp. In fact, five battalions were still there. 'Great silence was to be observed and not a man to show himself on any account but to lay conceal'd in their Posts to try once more if the Enemy would attack us.'[7] Montcalm was not taken in, and, true to his policy, attempted no offensive movement. Townshend covered the final withdrawal with Bragg's (the 28th Foot) and the Light Infantry; at this stage Monckton embarked his troops from Point Lévis and made a feint towards the St Charles River end of the French position, to deter Montcalm from interfering. The French commander still remained quiescent; observers in both camps thought he missed an opportunity.[8] Thus one of the British Army's great successful evacuations passed into history. Carefully planned, and most skilfully executed by the navy, it was a predecessor of Gallipoli; though the French, unlike the Turks in 1916, were well aware of what was going on.

The main strength of Wolfe's army was now collected on the south shore about Point Lévis, and orders were issued on September 4th for the beginning of the move above the town. That night the flat-bottomed boats with the army's 'light baggage' went up past Quebec successfully. On the evening of the 5th Murray marched up with four of the line battalions, the Light Infantry and the Louisbourg Grenadiers, crossed the Etchemin River and embarked in the squadron above the town (where one battalion, the 3rd Royal Americans, had long been). The following day Monckton and Townshend with three more battalions did the same. The ships were painfully crowded. That evening Admiral Holmes, who had been below Quebec since August 25th, came back and hoisted his flag again in the *Sutherland*; with him came General Wolfe. Carleton with the 2nd Royal Americans was left to protect the Isle of Orleans, and Burton with the 48th to hold Point Lévis.[9] A great part of the brigadiers' plan had now been carried out. The whole direction of the operations had been changed. The army had been concentrated and moved above the city. The way was open now for the execution of the rest of the plan – the descent to cut Montcalm's line of communication between the Jacques Cartier and Cap Rouge Rivers.

This was very nearly done on September 9th, and the evidence indicates that only bad weather prevented it. On the 7th the squadron was off Cap Rouge, and Bougainville's men, including the cavalry, watched it in force from the shore. That morning Wolfe and the brigadiers met on board the *Sutherland*, and an order of battle was drawn up; the units at hand were organized into three brigades, and instructions were given for formations in various contingencies. If the army engaged in two lines, Townshend's brigade would form the second; if in one line, then each battalion would keep a quarter of its strength in reserve in rear of it. The order incorporating these decisions remarked with notable vagueness, 'When the coast has been examined, and the best landing-places pitched upon, the troops will be ordered to disembark, perhaps this night's tide.' Obviously a final decision was yet to be made. But later in the day, while a feint at landing was executed at Cap Rouge to bother the French, Wolfe and the brigadiers went up the river to reconnoitre as far as Pointe-aux-Trembles. It should be noted that during the night Saunders' boats made a demonstration at Beauport 'to faver the proceedings of Gen$^l$ Wolfe above the town'.[10]

The 8th of September was a day of solid rain. It is evident that a decision as to the place to land had now been reached, and this day orders were issued. Not unnaturally, they do not mention the point of attack; but the so-called 'Journal of Major Moncrief' (which clearly is actually the journal of Major Mackellar, the Chief Engineer, and therefore an important document) [11] says that the General had 'fixed upon a place a little below *Pointe aux Trembles*'; and Murray in a letter to Townshend written the following month speaks retrospectively of Wolfe's 'Scheme of landing between point au Tremble, and St. Augustin'. Admiral Holmes says the plan was to land 'about four Leagues above the Town',[12] and Holmes was certainly in a position to know. St Augustin is about twelve miles from the city walls; and for roughly five miles above it, to a point just below Pointe-aux-Trembles (now Neuville), the shore, in contrast with the situation both above and below, is low and suitable for landings. The orders contain detailed instructions for a feint at Pointe-aux-Trembles itself by the Royal Americans and the Light Infantry; the commanding officer was 'to put on an appearance of intending to land at that point'. The actual landing below was to be executed by five battalions, which were to be followed ashore as soon as possible by the rest of the army, including the two units that had executed the feint. But the weather was so bad that a signal was arranged to postpone the operation in case there was no improvement. And later on the 8th, it seems, while the miserable soldiers on the packed ships watched the leaden skies, General Wolfe —

so Townshend's journal tells us — 'went a reconoitering down the River'.[13]

The rain went on; and at half past one in the morning of the 9th the signal of postponement was made.[14] Subsequently an order was issued stating that, 'As the weather is so bad that no military operations can take place, and as the men are so excessively crowded in the transports, and in the men of war, so as to endanger their health', over 1,500 of the troops were to be landed at St Nicholas on the south shore, 'in readiness to embark at the first signal'.[15] The long downpour had undoubtedly turned the ground into a quagmire. It has nevertheless been pointed out that this might have been considered an opportunity for the British; for while they could move freely by water, Bougainville's movements on shore would be seriously hampered, and had they landed he could not have hoped to be on the spot to oppose them.[16] Be this as it may, the operation was postponed, and as it turned out cancelled. It is possible that something Wolfe had seen on his reconnaissance down the river influenced the postponement. Up to now he had followed the brigadiers' plan. From this point he abandoned it, and the final tactical decision as to where to land was his alone.

The information we have about Wolfe's reconnaissances is exasperatingly slight (how one regrets, here as elsewhere, his decision to destroy his journal!). There is no source but Townshend for the one on the 8th, and Murray's biographer, General Mahon, argues, not particularly convincingly, that it did not take place. On the 9th, Mackellar records, Wolfe 'found out another place more to his mind, and laid aside all further thoughts' of Pointe-aux-Trembles. Did the General go down the river both days? Or are Townshend and Mackellar really talking about the same reconnaissance? It does not greatly matter, for the result is clear.

It was on the 9th that Wolfe sent off his last report to his Government. It was addressed to Lord Holderness, one of the Secretaries of State, and it is composed in the same tone of almost entirely unrelieved discouragement as the letters to Pitt, Saunders and Mrs Wolfe. He describes again his consultation of the brigadiers, and their plan, designed to draw the French 'from their inaccessible situation, and bring them to an action'. He concludes:

> I agreed to the proposal, and we are now here, with about 3600 men, waiting an opportunity to attack them when and wherever they can best be got at. The weather has been extremely un-favourable for a day or two, so that we have been inactive. I am so far recovered as to do business, but my constitution is entirely ruined, without the consolation of having done any considerable service to the State, or without any prospect of it.[17]

If Wolfe had formed his new plan at the time when he closed this dispatch, it would seem that he did not regard it with any special confidence.

The landing-place which Wolfe now selected was the Anse au Foulon, since known as Wolfe's Cove. It was close to, and just below, St Michel, where he had twice considered landing in July. If we disregard as merely tentative his three sugges-tions to the brigadiers for a Beauport operation – which a hostile critic might term his seventh, eighth and ninth plans – we may call the scheme for a landing near St Augustin, which he took from the brigadiers, the Commander-in-Chief's seventh plan. The Foulon plan was the eighth, and was to be the last.

How did Wolfe come to select the Foulon? We do not know. The claim has been made that Captain Robert Stobo, a colonial officer, who like Mackellar had been a prisoner at Quebec, made the suggestion. It has been pointed out, however, that Stobo was not present when the choice was made, having we know left the army before the city on September 7th. This would not, of course, preclude the possibility of his having planted the idea in Wolfe's mind earlier. Townshend wrote in his journal on the 10th, 'By some intelligence the Genl. has had he has changed his mind as to the place he intended to land, Heard that we had some Deserters from the Enemy's Camp ...'[18] On this very slender foundation General Mahon erected a tremendous structure of conjecture, a work of fiction, indeed, to explain the landing at Foulon. Bigot and Cadet, he says, in effect, desired the colony to fall, in order to prevent

investigation of their thieveries. They, or at any rate Cadet,
arranged for the Foulon to be unguarded; they arranged for
the French posts along the river to be warned that French
provision boats would be coming down on the night when the
British troops were dropping down to the Foulon; they
arranged for the movement of the provision boats to be cancelled without information of this being sent to the posts; they
arranged for Madame de Vienne, called by Mahon 'a lady of
notoriety and charm' (she was actually the wife of Bougainville's cousin, and he had lived at the Vienne house when stationed on the Beauport shore),[19] to decoy Bougainville away
from his post of duty on the fatal night; finally, they sent word
to Wolfe that a landing at the Foulon would not be opposed.[20]
This is such an ingenious and romantic tale that it seems almost a pity that there is nothing to support it. There is plenty
of evidence that Bigot and Cadet were rogues, but none at all
that they were traitors. If information from the enemy's camp
actually influenced Wolfe's choice of a landing-place, it appears
likely that it was merely a report that the Foulon was accessible and inadequately guarded. But it is at least possible that
there was no such information, and that Wolfe's decision was
based entirely on his own observations during his down-river
reconnaissance on the 8th or the 9th.

Whatever the grounds for it, Wolfe had made a decision by
September 10th; for on that day he made another reconnaissance of the place which is very well authenticated. He took
with him to 'Gorham's Post', just below the mouth of the
Etchemin, Admiral Holmes, Brigadiers Monckton and Townshend, Major Mackellar and some other officers. They disguised
themselves in 'grenadiers' coats' and 'coloured cloaths', which
did not deceive the vigilant French officer in charge at Sillery,
who watched them across the river through his telescope and
reported their proceedings; however, their planting stakes in
the ground led him to conclude that they were merely laying
out a new camp.[21] The Chief Engineer's account is worth quot-
ing:

> The place is called Toulon [sic]; they reconnoitred it from a ris-
> ing on the south side of the river, below the mouth of the Etche-

mins river . . . as the place is laid down upon the plan [presumably Mackellar's great plan of the Quebec area made later], it requires little or no description, but it must be observed that the bank which runs along the shore is very steep and woody, and was thought so impracticable by the French themselves, that they had then only a single picket to defend it. This picket, which we supposed might be about 100 men, was encamped upon the bank near the top of a narrow path which runs up from the shore; this path was broke by the enemy themselves, and barricaded with an abattis, but about 200 yards to the right there appeared to be a slope in the bank, which was thought might answer the purpose. These circumstances and the distance of the place from succours seemed to promise a fair chance of success.

It would be interesting to know just what passed between Wolfe and the two brigadiers at Gorham's Post that day. He must have pointed the Foulon out to them, but his exchanges with them and Murray during the next couple of days make it evident that he neither asked their opinion and advice nor informed them specifically of what he had in mind. It is a queer proceeding, and suggests how distant and formal the General's relations with his chief subordinates had now become.

Whatever one may think in other respects of Wolfe's choice of a landing-place – and it is a question we must discuss presently – it offered at least one important advantage over landing higher up the river, and one of which surprisingly little notice is usually taken. The brigadiers' plan had been far superior to Wolfe's earlier ones in the degree of concentration which it permitted. Wolfe's new plan allowed still more concentration, and of this he took full advantage. Operating at a distance up the river, he had not been able to avoid leaving considerable detachments to protect his hospital and stores on the Isle of Orleans and his Point Lévis batteries; operating close to the city, and therefore close to those places too, he was able to withdraw the two battalions from them and join them to his striking force. This added some 1,000 men to the force of 3,600 mentioned in the letter to Holderness, and would materially improve the British chances of success in the battle Wolfe hoped for. This was the more desirable as Wolfe had committed

a serious sin against the principle of concentration at the
moment of evacuating the Montmorency camp: the force under
Major Scott which he sent down the river on a mission of
destruction is said to have amounted to 1,600 men, including a
good many regulars and all the Rangers. These troops were still
absent when the battle was fought on the 13th.

A letter which Wolfe wrote to Burton of the 48th on September 10th [22] refers to the arrangements for bringing up the
troops from Orleans and Point Lévis, and declares specifically
the General's intention of making 'a powerful effort' at the
Foulon about four in the morning of the 13th. On the 11th
orders were issued for the re-embarkation of the troops at St
Nicholas the following morning: 'The army to hold themselves
in readiness to land and attack the enemy.' The troops were to
'go into the boats about nine to-morrow night, or when it is
pretty near high water'. The flat-bottomed boats would rendezvous abreast of the *Sutherland*, and when she showed 'two
lights in the main top-mast shrouds' they were to drop down
the stream. [23] But the orders, naturally, said nothing of the
actual objective; and Monckton, Townshend and Murray were
still in the dark – though Wolfe had, as we have just seen,
told the whole story to at least one battalion commander
already.

The Commander-in-Chief's motives in not taking the brigadiers into his confidence remain obscure. The reason given by
his supporters is 'security' – the importance of preventing any
warning reaching the enemy. Security is a fine thing, particularly in amphibious operations; but it can be overdone, and a
general who refuses to trust his most senior officers cannot
expect them to serve him efficiently or to keep up their own
morale or the army's. If Wolfe had not opened his mind so
fully to Burton one would have more respect for his reluctance
to inform Burton's seniors. As it is, the suspicion creeps in, was
he perhaps yielding to the temptation to put these captious
sprigs of nobility in their place? At any rate, on the 12th, only a
few hours before the time set for the operation to begin, all
three brigadiers addressed to the General a respectful request
for information: [24]

Sir

As we do not think ourselves sufficiently inform'd of the several parts which may fall to our share in the execution of the Descent you intend to morrow, We must beg leave to request from you as distinct orders as the nature of the thing will admit of, particularly to the place or places we are to attack; This circumstance, perhaps very decisive, we cannot learn from the publick orders, neither may it be in the power of the Naval Officer who lands the Troops to instruct us – As we should be very sorry no less for the publick, than our own sakes, to commit any mistakes, We are persuaded you will see the necessity of this application which can proceed from nothing but a desire to execute your orders with the utmost punctuality

> We are Sir
> Your most obedt. hble
> Servts.
> Robt. Monckton
> Geo. Townshend
> Ja. Murray.

Wolfe answered this polite inquiry from the men who had to win his battle for him with a less polite letter addressed to Monckton:

My reason for desiring the honour of your Company with me to Goreham's post yesterday [sic], was to shew you, as well as the distance wou'd permit, the situation of the Enemy, & the place where I mean't they shoud be attack'd; as you are charged with that duty, I shoud be glad to give you all further light, & assistance in my power – the Place is called the *Foulon* distant upon two miles, or two miles & a half from Quebec, where you remarked an encampement of 12 or 13 Tents, & an Abbatis, below it – you mention'd to day, that you had perceived a breast-work there, which made me imagine you as well acquainted wh. the Place, as the nature of things will admit off, I took Capt: Shads wh: me also, & desird the Admirals attendance, that as the former is charg'd by Mr: Saunders wh: conducting of the Boats, he might make himself as much a Master of his part as possible; and as several of the Ship's of War are to fall down wh: Troops, Mr. Holmes wou'd be able to station them properly, after he had seen the Place . . . It is not a usual thing to point out in the publick orders the direct spot of an attack, nor for any inferior Officer not charg'd wh: a particular duty to ask instructions upon that point. I had the honour to inform you to day, that it is my duty to attack, the French Army, to the best of my knowledge, & abilities, I have fix'd upon that spot, where we can act wh: most force, & are most likely to succeed, if I am mistaken, I am sorry for it; & must be answerable to his Majesty & the Publick for the consequences.

At the same time Wolfe sent a short note to Townshend, telling him that Monckton was charged with the first landing at the Foulon: 'if he succeeds, you will be pleas'd to give directions that the Troops afloat be set on shoar wh: the utmost expedition; as they are under your command: and when the 3600 men now in the fleet are landed, I have no manner of doubt, but, that we are able to fight & to beat the French Army; in which I know you will give your best assistance'.[25]

Both these letters bear the time 8.30 [PM] on the 12th. Soon after Wolfe closed them his men began climbing into the boats for their great adventure. The General had been encouraged by intelligence received from a French deserter, and during the day he had passed the encouragement on to the army in a famous order:[26]

The enemy's force is now divided, great scarcity of provisions now in their camp, and universal discontent among the Canadians; the second Officer in command is gone to Montreal or St. John's, which gives reason to think that General Amherst is advancing into the colony: a vigorous blow struck by the army at this juncture may determine the fate of Canada. Our troops below are in readiness to join us; all the light artillery and tools are embarked at the point of Levi, and the troops will land where the French seem least to expect it. The first body that gets on shore is to march directly to the enemy, and drive them from any little post they may occupy; the Officers must be careful that the succeeding bodies do not, by any mistake, fire upon those who go on before them. The battalions must form on the upper ground with expedition, and be ready to charge whatever presents itself. When the artillery and troops are landed, a corps will be left to secure the landing-place, while the rest march on, and endeavour to bring the French and Canadians to a battle. The Officers and men will remember what their country expects from them, and what a determined body of soldiers, inured to war, is capable of doing, against five weak French battalions, mingled with a disorderly peasantry. The soldiers must be attentive and obedient to their Officers, and resolute in the execution of their duty.

We must now turn our eyes back to the French camp.

Montcalm, as we have already seen, had no *flair* for penetrating his enemy's intentions; and in the last ten days of his life he wholly failed to do so. But it was not for want of activity or devotion. At three in the morning on September 2nd, while the British were in the midst of evacuating their Montmorency position, he wrote a celebrated letter to Bourlamaque: [27]

... The night is dark, it is raining; our troops, dressed and awake, are in their tents; the right and the city are particularly on the alert. I am booted and my horses saddled, this in fact is my usual way at night. A succession of interruptions, things to sign, visits from the Indians and councils with them, questions, small details, always notes to Messrs. de Vaudreuil, Montreuil and Repentigny, and trips to see the generalissimo. Then at last, I am able to take my ease in my house ...

... As for things here, I think Wolfe will act like a player of *tope et tingue*, who, after having played to the left of the tope, plays to the right and [then] to the middle. We shall do our best to see him off ...

This pretty clearly means that he expects Wolfe, having failed both above the city and at Montmorency, to strike next in 'the middle' – at the right of the Beauport lines or perhaps the city itself, those areas he mentions as particularly watchful. It would seem that this conception largely dominated Montcalm's mind to the end.

He was too good a soldier, it is true, to overlook the menace west of Quebec altogether. The movement of British troops above the city on the 5th and 6th was duly observed, as was the movement of boats up the river. On September 8th Montcalm wrote to Bourlamaque, 'This month will be very decisive for this colony. The enemy seems very much interested in

interfering with our communications above Quebec, and I think
he has it in for our ships. That area is always one of the most
critical on all counts.' There were not enough troops – above
all, not enough good troops – to cover the whole line that was
now threatened by the British force, rendered so dangerously
mobile by the fleet. Montcalm regrouped to meet the new situation. As soon as the British left Montmorency, 2,000 men were
moved from that flank to the right of the Beauport lines, and
Montcalm himself moved back to the centre, establishing himself at the de Salaberry house at Beauport 'to be in full view
and within range of everything'. To give flexibility to his dispositions, on September 4th he stationed the battalion of the
Régiment de Guyenne just east of the St Charles, near the
bridges, 'to move wherever it might be needed, even above
Quebec if necessary'.[28]

In the new and fluid situation, however, some further
measure seemed needed to support Bougainville; and on the
5th Montcalm moved the Guyenne battalion across the St
Charles and placed it under Bougainville's command. It camped
overnight in the area of the Plains of Abraham, quite close to
the Foulon. Montcalm, however, was clearly anxious to ensure
that the battalion would continue to be available as a mobile
reserve for use either above or below Quebec; and although he
told Bougainville in the first instance that he could use it as he
saw fit, a few hours later he sent through Montreuil a further
message that it was to be kept in reserve on the main road
adjacent to St Michel and Sillery. On September 6th the battalion was sent back to its former camp east of the bridge. It
has been argued that this movement was ordered by Vaudreuil
contrary to Montcalm's advice; but there is nothing in the
records to support this. The two men seem to have conferred
together, and for once there is no evidence of disagreement.

Since a French regular battalion had thus been stationed
momentarily in a position where it could have ruined Wolfe's
plan, it is not surprising that after the plan had succeeded this
incident should have become a focus of hearsay and ultimately
of legend. In English-speaking Canada today few stories are
more firmly established in the textbooks than the tale that on

the day before Wolfe landed at the Foulon Montcalm ordered the Guyenne battalion back there, but that Vaudreuil reversed his order with the remark, 'We'll see about that tomorrow.' In French Canada one is likely to encounter the precisely opposite story, stemming from the statement in Vaudreuil's dispatch: 'I was counting heavily upon the Guyenne battalion; I thought it was still on the heights of Quebec, but M. de Montcalm had recalled it, the same day [the 12th] at nightfall, without informing me.' [29]

Faced with contradictory accounts like these, the bewildered reader may well ask which is true. The answer seems to be, neither. There is absolutely no evidence to support Vaudreuil's assertion; and since his account would involve a double movement of the battalion – from its camp near the St Charles to the heights (usually called by the British the Plains) of Abraham, on some date after the 6th, and back again on the 12th – which could not have escaped being seen and recorded, it seems safe to assume that things did not happen as he tells them. Whether he lied – as some people are quite ready to believe – or whether, shaken as the old man was by a succession of terrible events, he had convinced himself that what he said was true, or whether his account is a badly confused version of something that actually did happen, can be left for the reader to decide for himself.

For the reverse story – the story of Vaudreuil's 'We'll see about that tomorrow' – there is evidence, but it is slight and weak. It consists entirely of a brief and bald entry under the date September 12th in the diary of Father Récher, the parish priest of Quebec, which came to light in 1903.[30] Récher does not seem to have had the sort of 'contacts' that would enable him to have first-hand knowledge of the matter, and indeed it is hard to imagine anyone much less likely to know what went on between Vaudreuil and Montcalm. There is absolutely no other evidence for the tale. It is true that the Chevalier Johnstone, Lévis' aide-de-camp whom he had left with Montcalm, and the artillery officer Montbeillard who at this time was keeping Montcalm's journal,[31] both assert that orders had been given to move Guyenne to the heights and had not been carried

out. But neither mentions Vaudreuil in this connexion; Johnstone blames Montreuil. And as we shall see, there is yet
another story.

On balance, although some element of doubt remains, it
seems likely that Guyenne never moved after the 6th; perhaps
there was not even a proposal to move it. The tales that were
told may have been the products of inaccurate recollection and
hearsay, working upon the known, undoubted and dramatic
fact that a week before Wolfe's landing at the Foulon a powerful French force had been stationed almost at that very spot,
and immediately withdrawn. One thing at least is evident. The
story of Vaudreuil's interference with Montcalm's dispositions
at this moment, so widely circulated by a succession of writers
beginning with William Wood, rests on the flimsiest founda-
tions and should probably be forgotten.[32]

During those fateful days while Wolfe was working out his
plan and the British brigadiers were wondering when he would
condescend to reveal it to them, the French leaders were
watching their enemy's movements with desperate concentration and utterly failing to fathom their meaning. Montcalm
was worried about the up-river sector, but apparently more
about the more distant area than that close to Quebec. He had
written to Bougainville on September 1st, 'I am always afraid
that the English will try to establish themselves somewhere
to cut our communications; take care at Jacques Cartier and
Deschambault.' On the 10th he comes back to the subject:
watch out or they will steal a march on you and come down
on 'Jacques Cartier or even Deschambault where they have
been already'. (One remembers him riding off at the head of
the grenadiers when the news came of the raid on Deschambault in August.) Then he writes, very significantly – and, to
the officer in charge of the right, very imprudently – 'M. de
Vaudreuil is more anxious than I am about the right'. And again
he says, 'Take care at Deschambault.' One remembers, too,
that Montreuil had written to Bougainville on behalf of Montcalm on the 5th, urging him always to be ahead of the enemy
– 'that is, higher up than they are'.[33] In the light of Wolfe's
new plan, this was unfortunate advice.

Montcalm, it is pretty evident, relied heavily on the cliffs for the security of the area immediately west of Quebec. Vaudreuil, after the fall of the city, exerted himself to prove that he had seen the danger here, but that Montcalm had scoffed at it. He produced two letters Montcalm had written to him. One, dated July 29th, contains the famous phrase (which William Wood actually more than once attributed to Vaudreuil!), 'We don't need to believe that the enemy has wings'; but this, contrary to Vaudreuil's implication, clearly implies apprehension of a direct amphibious attack on the city, not a landing near the Foulon. The other is undated and does refer to the Anse des Mères area, close to the Foulon; and in it Montcalm does say, 'I swear to you that 100 men, well posted, could stop the whole army and give us time to wait for daylight and then march to our right to that sector.'[34] This statement was true enough; 100 alert and determined men at the Foulon could have brought Wolfe's scheme to ruin.

In spite of his worries about Jacques Cartier and Deschambault, it appears that Montcalm still thought the Beauport lines the point of main danger. Writing to Bougainville on September 5th about the westward movement of 'almost everything in the Point Lévis camp', he added, 'M. Wolf is just the man to double back.'[35] He feared that all the activity above the city was merely a feint. The best evidence of this is the fact that he himself remained at Beauport. Had he believed that the main blow was most likely to fall west of Quebec, he would undoubtedly have gone thither. But he stayed at Beauport; and he was on the Beauport shore, anxiously expecting an attack there, on the morning of the 13th when Wolfe landed at the Foulon.

This reminds one of a passage in the diary of Mackellar ('Moncrief'). The Chief Engineer, mentioning that the British had contact with a picquet of Guyenne near the Foulon after the landing on the 13th, adds that they heard later that the whole battalion 'was to have come upon this ground the night before', but was prevented by 'some lucky incident': 'some say they were detained by the French general himself, upon receiving intelligence by a deserter that there was a descent to be made that night upon the coast of Beauport'.[36] This is hearsay, but it is interesting. Is it possible that it is true, as Johnstone and Montbeillard indicate, that orders had been issued to Guyenne to return to the Foulon? And is it possible that the orders were not carried out because Montcalm himself changed his mind? And that a garbled memory of this is the basis of Vaudreuil's statement about Guyenne? We shall probably never know what really happened.

Vaudreuil, even though we have Montcalm's word for it that he was more anxious about the right than the General, had not fathomed Wolfe's intention. On September 8th he wrote Bougainville that the British could have only two possible objects — a diversion, or to establish themselves 'up above' (en haut), presumably above Cap Rouge; he thought the former more likely. On September 9th he wrote to Lévis that there were now twenty-two sail above Quebec: 'The object of the English is probably to effect a great dispersion of our forces.' On the 12th, the day before Wolfe attacked, he wrote again: 'The English vessels remain in the Cap Rouge area; they go up and down almost simultaneously, which indicates that they have no settled object.' He added that the departure of the fleet could not be delayed much longer.[37]

Bougainville had been reinforced; two light field guns were sent to him on the 7th, and Vaudreuil later asserted that he had about 3,000 men for his task, including the detachments stationed at various vulnerable points along the shore. One of these detachments was M. de Vergor's 100 men of Quebec and Montreal at the Foulon. Bougainville's mobile striking force, the élite of his corps (and of the army), consisted of the grenadier companies of the five regular battalions, a picquet from each of those battalions, the 200 cavalry, 250 volunteers under Captain Duprat, the 'reserve of Repentigny' (a body of selected Canadians) and four or five hundred Indians. Vaudreuil on September 6th calculated the strength of this flying column at 1,085 men.[38]

This column had the exhausting task of following the British ships wherever they went. Actually, however, the amount of movement by the ships in the days just before Wolfe's landing seems to have been exaggerated. The *Sutherland*'s master's log shows that she did not weigh anchor between the late afternoon of the 9th and the morning of the 13th, and the *Lowestoft*'s indicates only minor movements.[39] It is possible, though rather improbable, that not every movement was recorded. Bougainville was clearly responsible for all the posts and troops west of the walls of Quebec. Clearly also, however, his attention was devoted in practice to the mobile column and to watching the ships; the posts nearest the city were left to their own devices. What the situation demanded was the presence of an active senior officer to inspect and supervise those posts on behalf of Bougainville, or on behalf of Montcalm; but the personnel and organization of the French army were unequal to providing such an officer.

In Quebec and the Beauport camp the food situation was worse than ever. The flour from France was exhausted, and only the fact that there had been an early and bounteous harvest in the district of Montreal made it possible to feed the army at all, even though it had been put on short rations. The arrival of provisions from up the river was a matter of importance to every individual at Quebec, and this fact was to play its part in the drama now about to begin. Wolfe had heard from a deserter that the enemy army was eating 'bread made of new wheat', and the knowledge that it was in such straits encouraged him as he planned his desperate venture.[40]

As the final crisis approached, the two opposing commanders, as we have seen, both viewed their prospects pessimistically. And both were very much alone. A commander-in-chief always occupies a solitary pinnacle, and there were special solitudes for Wolfe and Montcalm. The Englishman, with relations strained between himself and his brigadiers and Carleton, was peculiarly isolated; one gets the impression that his close associations were limited to his two aides-de-camp and Isaac Barré, who seems to have remained friendly to him to the end. To Ralph Burton he was 'yours affectionately',[41] but Burton had his battalion to command. As for Montcalm, he found the officers with him at Beauport neither especially competent nor particularly congenial. He wrote both

Bourlamaque and Lévis saying that he wished they were with him.[42] Montreuil he praised without enthusiasm, and Poulhariez, one of the lieutenant-colonels, seems to have been on terms of friendship with him; the other officers about him, he told Lévis confidentially, were 'nothing'. Brigadier Sénezergues, his senior subordinate at Beauport, he simply does not mention, and the silence is eloquent. And, like Wolfe, he was unwell: 'My health is going to pieces', he told Bourlamaque on September 8th. Nevertheless, for all his chronic pessimism, he was not quite without hope; the season was far spent, perhaps the British would have to take themselves off, and Quebec and New France would be reprieved for one more year. 'What are your plans for a place to live this winter?' he asked Bourlamaque on the 11th. 'Quebec, in truth, will not be habitable ...'[43] But the choice was not to rest with Bourlamaque, and both Montcalm and his British antagonist were almost finished with worries about health or habitation.

# CHAPTER SEVEN

## The 13th of September: Approach

---

On September 12th, while Wolfe was making the final dispositions for that night's enterprise, the French, unfortunately for
themselves, were making some routine supply arrangements
which were to render the enterprise a great deal easier.

During the day the *munitionnaire* Cadet wrote to Bougainville at Cap Rouge asking him to do everything possible to pass
a convoy of provision boats down the river to Quebec during
the night; if this could not be done, then Cadet would have to
send carts to Cap Rouge for the food next day – 'but if it came
by water, that would save us a great deal of trouble'.[1] As part
of the plan, Bougainville's posts were warned that the boats
would be attempting the dangerous trip down the river past
the British ships, and that it was important to avoid any action
that would give them away. But, for some reason that does not
appear, the convoy movement was cancelled; and word of the
cancellation was not sent to the posts.[2] It is really not surprising that some writers should have suggested that this train of
events was the result of treachery; but there is no evidence
that it was due to any cause except gross negligence. It was to
make a great contribution to the fatal outcome. It would seem
that a heavy responsibility rests on Bougainville; for the boats
were to depart from Cap Rouge, where he was, and he cannot
have failed to know of the change of plan.

Wolfe's letter to Burton had said, 'Tomorrow the troops
re-embark, the fleet sails up the river a little higher, as if
intending to land above upon the north shore, keeping a

convenient distance for the boats and armed vessels to fall
down to the *Foulon* . . .' It seems unlikely that the upward feint
here suggested was ever made, for it is not recorded either in
the ships' logs or by Admiral Holmes, although Townshend's
draft dispatch after the battle does speak of 'some little movement of y^e ships made by Admiral Holmes to draw the attention of y^e Enemy up y^e River'. But there was certainly a most
useful feint on the opposite flank, opposite Beauport. The
boats of the main body of the fleet assembled off Point Lévis
manned and armed; and the *Stirling Castle*'s log says, 'Att 11
they put off from thence and keept rowing between Bowport
and mouth of Charles River.' This demonstration continued
until four in the morning – the hour of the Foulon landing.[3]

According to the *Sutherland*'s log, the troops in the ships
began embarking in the boats at nine o'clock; other sources
make it later, which seems more likely. In any case, the tide at
Cap Rouge, off which the squadron lay, did not begin to ebb
that morning until about 1.35 AM. At two o'clock or a little
later the boats cast off and dropped down the river with the
current and the tide. 'Fine weather, the night calm, and silence
over all.' So wrote a member of the forlorn hope in the leading
boat. The moon had risen about ten, but she was in her last
quarter and by that much the less likely to betray them.[4]

The plan for the movement was simple and effective. The
'first flight' of some 1,800 troops dropped down in the boats,
which had the best chance of escaping observation. They were
followed, half or three-quarters of an hour later, by the armed
sloops and vessels with stores and ammunition, and about
three o'clock by the *Lowestoft*, *Squirrel*, *Seahorse* and some
other vessels, all full of troops. This was the second flight, to
be landed by the boats that had put the first ashore, while the
ships would lie off to give cover. The third flight – Burton's
and Carleton's men from Orleans and Point Lévis – were to be
on the south shore opposite the Foulon, whence they would be
ferried over as soon as boats were available. Only one ship,
the big *Sutherland*, was to remain finally at Cap Rouge; Holmes
shifted his flag to the *Lowestoft* to watch and supervise the
landing operation.[5]

Colonel Howe's Light Infantry were in the van. In the first boat was a picked detachment of twenty-four volunteers commanded by Captain Delaune; theirs was the task of leading the attack at the Foulon.[6] Wolfe himself is said to have been in one of the leading craft (there is nothing to support the story that he was in the same one with Delaune). Captain James Chads of the *Vesuvius* fire-ship was the naval officer charged with the landing arrangements, and it is evident that he did his work well.

Of all the tales and legends about this campaign, none has been more popular or more durable than the one relating to Wolfe and Gray's *Elegy in a Country Churchyard*. Parkman tells it in the traditional form, making the General recite the lines in a low voice as his boat slips down the dark stream bearing him to death and immortality:

> The boast of heraldry, the pomp of pow'r,
> And all that beauty, all that wealth e'er gave,
> Awaits alike th' inevitable hour.
> The paths of glory lead but to the grave.

Then, as the recital ends, the General says, 'Gentlemen, I would rather have written those lines than take Quebec.' (And the historians adds, 'None were there to tell him that the hero is greater than the poet.')

Did this really happen? The answer seems to be that the tale has more foundation than most of the Quebec legends, but that the incident did not take place as the boats moved down the river in the early morning of the 13th. Wolfe had issued orders enjoining strict silence. There are cases on record of generals who disobeyed their own orders when it suited them – but hardly in circumstances like these.

The story was told by John Robison, who lived to be Professor of Natural Philosophy in the University of Edinburgh, and who in 1759 was in the fleet as a sort of tutor to a young naval officer and was 'rated as a midshipman'. Unfortunately he never wrote it down himself, or if he did the writing has not survived; but he was fond of telling the tale, and several people to whom he told it did set it down. Their versions differ; but the two earliest ones between them give us an intelligible account. One, by John Playfair, says that Robison was 'on duty in the boat in which General Wolfe went to visit some of his posts, the night before the battle', and heard the General repeat 'nearly the whole' of the *Elegy* 'to an officer who sat with him in the stern of the boat', adding that 'he would prefer being the author of that poem to the glory of beating the French to-morrow'. The other, by William Wallace Currie, reports Robison as being in a boat 'very near the one General Wolfe was in', the night before the attack, when as yet nothing was definitely known of the General's intentions. 'A gentleman was repeating Gray's Elegy to the latter, and Mr Robison heard him (the General) say, "I would rather have been the author of that piece than beat the French to-morrow;" and from this remark guessed that the attack was to be made the next day.'[7]

These seem to place the episode in time – not during the trip down the river early in the morning of the 13th, but on the evening of the 12th. (It is true that the second version says, 'The boats were ordered to drop down the St Lawrence', but once the final voyage had begun Robison would need no hint from Wolfe to let him know that the attack was about to take place.) As to whether Robison was in the same boat or not, and whether it was Wolfe or 'a gentleman' with him who recited the poem, the reader may take his choice. The Currie version seems to carry a certain conviction, simply because it is somewhat the less dramatic, and by that much the less likely to have been manufactured or imagined. And it must be said that the story in general is not out of keeping with the tone of melancholy which is so marked in almost all of Wolfe's final letters. To add a final note of romance, early in the present century there came to light a copy of the *Elegy* inscribed 'From K.L. *Neptune* at Sea' and containing annotations said to be in Wolfe's handwriting. 'K.L.', it is assumed, was Katherine Lowther, to whom Wolfe was engaged.[8] (The lady, it may be recalled, later became Duchess of Bolton. Of her relations with

Wolfe we know next to nothing, for not a single letter that passed between them has survived.)

The Marquis de Vaudreuil asserted that Wolfe had been informed of the order to the French posts about the provision boats by two deserters from the Royal-Roussillon regiment. These were doubtless the two whom the log of the *Hunter* sloop, then lying off Sillery, notes as coming aboard in a 'canoe' at 11 PM. Whether the information they gave reached Wolfe before the operation was launched seems questionable, but Mackellar ('Moncrief') says that a Light Infantry officer in one of the leading boats got it from the *Hunter* 'by accident'. (According to the Light Infantryman in the first boat, the *Hunter* took the boats for enemy craft, 'not being apprised of our coming down'.[9] The latter statement is improbable, but it is very likely that the *Hunter*, expecting both the French and British boats, was momentarily uncertain which those carrying the Light Infantry were.) If the officers in the British craft did have the story about the provision boats, it helps to explain what followed.

As every schoolboy knows, or used to know, the British boats did not reach their objective without being challenged. There are many contemporary versions of the story of the challenge or challenges; they come from both sides and there are a number of variations. It is hard to say when or where the boats were first challenged, but it seems likely that they were close to the Foulon before any sentry shouted at them. It can be said with confidence, however, that one detail which is found in Parkman and in dozens of other books cannot be true. The French sentry asks the French-speaking Highland officer his regiment, and the Highlander replies *De la Reine*. Now the Régiment de la Reine was on Lake Champlain with Bourlamaque, and that alleged reply would have given everything away. (Vergor's own account says that the reply was *Marine* – which makes much more sense. It seems just possible that in some manner *Marine*, passing from mouth to mouth and mind to mind, became corrupted into *De la Reine*.) Townshend, as so often, gives us in the quaint English of his notes some pictures-que details, and quite likely the most accurate account:

... when ye first corps for disembarkation was passing down ye
N: Side of ye River & ye french Centries on ye bank's challeng'd
our boats, Captn Frazer who had been in ye Dutch Service &
spoke french – answered – la france & vive le Roy, on which ye
French Centinels ran along ye Shore in ye dark crying laisser les
passer ils sont nos Gens avec les provisions ...

The French versions are very similar to this. Says Bigot, 'Four
different sentries contented themselves with shouting to them,
*Qui vive?* They replied, *France*, and were allowed to pass without being recognized.' The French – more inefficiency – had
arranged no password.[10] The *Army List* tells us, incidentally,
that there were three Captain Frasers in the 78th Highlanders:
Simon, Alexander and James.

At the Anse au Foulon the cliffs rise roughly 175 feet above
the St Lawrence. The cove was formed by a geological fault
which crosses the river at this point. A rivulet coming from the
west descends the cliffs here and flows into the river. From the
stream's east bank a path – not a 'winding' path as so many
books would have it – ran transversely upwards across the face
of the cliff. The French officer La Pause, who inspected it
earlier in the summer, described it as 'a path on which two men
can descend abreast'.[11] That it was a good and usable track is
proved by the fact that a few guns were hauled up it that morning, and many were hauled up it in the course of the next few
days. This path still exists; anyone who doubts it can convince
himself by comparing the plans drawn by the Royal Engineers
who served under Wolfe and Murray in 1759–60, the great survey of the Quebec area executed by their successors just over a
century later, and the maps produced by the Royal Canadian
Engineers of our own times. The generations have transformed
it into a motor-road, and it is doubtful whether many of the
Quebecers or the tourists who drive up its steep gradient today
realize that they are on the path up which Wolfe's guns were
dragged 200 years ago.

The foreshore has been greatly altered, by the construction
of a road and railway tracks and, in the present century, of the
Wolfe's Cove Dock where the great transatlantic steamships
lie. A Canadian Pacific Railway tunnel breaks through the cliffs

not far from the point where Wolfe and Delaune must have leaped ashore. Yet apart from such disturbance as was caused by the construction of the tunnel and the process of developing the path into the modern road, it seems likely that the cliffs themselves have changed comparatively little since 1759.

It is difficult to be certain precisely what Wolfe's plan was; but from the little first-hand information he has left us it seems likely that he intended the leading troops to attack straight up the barricaded and entrenched path. In his letter to Monckton on the 12th [12] he wrote,

> I have desired Mr Holmes to send the Boats down, so that we may arrive about half an hour before day, as you desired; to avoid the disorder of a night attack; & I shall be present myself, to give you all the aid in my power. The Officers who are appointed to con-duct the divisions of Boats, have been strickly enjoin'd to keep as much order & to act as silently as the nature of this service will admit off, & Capt Shads will begin to land the men a little this side of the naked rock, which you must remember to have seen, within which (to the Eastward) the Enemy is posted.

The largest display of 'naked rock' today is on the bold shoulder of cliff forming the western side of the Cove, which is almost bare of vegetation from top to bottom. If this is the feature spoken of by Wolfe — and it seems quite likely — it would appear that the General intended to put the Light Infan-try ashore somewhat above the Cove, doubtless with the idea that here the landing was least likely to be observed. The troops would then move to their right, cross the streamlet (which would not be a serious obstacle) and rush the path. It is notable that virtually every British contemporary account, including Townshend's official dispatch, states that the run of the tide carried the boats considerably farther east than the point where the landing was intended; and since there seems little doubt that the troops actually went ashore only a short distance below the path the interpretation here suggested seems at least plausible.

It is true, as we have seen, that Mackellar in his account of Wolfe's reconnaissance on the 10th refers to the accessible

slope to the east of the path, 'which was thought might answer
the purpose'. But it appears from various references that
Mackellar's journal was revised after the fall of Quebec; and it
may be that this passage reflects the influence of hindsight.
But it is best to admit that the documents, in this as in many
cases, give us no basis for certainty.

In the last half-hour of darkness, as planned, the boats
grated on the gravel under the shadow of those frowning cliffs.
There seems to be no eye-witness to tell us what happened on
the beach at that moment; no account by Howe or Delaune or
Chads has survived, Wolfe of course left nothing, and the bold
Light Infantryman is sadly vague; he does seem to suggest,
however, that there was a parley with a sentry, who, uncertain
whether or not to accept Captain Fraser's explanations, sent
for his officer, 'who had reason to suspect us, ordering all his
sentrys to fire upon us; but by this time the aforesaid volunteers
was up the eminence, and a part of the Light Infantry following'. According to Knox, the French-speaking Scot represented
himself as commanding a French detachment which had been
sent to take post at the Foulon, and ordered the bewildered
and uncertain sentry to go to his guard and call off the other
sentries. Knox says the resourceful Highlander was Captain
Donald McDonald; and there was an officer of that name in the
78th. Quartermaster-Sergeant John Johnson of the 58th tells
us that as Wolfe 'leaped out upon the beach' he looked up and
said, 'I don't think we can with any possible means get up
here, but however we must use our best endeavor.' [13] Unfortunately, there is no reason to believe that Johnson was there,
and as we shall see a rather better authority indicates that
Wolfe was not among the very first to land.

Townshend's rough notes again come to our help. Townshend was not there either, but as the officer in effective command at the end of the battle he had all the information in the
army at his disposal, and it cannot be doubted that he would
be interested in knowing just what had occurred. The passage
is even more untidy than usual, but its general meaning is
clear. He indicates that the landing took place 'considerably
below ye place of attack':

. . . Col Howe (now Sir William) found he was below it, & Major Delauney a very active & enterprizing Officer who had a command in ye light Corps, saying ye place was higher up ye River – & ye Colonel knowing ye Consequence of ye Enemie's perceiving at day light our situation & being reinforc'd, he ordered ye officer to attack where proposed & very gallantly himself scrambled up the rocky height in his front by which he turning to his left he attack'd & drove ye enemy from their position & most happily facilitated ye success of ye former up a narrow precipice with an abbatis & a battery just over it – which was firing on ye [ships?] just at daybreak.

Note that there is no mention of Wolfe (but Townshend would certainly not have gone out of his way to give credit to *him*). The picture we receive is that of a moment of uncertainty, a hasty reconnaissance and whispered consultation on the dark beach, and then Colonel Howe's decision to attempt to scale the cliff directly in front – something that had been no part of the plan – while Delaune and his party turn west to go for the path (the 'narrow precipice with an abbatis'). Howe is remembered in history chiefly as a too-leisurely British Commander-in-Chief in the American Revolution; let us not forget the bold young colonel who opened the door to Wolfe's army on the cliffs above Quebec.

Where did all this take place? Vergor's little camp was near the top of the path, exactly where it seems impossible to say. Howe turned 'to his left' to attack it. This, plus examination of the ground, tells the story. But the examination of the ground is important.

On the basis of the accounts that have been quoted, it might seem probable that the place where Howe made his climb was a spot some 400 yards east of the top of the Foulon road, where the hill, though high and steep, is clothed from bottom to top with bushes and small trees. This theory does not survive experiment on the spot. What a casual look at the cliff does not reveal is the nature of the surface. The whole face of the hill is covered today with small fragments of shale which constantly give way under the climber's feet; he can make progress only by pulling himself up by the trees and bushes, and when these fail him he sticks. (Admiral Saunders in his report to the Admiralty told how the soldiers 'were obliged to pull themselves up by the Stumps and boughs of Trees that cover'd the Declivity'; this phrase caught the eye and the imagination of Horace Walpole. Anyone who climbs these slopes east of Wolfe's Cove soon realizes that the Admiral was well informed.) It seems rather unlikely that the face of the hill was very different in 1759 – geologists laugh at two centuries – though it is of course impossible to be certain. One investigator, at least, was forced to the conclusion that to climb it at this point was impracticable in the dark for soldiers carrying their arms and ammunition.

The deduction seems to be that the ascent must have been farther west, closer to the Cove, where the slopes are easier and the cliff lower. Here the hill appears from below to be a relatively easy proposition; Professor Waugh wrote that the climb was 'well within the powers of any able-bodied person between the ages of ten and seventy'. Assuming that this is the area he means, it seems possible that he did not test his proposition by actual experiment. Those who do so, starting just east of the present railway tunnel and reaching the summit just east of the top of the Foulon road, will find the climb practicable but still tiring, for the surface here is the same shale as farther east, and here too a climber gets up only with the help of trees and shrubs. It may be that it would be easier after a prolonged spell of dry weather, when the soil under the shale would be firmer; but there was a great deal of rain in the first half of September 1759. My own experience left me convinced that the climb must have taken place in this area immediately east of the path, which a plaque at the top of the road seems to indicate as the traditionally accepted place; it also left me with a healthy respect for Howe and his men.

It is likely that only the leading companies of the army scaled the face of the cliff in this manner; but if we can take literally Admiral Holmes' statement, 'The General and the first embarkation of Troops climbed the Precipice and gained the Top of the Hill without any remarkable opposition', General Wolfe, sickly though he was, may have done the climb. Whether that excellent Royal Engineer, Mackellar, was early on the ground himself we do not know; in any case, he wrote a clear account [14] which we cannot do better than quote. The Light Infantry, he says, 'actually landed without being once fired at':

> The battalions under Brigadier-Generals Monkton and Murray landed immediately after them, and then the enemy's picket took the alarm and began to fire. Three companies of light infantry were immediately ordered to get up the bank to the right of the pathway, as they could, and to give a signal when they got up, upon which the remainder of the light infantry were to force the pathway, and attack the picket in front; but after a little firing, that picket was dispersed by these three companies only, the captain was wounded, and with about half his picket taken prisoners; the remainder made their escape along the edge of the bank towards the town, and with some small flying parties posted there kept firing upon some of our boats, which had by mistake dropped down too far that way, where the general was obliged to follow in his own boat to order them back. The battalions were formed upon the beach, as they landed, and now began to get up the bank and form above . . .
>
> The general being now landed gave orders to despatch the getting up of some troops still remaining below, and a guard being left to cover the remainder of the landing, got up the bank about clear daylight . . .

The implication seems to be that, Vergor's men once disposed of, the main body of the British force was able to move up the path; and this is specifically stated in the legend accompanying the engraving of the drawing of the affair made by Wolfe's aide-de-camp Hervey Smyth ('by this Road, afterwards mended, the remainder of the Army came up').

It is traditional to abuse Vergor. It is always asserted that he gave up Fort Beauséjour to the British in 1755 in a cowardly if not a treacherous manner, and escaped punishment through the influence of Bigot; yet the Governor of Cape Breton at the time expressed the opinion that he had done as much as his means allowed.[15] He is always accused of having allowed a large proportion of the men of his detachment to go home to

work their farms, on condition that they would do some work
on his own; but this seems to depend entirely on one doubtful
anonymous source, the gossipy *Mémoires sur le Canada*,[16]
whose author says Vergor's post was at Cap Rouge! Vergor
cannot have been much of an officer, or his post would have
been more alert; but as we have already suggested, some of
the responsibility for the surprise would seem to rest with
Vergor's superiors, who failed to ensure that the Foulon detachment and the other posts along the river were properly
supervised or that the detachments manning them did their
sleeping in the daytime and stood to their arms at night – the
procedure appropriate to the circumstances. La Pause says
of these posts, 'Senior officers did not visit them at night and
no one kept an eye on this area.'[17] We do not even know for
certain that Vergor and his men were asleep. It would seem, at
any rate, that at least one sentry was awake, and that it was
Fraser's (or McDonald's) cock-and-bull story, told in convincingly good French, that prevented an effective alarm being
given earlier. And we know that Vergor did send an orderly
off to warn the city.

Whoever was to blame, the improbable thing had happened.
A succession of long chances had all turned out in Wolfe's
favour. The supreme crisis of his plan had been surmounted.
A check at the Foulon would have ruined everything; but with
his little army safely landed and successfully deployed at the
top of the Foulon cliffs, he could face the next stage with com-
parative confidence.

The landing had not been carried out entirely without loss.
As soon as the French in the nearby posts realized what was
happening, the Samos battery west of the Foulon opened fire on
the ships and boats, and did some harm; the *Lowestoft*'s log
records one seaman killed, the *Squirrel*'s a certain amount of
damage to the ship; and small-arms fire from the banks caused
some casualties – Captain Knox says there were eight in his
boat. Townshend's notes mention that his men's boats shel-
tered behind the ships 'which ye Enemy was battering'. Once
well ashore, Wolfe sent Murray to deal with the battery. He
shortly recalled him, on seeing the French army beginning to

arrive from Beauport; but the threat was enough to cause the French to spike their guns and decamp, and the Light Infantry soon took possession of the battery.

There is some reason to think that Wolfe was slow to believe fully in his own success. Thirteen years later – rather too long after the event for the story to be very satisfactory evidence – Isaac Barré, Wolfe's good friend and supporter, told an inquirer (who seems to have been put up to it by James Murray) that subsequent to the first disembarkation and just after Wolfe had 'got on the hights', the General ordered Barré to return to the boats '& Stop them a little 'till he had an Oppertunity of knowing the Ennermy's Strength . . . & whether they might not be in Numbers sufficient to prevent his establishing himself.' Barré went back and found the boats alongside the transports 'and actually full of Troops ready to come on Shore'. He explained that, 'thinking from the knowledge he had of M$^r$. Wolfs Intentions, that the orders he had received were in consequence of his not expecting the Troops could be got landed so soon', he 'took the Liberty seeing Things thus situated, not to deliver the Orders he had received, but suffer'd the Troops to land as fast as possible & went & Reported it to Gen$^l$. Wolfe, who was much pleased to find himself Established on Shore with his Army sooner than he expected'.[18] Had the French been more alert and energetic, Barré's intelligent action might have made the difference for the British between victory and defeat. As things were – assuming that his memory was good and that he was accurately reported – it probably made no great difference.

As the British regiments landed and gained the summit of the cliffs, Wolfe formed them in line with their backs to the river, their right to the city and their left to Sillery. No doubt he feared an immediate French attack; but none materialized, and Wolfe himself, it appears, undertook a reconnaissance towards the town to choose the best ground to take up. The first landing had been about four o'clock; and according to Mackellar the last units – Burton's and Carleton's men from the south shore – joined the main body about eight.

Two hundred years later, the efficiency with which Wolfe's

daring plan had been executed by his regiments and the navy
still commands our admiration. Admiral Holmes had been
deeply worried by the responsibilities it laid upon him – 'The
most hazardous and difficult Task I was ever engaged in': [19]

> For the distance of the landing Place; the impetuosity of the
> Tide; the darkness of the Night; and the great chance of exactly
> hitting the very Spot intended, without discovery or alarm; made
> the whole extremely difficult: and the failing in any part of my
> Disposition, as it might overset the General's Plan, would have
> brought upon me an imputation of being the Cause of the Mis-
> carriage of the Attack . . .

No naval operation is more difficult and more hazardous, even
in the twentieth century, than landing troops in darkness on a
hostile shore with precision as to time and place. But for all
Holmes' apprehensions, there was no serious 'failing in his
dispositions'; the only hitch was the fact of the troops being
landed a little farther east than was intended, the result of the
speed of the tide; and the effect of this was repaired by the
resourcefulness of the army.

The credit is of course due primarily to the sailors. The
service which Wolfe had so often abused had served him mag-
nificently. The plan for the approach and landing – we do not
know whether it was made by Wolfe or by Holmes, or by the
two in consultation – was very sound, and it was most skilfully
executed. It is obvious that the boat work was extremely well
organized; the three successive flights of troops were lifted
and landed wih striking rapidity and smoothness. The army
did its part with a dexterity and boldness that matched the
navy's. This night's work fully supports the reputation of the
enterprise as a classic of combined operations. It was a professional triumph.

Very different – tragically different – is the story on the other
side. It begins with the fatal blunder about the provision boats,
and it goes on just as badly. In spite of all the firing that took
place around the Foulon immediately after the first landing,
hours passed before Montcalm and Vaudreuil, in the camp on

the Beauport shore, fully realized what had happened. For all Vaudreuil's disclaimers, it is hard to avoid the conclusion that this is basically due to a conviction in the minds of all the French leaders that no large-scale landing was possible in the Foulon area.

It was a disturbed night at Beauport; the feint made by Saunders was highly effective. Perhaps it is well to quote the account in Montcalm's journal, written by the artillery officer Montbeillard:

> ... In the evening I went to the quarters of M. le Marquis de Montcalm, who ordered me to move two field pieces next day to the height at the [Beauport] ravine to replace those that had been sent to M. de Bougainville. We walked for a long time, visiting our entrenchments; and the more I looked at them the more I was persuaded that the enemy would not attempt an attack upon them.
>
> *The 13th.* An hour after midnight M. du Mahe [Dumas] sent me word that a great noise of boats had been heard and that the troops were moving into the entrenchments. I immediately mounted, rode along the line and had the batteries put in readiness.
>
> Towards three o'cloock a patrol canoe arrived which assured us that the boats were on the edge of the Canardière bank. I moved a small gun to that point, and the Quebec militia advanced on to the beach. Another canoe was sent to get news of the enemy. It was a considerable time away and came back without seeing anything. The city then made the pre-arranged signal to indicate that something had happened. A little before day some musket-shots were heard above Quebec; we had no doubt that a convoy of provisions we were expecting had been discovered and perhaps captured. By what fatal circumstances, when the city signalled, did no one send to find out what had happened, and why was the Regiment of Guienne, which it had been decided should encamp on the heights above Quebec, still in our camp?

At dawn, says Montbeillard, a badly frightened Canadian, one of Vergor's men, arrived at the Canardière (just east of the St Charles) and reported that the enemy was on the heights; but 'We knew so well the difficulties of penetrating at that point, ill defended though it was, that people did not believe a word of his man's story, thinking that fear had turned his head.' Montbeillard was about to turn in — against a background of popping shots above the city — when he saw detachments of French troops making for the heights, and put aside all thought of sleep.

Just when or how Montcalm first heard of the landing is not clear; perhaps it was from the same fugitive mentioned by Montbeillard, or another. Vaudreuil claims that the General knew before he did, and did not bother to inform him. Vaudreuil himself learned of the attack, he says, by a note from the Chevalier de Bernetz, the commandant of the Lower Town and temporarily of the whole city. This queer little missive has been preserved.[20] In it Bernetz says he has learned by an orderly from Vergor that the British have landed at the Foulon; he thinks, however, that they have re-embarked, since musketry is no longer heard! He also says, quite inaccurately, that there has been an attack on the Lower Town, and remarks that the commander of the Guyenne battalion — the general reserve — 'cannot make too much haste'. The note was written at a quarter to six.

An hour later Vaudreuil sent to Bougainville a letter which breathes perplexity and irresolution.[12] Here it is:

I have received, Monsieur, the letter you did me the honour to write with the deposition of the prisoner or deserter attached. I have passed it all to M. le Marquis de Montcalm. It seems quite certain that the enemy has made a landing at the Anse au Foulon. We have put a large force (*bien du monde*) in motion. We hear a certain amount of shooting (*quelque petites fusillades*). M. le Marquis de Montcalm has just left with 100 men of the Government of Three Rivers as a reinforcement. As soon as I know for certain what is going on I shall inform you. I am anxious to have news of you and to know whether the enemy has made any attempt on your side.

I have the honour to wish you good day.

At a quarter to seven.

Your messenger will see M. de Montcalm in passing and will be able to give you news of him.

Vaudreuil.

The enemy's forces seem considerable. I do not doubt that you will be attentive to his movements and follow them. I rely on you for this,                              V.

Nearly three hours after the first landing, it is evident, the situation was still not clear enough to the Governor to make him feel safe in issuing a firm order to Bougainville to march towards Quebec. But Montcalm was riding to his last battlefield.

The Chevalier Johnstone, a Scots Jacobite who was aide-de-camp to Lévis and at this moment was serving Montcalm in a similar capacity, in his *Dialogue in Hades* puts into Montcalm's mouth the complaint that he did not choose the ground on which he fought the battle now imminent. He would, it is suggested, have preferred to march by Lorette and Ste Foy, join Bougainville and attack Wolfe from the west, pushing him back against the city; but by the time he heard of the landing the army was already on the Plains of Abraham or en route thither. There might have been much to be said for the course suggested, but there seems to be no other evidence to support Johnstone. Also, in view of the inadequate armament of the city walls, it is doubtful whether Montcalm would have dared leave Quebec uncovered. It is the case, however, that Lévis' journal – not a first-hand source, but probably based on information from the best-informed survivors – states that Montreuil was first to learn of the landing, from a fugitive. Montreuil, it says, ordered the Guyenne battalion, and the duty picquets of the other battalions, up to the heights before Montcalm was notified; the General then ordered the rest of the army to follow. By seven in the morning the troops from the Beauport camp were beginning to stream across the bridges.

Well might the author of the *Journal tenu à l'armée* comment bitterly on 'the mixture of misfortune and disorganization in our service' which prepared the French catastrophe, and on the extraordinary inadequacy of the communications provided between Bougainville's various posts, and between those posts and Montcalm's camp. As a result of this, the troops at Beauport, having manned the entrenchments a good part of the night, were dismissed to their tents at daylight, when the British were already landing at the Foulon in large numbers![22] In the early hours of September 13th an extremely efficient military machine clashed with a very inefficient one, and the consequences cannot be called surprising.

It was in a mood of shocked depression that Montcalm rode across the St Charles towards the heights where the line of scarlet shone in the morning light. Apparently Major Malartic was beside him on that grim ride. A fortnight later he wrote that he had never seen the General so melancholy. Ordinarily a free and vivacious talker, now he said not a word: 'it seemed as though he felt his fate upon him'.[23] One can well understand it, for Montcalm had been outwitted and out-generalled. His dispositions had failed. While he was watching the beach at Beauport, Wolfe had struck at a place where no blow had been expected. Nothing was left now but for Montcalm to take the chance of a desperate stroke in the open field against an army far better than his own.

# CHAPTER EIGHT

# The 13th of September: Battle

Having made his reconnaissance in the direction of the town, and presumably selected the ground he proposed to occupy, Wolfe moved the part of the army which was formed in line above the Foulon path off to the eastward along the cliff edge.[1] (There is really nothing to sustain Doughty's queer notion, based on a French account,[2] that it fetched a long circuit round by the Ste Foy road.) On coming opposite to the chosen position, it deployed to the left and stood in line of battle facing the city. It was now on the area of generally flat and open ground then commonly called the Plains – or the Heights – of Abraham; though the lands actually held by the seventeenth-century pilot Abraham Martin seem to have been considerably nearer the city than the ground taken up by Wolfe.[3] Knox tells us that this ground was occupied about six o'clock in the morning, and adds that the line as first formed consisted only of three battalions and the Louisbourg Grenadiers; but as more units came up Wolfe revised and extended it.

In the end, six battalions and the Grenadiers formed the battle-line. On the right, above the St Lawrence, drawn back to deal with the French sharpshooters in the bushes by the cliff-side, was the 35th; next came the Louisbourg Grenadiers, and in order the 28th, 43rd, 47th, 78th (Fraser's Highlanders) and 58th. Evidently in order to cover the long front across the plateau stretching towards the St Charles, the line was formed only two deep instead of the three then usual. In reserve in rear, extended on a wide front, was the 48th. Monckton, as

senior brigadier, commanded the right of the line, Murray the
left. As the battle developed and a threat by the French militia
and Indians appeared on the left, Townshend deployed the
15th Foot and the two battalions of Royal Americans, as they
arrived, *en potence* (at right angles to the main line) to counter
this. Later the 3rd Royal Americans were detached to protect
the landing-place at the Foulon, primarily, no doubt, against
the possibility of attack by Bougainville; and Howe's Light
Infantry offered additional protection to the rear of the British
army.[4] While these arrangements were being made, the navy
was performing one final service for Wolfe. The sailors were
dragging up the Foulon path two light brass 6-pounder guns,
which the Royal Artillery was shortly to bring into action with
great effect.

About these British dispositions there is very little doubt or
uncertainty. When we turn to the French side it is different. The
records are vague and full of disagreement. The basic problem
is, how many troops were left in the Beauport position, and
who was responsible for this? Vaudreuil's detractors blame him
for holding back troops that should have been sent to the
battlefield, for fear of a sea-borne attack, even at this late hour,
on the Beauport lines. Vaudreuil claims that he ordered forward the whole army except the guards for the batteries and
the St Charles *tête de pont* – and asserts that some militia (he
does not say which units or how many) were held east of the
St Charles on orders from Montreuil. Perhaps we might quote
the account of that relatively independent witness, the author
of the *Journal tenu*:

> Our army at Beauport had for some days been reduced, by the
> corps detached from it, to about 6000 men. To guard the camp
> were left the two battalions of Montreal, comprising about 1500
> men, which nevertheless advanced as far as the River St. Charles
> when M. de Vaudreuil went to the army. According to this cal-
> culation, then, M. de Montcalm could concentrate only about
> 4500 men.

This is probably not far from the truth, especially as Montbeillard states the number of men left in the camp as 1,400.

However, there is plenty of evidence that some of the troops of
the Government of Montreal (whose total strength Montcalm
had stated in July as 3,800) [5] were on the battlefield. And there
seems no doubt that, except possibly for a few *troupes de la
marine*, no regular soldiers were left in the camp; and the
regulars were the most important part of the army for the
business now in hand.

The various French – and British – accounts agree moder-
ately well on the composition of the French battle-line as
Montcalm finally formed it. On the right, nearest the St
Charles, a large number of Quebec militiamen and Indians, in
advance of the main French position, harassed the British left
flank from the bushes along the edge of the hill. In addition the
Government of Quebec probably provided a unit of the actual
battle-line here. And Vaudreuil states that there were also
some Montrealers on this flank. Then came the five gallant
little battalions of French regulars, from right to left La Sarre,
Languedoc, Béarn, Guyenne, and Royal-Roussillon, all in the
white uniform of the French Line (many distinguished authors
to the contrary, Royal-Roussillon did *not* wear blue). To the
left of the regulars were the Governments of Montreal and
Three Rivers; and, as on the other flank, in advance along the
declivity above the St Lawrence was a cloud of Canadian and
Indian snipers.[6]

To establish the ultimate French formation is not so easy.
Several British diarists speak of the French as advancing in
three 'columns' – that is, deep masses, the companies formed
one behind another, as distinct from extended lines. But Malartic, a competent soldier who was in the thick of the fight,
attributes the French defeat precisely to the fact that they did
*not* adopt such a formation.[7] Brigadier Townshend, speaking
from the viewpoint of an officer of the opposing army who had
ample opportunity to collect information later, says that Béarn
and Guyenne, in the centre, formed a column, but implies that
the right and left wings were in line. This may probably be
accepted, and it seems likely that there were considerable dis-
tances between the three bodies.

Much has been written about the strengths of the opposing

armies. Knox published a return indicating that the British on
the field numbered 4,828 all ranks. But the return accompanying Townshend's official dispatch – which ought to be the
most reliable source – makes the total only 4,441.[8] The larger
figure accords rather better with Wolfe's calculation of 3,600
as the strength of the troops embarked in the fleet above the
city; but perhaps it is best to use the official one. As for the
French, there is nothing remotely resembling a return, only
individual estimates. These range from 2,500 in Malartic's
journal (but the same writer says 'over 3000' in a letter to
Bourlamaque)[9] up to 4,500, as we have seen, in the *Journal
tenu à l'armée*. British estimates of the French strength also
vary widely. Knox's figure of 7,520, communicated to him 'by
an intelligent Frenchman', seems very high. Townshend's is
only 3,440. It is apparent that, quite apart from the 800 men
sent away with Lévis and the force of something less than
3,000 with Bougainville, there had been considerable wastage
in the French army; prisoners told Wolfe early in August that
1,500 Canadians had deserted.[10] If we accept the *Journal tenu*
figure of 4,500 for the strength on the battlefield, we shall
probably not be far wrong. It seems likely that the two opposing armies were very similar in strength. But they were very
different in quality. Wolfe's men were all regulars; whereas
Montcalm had estimated the strength of his five battalions of
*troupes de terre* at 2,900 at the beginning of the campaign,[11]
and large numbers of these had been detached or had become
casualties in the meantime.

It is interesting to attempt to relate the battlefield to the
modern topography. The best means of doing this is by reference to the contemporary plans made by the British engineers
(the French seem to have made no plans whatever). It is worth
reminding the visitor to Quebec that the present Battlefields
Park covers only a small portion of the actual field; the British
and French lines were astride the Grand Allée, and a great
part of the action took place on ground now covered with
buildings. It is useless to try to locate the events to within a
few yards; but it is evident that the right of the British line lay
in the close vicinity of the modern Prison. Montcalm's line

before his final advance was on the high ground then known as the Buttes à Neveu (marked today by the Martello towers built early in the nineteenth century). Only a scant quarter-mile separated the two armies. When the French attacked, the main clash took place somewhere in the area of De Salaberry and Cartier Streets.

We have so far said nothing about Colonel de Bougainville, except to quote the peculiar letter sent to him by Vaudreuil. The question of his doings is important and interesting.

Considering the significance of the matter, it is extraordinary how little first-hand evidence there is concerning the actions of Bougainville on the night of September 12th/13th. His biographer is unable to throw any light on them at all.[12] This has not prevented many authors from writing about them in detail. Notably, Doughty (who appears to have been able to convince himself of almost anything) assures us – chiefly, it seems, on the basis of a muddled reference by Foligné, who was in command of one of the Quebec batteries, and not in a position to have first-hand knowledge of the matter – that Holmes' ships went up to Pointe-aux-Trembles that night, and that Bougainville followed them there. He adds that even if some of Holmes' vessels went downstream, it was still Bougainville's duty to follow 'the larger vessels' west.[13] But as we have seen there is very little indication that Holmes made any upstream feint; while as for the 'larger vessels', Holmes' detailed account and their own logs make it quite clear that the largest of all, the *Sutherland*, remained at anchor at Cap Rouge, while the next in size, the frigates and sloops, dropped down the river carrying troops for the landing.

The fact is that there is no good evidence of any movement on Bougainville's part on the night of September 12th/13th. Apart from a brief and uninformative memorandum of the campaign as a whole,[14] only one account written by himself seems to have survived, and none of his apologists is acquainted with it. It is a letter written to Bourlamaque five days after the battle, and so short that it is easily quoted:[15]

You know, Monsieur, the details of our unlucky adventure, the loss of our general, of the finest position in the world, and I may almost say, of our honour. A man allowed himself to be surprised at the Anse des Mères; I was at Cap Rouge (*je suis au cap Rouge*). The enemy landed at midnight, I was informed only at eight o'clock. M. de Montcalm marched against them and considered himself obliged to attack without waiting for me; when I got close enough to come into action, the army had been routed, and all the enemy's forces turned on me . . .

(After this, it is perhaps unkind to quote Doughty: 'Bougainville was not at Cap Rouge ... Had Bougainville been at Cap Rouge at this time, it could only have been by disobedience of orders.')[16] If Bougainville had really made any movement up the river, it is incredible that he should not have mentioned it. And it is worth recalling that the static posts along the river, including those at Samos and the Foulon, were under Bougainville's command; he is therefore answerable for the failure to make adequate arrangements for passing information of the attack. He was an able man, but his military experience was scarcely equal to the high rank he held and the heavy responsibilities that rested upon him. Vaudreuil says that Bougainville saw the vessels going down the river, 'and nevertheless remained at Cap Rouge, although there was then only one ship anchored there'. Bougainville refrained from mentioning the matter in his letter to Bourlamaque, so we have no real information as to why he failed to act. One thing is pretty clear: since he evidently had not left his station that day, and since it appears that there had been little activity by the British ships for some days past, the traditional explanation, that his men were worn out by constant marching and counter-marching in pursuit of the squadron, will not hold water.

One of the oft-repeated stories concerning the Battle of the Plains relates to Montcalm's artillery. He sent, we are told, to the Chevalier de Ramezay, in command of the Quebec garrison, to ask for 'twenty-five field pieces which were on the Palace battery'; but Ramezay would give him only three. Parkman tells this story, and almost every author since his time has echoed it; but one searches the contemporary records in vain for evidence to support it. And one discovers in the process that de Ramezay was not in Quebec at the time of the battle! He was absent through illness, and returned to duty only later in the day. The tale about his refusing the guns seems to rest entirely upon the authority of Johnstone's *Dialogue in Hades*.[17] This account of the battle in the form of an imaginary conversation between Wolfe and Montcalm was, one suspects, written long afterwards, and it scarcely deserves the importance as a source which many historians have accorded it. There is no hint of any such incident in any of the accounts by Frenchmen who were there. It is hard to believe that if it had really happened it would not have been mentioned by Montbeillard, Montcalm's diarist, who was in charge of the guns on the field of battle; Montcalm would certainly have told Montbeillard and Montbeillard would certainly have recorded it. But the artilleryman merely says, 'They had sent us some [guns] from the city', and goes on to describe how he placed them. There is no note of complaint here or in any other diarist's account.

In any case, the twenty-five field guns seem to have existed only in Johnstone's imagination. One version of the *Dialogue* [18] calls them brass guns, another [19] omits the adjective; one calls them 'two or three pounders', another 2-pounders. No such group of guns appears in the detailed statement of guns surrendered with Quebec on September 18th.[20] There are only eight brass guns of any sort on the list, and only two brass 2-pounders. There are only two field carriages for 2-pounders; there are also, however, fifteen for 4-pounders and seventeen for 6-pounders, and there are numerous iron guns of these last calibres. (Nothing is said of the carriages' condition.) It might thus have been possible to get together twenty-five field guns in Quebec, but not guns of the sort described by Johnstone; and there is nothing in the contemporary records to suggest that there were either gunners to man them or teams to draw them. They could of course have been manhandled.

As it was, the French out-gunned the British on the battlefield, though it is hard to establish how many guns they had. Montbeillard, the person best able to tell us, is vague. He says he 'detached' two guns from the left to the right, and later he speaks of the 'pieces' on the left, which suggests a minimum of four. Foligné says there were five guns.[21] At any rate, there were more than the British two. Whether they were as well served is perhaps doubtful.

Another of Johnstone's stories, which has been just as widely circulated as the one about the guns, has just as much, or as little, evidence to support it. He says that Montcalm assembled a council of war on the battlefield, and that every member of it favoured attacking at once. No other source mentions any such thing. Montreuil, who according to Johnstone argued in the council for attacking in columns instead of in line, makes no reference to it in the letter to Lévis in which he describes the battle.[22] Montcalm doubtless had some informal discussion with the senior officers, but it is almost incredible that he could have called a formal council without its being in some way recorded. There is nothing to indicate that Montcalm was ever in any doubt as to what he had to do; the decision to attack, right or wrong, was his own.

While the French force was concentrating and Montcalm was ranging it in order of battle, fierce and sanguinary skirmishing was going on. The French had pushed parties of colonial regulars and militiamen forward, in the centre as well as on the flanks, and these were exchanging shots with the British. The fighting was especially fierce on the St Charles side, where the British occupied a couple of houses which seem to have changed hands at least once. Montbeillard's guns came into action here, and one of the houses was set on fire by one side or the other. French and British alike suffered casualties by artillery fire during this phase.[23]

It was a long way from the centre or left of the Beauport lines to the Heights; but by half past nine, according to Malartic, all the units mentioned above had arrived on the ground. About this time Montbeillard passed from the right to the left on one of his artillery errands. He writes:

I paused a moment with M. le Marquis de Montcalm, who said to me: 'We cannot avoid action; the enemy is entrenching, he already has two pieces of cannon. If we give him time to establish himself, we shall never be able to attack him with the sort of troops we have.' He added with a sort of shiver, 'Is it possible that Bougainville doesn't hear all that noise?' He left me without giving me time to say anything in reply, except that we were very thin on the ground.[24]

The moment had almost come. As Montbeillard stood by his guns on the left, he suddenly saw that the French battle-line was in motion, 'M. de Montcalm at its head and on horseback'.

Many books assure us that Wolfe had put on a new uniform which rendered him an obvious mark for enemy sharpshooters; but for this as for so many other stories one looks in vain for support in the contemporary records. But that he exposed himself recklessly cannot be doubted. He was active in the forefront as the skirmishing proceeded. Mackellar says, 'The general moved about everywhere, but after the action began kept on a rising ground where our right stood, from whence he had a view of the whole field.' Townshend in his notes tells how just before the French advance Wolfe 'came towards ye left', and finding all well there returned to the centre. The fire of the French skirmishers was deadly enough to lead Wolfe to order his troops to lie down,[25] and they doubtless lay on their arms until it became obvious that the French were about to advance.

It was about ten o'clock when Montcalm gave the order to march. (Practically all the ships' logs give this as the time when the noise of the general action was heard.) The ensigns let the big silk colours fly; the drums rolled out the charge; across the intervening space the British heard a deep-throated cheer. No doubt the gayness and the gilt of the five French battalions had suffered somewhat during the long summer of campaigning; yet they must still have been a gallant sight as they moved down the slope in their white uniforms. *De bonne grâce* – so say both Montreuil and Malartic – the mingled array of regulars and militiamen went forward to fight for the colony and the King.

The French advanced at a run – 'much too fast', Malartic told Bourlamaque. They paid now for Montcalm's error of judgement in incorporating a body of militia in every regular battalion. The formation began to fall to pieces immediately. 'We had not gone twenty paces,' writes Malartic, 'when the left was too far in rear and the centre too far in front.'[26] At half-musket-shot from the British the shaky line came to a halt to fire an unsteady volley; the same witness says, 'the Canadians who formed the second rank and the soldiers of the third fired without orders, and according to their [the Canadians'] custom threw themselves on the ground to reload. This false movement broke all the battalions.' (It is not easy to load a muzzle-loader in the prone position; but Malartic is presumably writing about things he saw.) Montbeillard gives a slightly different account. He says, 'The French and Canadian front rank had gone down on one knee [to fire] and lay down after the volley.' Knox's version is that the French began to fire when 130 yards from the British. He indicates that they continued firing until they came within forty yards; but the French accounts suggest that many of the troops never advanced beyond the point where the firing began. Malartic's journal says that the men who lay down went to the right about the moment they picked themselves up.

The scarlet line of British infantry stood impassive. 'General Wolfe', Quartermaster-Sergeant Johnson recalled many years later, 'had given positive Orders, not to fire a Shot until the Enemy should be within Forty Yards of the point of our Bayonets.' (There are various accounts of the actual range at which fire was opened, and it is interesting that Townshend said sixty yards in the draft of his dispatch,[27] but changed this to forty in the final version.) The British guns tore the French formation with their grape-shot, but the muskets – each loaded on Wolfe's instructions 'with an additional ball' – remained silent, the disciplined soldiers waiting for the word. Nevertheless, the schoolbook story of the single crashing volley that finally came – the 'most perfect volley ever fired on battlefield', says Sir John Fortescue's *History of the British Army* – is an over-simplification. The French witnesses do not speak of such a volley; Montbeillard says that the British replied to the French discharge with 'a very lively platoon fire' – that is, a fire by platoons in succession. Knox does tell us, however, that the British units in the centre, 'being little affected by the oblique fire of the enemy', did fire like a single cannon-shot. There was no way of coordinating the firing of a single volley across that long line. No doubt each individual battalion commander judged the distance and gave the word himself. Nor did the British stand fast as long as has been reported. It seems likely that their first fire was by platoons; that the units after firing moved a few yards forward to get clear of the smoke; and that the 'general' volley came then. Here is the version given on the great engineers' plan signed by Mackellar [28] – probably as good a short contemporary account as exists:

> The French Line began the charge about nine [we have seen that it was probably about ten] advancing briskly and for some little time in good order, a part of their Line began to fire too soon, which immediately catch'd throughout the whole, then they began to waver but kept advancing with a scattering Fire. – When they had got within about a hundred yards of us our Line movd up regularly with a steady Fire, and when within twenty or thirty yards of closing gave a general one; upon which a total route of the Enemy immediately ensued.

Several accounts say that the French right broke first, and that the left stood longest.

Of one thing there is no doubt. The French fire had been ineffective – much less effective than that of their skirmishers earlier; but the British musketry, at that close range, was deadly in the last degree. In one brief spasm of firing Brown Bess blew Montcalm's army into ruin. The whole desperate encounter lasted only a few short minutes; and at the end of it the men of the French force who were still on their feet were in flight towards the city, and the British line had been launched in pursuit.[29]

At this moment Wolfe met his fate – a fate which he had done nothing to avoid and may even have deliberately courted.

Nearly four years before he had written a prophetic letter to his mother: [30]

> I reckon it a very great misfortune to this country that I, your son, who have, I know, but a very modest capacity, and some degree of diligence a little above the ordinary run, should be thought, as I generally am, one of the best officers of my rank in the service. I am not at all vain of the distinction. The comparison would do a man of genius very little honour, and does not illustrate me, by any means; and the consequence will be very fatal to me in the end, for as I rise in rank people will expect some considerable performances, and I shall be induced, in support of an ill-got reputation, to be lavish of my life, and shall probably meet that fate which is the ordinary effect of such conduct.

Perhaps he thus fell a victim to the spur of fame. Perhaps he deliberately exposed himself. It might seem strange that a young general with a brilliant career before him, and a man engaged to be married, should invite destruction; but as we have already suggested he may well have come to believe that he had only a short time to live in any case, and have thought a quick and glorious death on the battlefield, in the moment of a victory which – now he had brought the French to action – he had every reason to expect, far preferable to a lingering and painful illness. But these are only speculations, for apart from this letter – and perhaps also that other letter, to Amherst, in which he spoke of sacrificing 'even my Life' – we have no way of looking into his mind.

Almost every book tells us that Wolfe was struck three times: first, in the wrist, which he bandaged with a handkerchief; secondly, in the groin; and thirdly, and fatally, in the right breast. But Townshend's notes mention only wounds 'in ye hand' and in the breast. The story of the three wounds probably derives from a letter, apparently from a naval officer, published in the *Gentleman's Magazine* for December 1759; this says that Wolfe 'first received a musket ball thro' his right wrist, which tore the sinews much, but he wrapped his handkerchief round it, and marched on. The next he received was in his belly, about an inch below the navel, and the third shot just above the right breast.' It is quite incredible that a man could be shot in the stomach and disregard it ('he seemed scarcely to feel it', says Waugh!); we may conclude either that this wound did not happen, that it was inflicted by a spent bullet, or that it was simultaneous with the wound in the chest.

There is a story that Wolfe was shot by a British deserter – who afterwards confessed at Crown Point when about to be executed for desertion. The tale, though rather improbable, is certainly not impossible. (Knox tells us that a deserter from the Royal Americans was found wounded on the field and promptly court-martialled and shot.) But it seems to have been recorded only a long time afterwards.[31] The General was on the right, in front of the 28th Foot and the Louisbourg Grenadiers; and Townshend says that he suffered his death-wound as he led these corps into the charge. The probability is that he fell a victim to a French or Canadian marksman among the bushes on the edge of the hill above the St Lawrence.

The death of Wolfe has been the subject of what is 'probably the most famous of all historical paintings'[32] – and, as history, certainly one of the very worst. The General's senior officers assuredly did not gather round him in a picturesque group as depicted by Benjamin West; all the evidence is that not more than four people were with him when he died. The *Gentleman's Magazine* the month after the battle recorded a version of his last words: '*Support me*, said he to such as were near him, *let not my brave soldiers see me drop. – The day is ours – keep it.*' Captain Knox went to great trouble to collect information about Wolfe's last moments from those who were with him, and his account is famous and quite possibly accurate:

. . . he desired those who were about him to lay him down; being asked if he would have a Surgeon? he replied, 'it is needless; it is all over with me.' One of them then cried out, 'they run, see how they run.' 'Who runs?' demanded our hero, with great earnestness, like a person roused from sleep. The Officer answered, 'The enemy, Sir; Egad they give way every-where.' Thereupon the General rejoined, '*Go one of you, my lads, to Colonel Burton–; tell him to march Webb's regiment with all speed down to*

> *Charles's River, to cut off the retreat of the fugitives from the bridge.*' Then, turning on his side, he added, '*Now, God be praised, I will die in peace*: ' and thus expired.

Certainly Wolfe did not live long after receiving his fatal wound. The master's log of the *Lowestoft* tells the tale:

> At 10 our troops began a general action with the French. ½ past 10 was brought on board General Moncton wounded and several officers. At 11 was brought on board yᵉ corps of General Wolf . . .

Only a few minutes after Wolfe's fall, it would seem, Montcalm too was mortally hit. Montreuil says — and no eye-witness contradicts it — that he was wounded during the retreat, no doubt as he was swept along by the mob of fugitives. Colonel Williamson, Wolfe's artillery commander, asserted that he fell a victim to grape-shot from one of Williamson's 6-pounders;[33] and it is quite possible that Montcalm, a prominent figure on his charger, was deliberately sniped by the British gunners. According to Malartic, his wounds were in the lower part of the stomach and the thigh. Montbeillard saw him ride painfully back into the city, three soldiers holding him in the saddle. He was beyond help, but he was not to relax his hold on life until early the following morning.

The short violent clash between the two firing-lines was not quite the end of the battle. The Highlanders sweeping forward with their broadswords, and the English regiments with their bayonets, did some execution among the fleeing French (though Ensign Fraser recorded that they never caught up with the main body). That the pursuit was less effective than it has been represented is evidenced by the fact that the British captured only two guns and not a single colour. And the pursuers did not have things all their own way. This was particularly the case on the northern flank. Here, just east of the ground on which Montcalm had formed his line, was a considerable wooded area. Under its cover and that of the hill sloping down to the St Charles, some hundreds of Canadians made a stand which checked the British for some time. Fraser describes how the 78th, after carrying the pursuit almost to the city walls, were led by Murray by a circuit through the woods back to the battlefield, where they became engaged in a sanguinary fire-fight with the Canadians on the edge of the Côte d'Abraham overlooking the General Hospital. The enemy, he says, 'killed and wounded a great many of our men, and killed two Officers, which obliged us to retire a little, and form again'. Only when the 58th and the 2nd Royal Americans came to the High-landers' aid were they able to drive their antagonists down the hill and over the St Charles. In this phase the British also suf-fered somewhat from the fire of the hulks in the mouth of the St Charles.[34] These circumstances enabled the author of the *Journal tenu* (who must certainly have been a Canadian) to re-mark cattily, 'the rout was not complete except among the regular troops'; and indeed there seems little doubt that it was the local militia, fighting from cover in their traditional manner, who made it possible for the beaten army to make good its escape across the bridges to the Beauport camp.

The clash between the little armies had taken a considerable toll in life. The British casualties are returned by Townshend as 658 all ranks, of whom 58 were killed. The loss was heavy in the senior ranks, Monckton, Carleton and Barré all being wounded. The regiment suffering most was Fraser's High-landers, with 168 casualties. On the French side, Vaudreuil reported the loss of 'about 600' men in addition to 44 officers.[35] It seems strange that the beaten army should not lose more heavily than the victors, and the Governor may have under-stated; Townshend estimated the French loss as high as 1,500 men. Yet it must be remembered that the British casualties were heaviest during the skirmishing before and after the main encounter, whereas those of the French were chiefly suffered during that encounter itself; so it is possible that Vaudreuil's figures were not far from the truth. Like the British, the French lost heavily in senior officers; in addition to Montcalm, the two officers next in seniority, Sénezergues and Fontbonne, were both mortally wounded.

Vaudreuil arrived on the heights at the end of the battle. He had, he says, sent Montcalm a letter urging him not to attack prematurely, but the General disregarded it. The Governor does not explain why he himself was so late on the ground. He claims that he rallied 1,000 or more Canadians, who maintained for some time a fire which served to cover the retreat of the right wing of the army, commanded by Dumas.[36] It was doubtless Dumas' men who had inflicted such heavy losses on the Highlanders.

Bougainville, we have seen, was apparently even later than Vaudreuil. He arrived near the battlefield only after the battle was over. Townshend, who had taken command of the British force after Wolfe's fall and Monckton's wound, moved two battalions and two guns to oppose him. Bougainville at once withdrew, and Townshend let him go. In his dispatch he expresses the hope that he will not be blamed for not 'risking y^e fruit of so decisive a Day' by pursuing a fresh enemy who might be found posted among 'Woods & Swamps'. Neither commander showed any disposition to be bold at this moment. It is likely, however, that Bougainville's appearance, and his continued presence nearby, helped to deter Townshend from making any attempt to complete the victory by following the main French force across the St Charles. Townshend's rough notes, indeed, describe how he found himself in the first instance with only one battalion to confront Bougainville, and was embarrassed by the fact that the artillery had 'brought wrong ammunition'; but he 'maintained his position till reinforced by y^e return of some of y^e scatter'd forces, from the pursuit', whom he had sent his aide-de-camp to collect.

Those who wish to know the reasons for the British victory have not far to seek. The Battle of the Plains was an encounter between an army of professionals and an army largely composed of amateurs. Since it was fought under quasi-European conditions (Malcolm Fraser called it 'the first regular engagement that ever was fought in North America'), the result could have been anticipated, as indeed it had been fully anticipated by Wolfe. Discipline and training had their due effect. This was the fundamental factor. It has been argued that superior armament played an important part. No doubt it had some influence (one recalls Murray's comment about the evident

French fear of 'the English Musket' at Deschambault); but it was a secondary one. The regular soldier, whose advent in America in Braddock's campaign four years before had been so inauspicious, had now emerged as king of the American battle-field.

A tactical error by Montcalm had contributed to the result. As Lévis said afterwards, a defeated general is always wrong (he might have added that a dead one is at a particular disadvantage). Vaudreuil could be depended on to blame Montcalm for the disaster; but many other people besides Vaudreuil felt that he had attacked prematurely. That he had to attack there is no doubt; there was almost no food in Quebec, and Wolfe was across the line of communication by which food could come. Even if the city had been provisioned, the state of the fortifications was such that no long defence would be possible. But he did not need to attack at ten o'clock instead of twelve or two. The French reports that the British were entrenching are not confirmed from the British side; and while Wolfe could certainly have used the extra time to bring up more artillery, the French also had additional guns available in the city, and in spite of the ill-attested story about the commandant holding them back it is hard to believe that Montcalm really could not have got some of them. Bougainville had with him the best troops in the French army, and to attack without them was to court disaster. It is highly probable that the French would have been beaten even if Bougainville had been present, so serious was the difference in military quality between the opposing forces; but his presence would have given them a better chance. And the more Montcalm could have worn down and weakened his antagonists before the action by the formidable skirmishing fire of his Canadian irregulars, the greater that chance would have been. But his natural impulsiveness apparently got the better of him, and he threw away the colony's slim hopes in a piece of gallant folly.

The British victory, on the other hand, was far from complete; for the greater part of the French army made good its escape across the St Charles, and as we shall see it got clear away to the west that night. The loss of Wolfe was a serious misfortune for the British. Whatever his failings as a strategist, he had held the army on the battlefield in the hollow of his hand; and if Knox's informant gave an accurate account of his last words, he had a sharp appreciation of the importance of preventing the French from getting across the St Charles bridges. There is nothing to back up Willson's statement that Townshend, on taking command, 'instantly rescinded' Wolfe's order to move the 48th down to the river; there is indeed no evidence that either Burton or Townshend ever heard of the order. (However, one of the diarists tells us that the two battalions used by Townshend against Bougainville were the 48th and the 35th; and this is quite probable.)[37]

But there was certainly a period when there was no effective command. Wolfe was dying, the second-in-command had been incapacitated about the same time that the General received his mortal wound, and there is no telling just how much time passed before Townshend heard that the command had passed to him and was able to assume it. The spectacle described by Fraser, of Murray marching about with the 78th, mopping up the remnants of the French on the field instead of moving rapidly to cut off their retreat, testifies to the absence of higher tactical control. When Townshend did take charge he concentrated on re-forming the army, which had fallen into disorder in the pursuit, making its position on the Plains secure, and dealing with Bougainville. The latter's appearance, as we have seen, seems to have been a serious complication. Perhaps Townshend did as much as he could do in the circumstances. But thanks to lack of direction at a critical moment an opportunity had been missed. The French army had been defeated but not destroyed; and another year's campaign was required to finish the task left incomplete on the famous 13th of September.

# CHAPTER NINE

## The Fall of Canada

Back in the Beauport camp, surrounded by the debris of the French army, the Marquis de Vaudreuil found himself at a loss. What was to be done now?

His first act was to send a note to Montcalm, seeking his advice. The dying General's reply, sent through his aide-de-camp, Marcel, was no more helpful than one would expect from a man in his condition. He offered Vaudreuil three choices: capitulate 'for the whole colony'; make a new attack on the enemy; or retire on the Jacques Cartier River.[1] The cloudy state of Montcalm's mind is reflected in the fact that he sent to the British commander, apparently this same evening, while the authorities of the colony were trying to decide whether or not to make an effort to hold the city, a letter beginning, 'Obliged to yield Quebec to your arms, I have the honour to beg Your Excellency's kindness for our sick and wounded ...'[2]

Vaudreuil now took the action natural to the period and the circumstances. He called a council of war, summoning to it Bigot and the surviving senior officers. It met early in the evening, the minutes being signed at six o'clock. Vaudreuil asked it to consider whether it was possible to make a new attack on the British. This was rejected in favour of a retreat up the river (the minutes say 'unanimously', but Bigot claims to have supported Vaudreuil in advocating a new attack at dawn). The officers emphasized the condition of the army after the lost battle, and the fact that the British were between it and its supplies.[3] Vaudreuil issued orders accordingly, and at nine o'clock the army moved off up the east bank of the St Charles, directed on Charlesbourg and the two Lorettes, the object being to march around the British and get in rear of them. It was, in Malartic's phrase, 'a forced march, with little order'; a flight rather than a retreat. Artillery, ammunition and food supplies were left behind, for want of transport. But the movement achieved its purpose. The army made good its escape without interference by the enemy, and the following day it was at Pointe-aux-Trembles on the St Lawrence, whence the flight was continued to the Jacques Cartier.[4]

Townshend offers no apology or explanation for his failure to prevent the French from getting away. He could hardly have hoped to seize the bridge or bridges before they could destroy them – except perhaps in the first heat and confusion of the pursuit, when he was involved with Bougainville; but in the words of the record of Vaudreuil's council of war, the St Charles was fordable 'almost everywhere at low water', and the water was low on the afternoon of the 13th.[5] Of course, the British troops were undoubtedly exhausted after a night without rest and a fierce engagement; they would have had to be driven hard to enable them to make another great effort that day. Only exceptional leadership could have compassed it. Wolfe, one suspects, might have done it; Townshend could not, or at any rate did not.

Vaudreuil did two things before he rode away with the fleeing army. He obviously felt unequal to carrying the military burden; and he wrote off to Lévis begging him to join him as soon as possible. And he sent de Ramezay, the commandant of Quebec, instructions that he was not to try to hold out until the city was taken by assault: 'thus as soon as food runs short he will hoist the white flag'. He even provided de Ramezay with draft articles of capitulation.[6] No special steps were taken to prepare the city for defence, the obvious assumption being that it could not be defended. The garrison consisted of the various scratch units already in the place; and little was done to move into the city the food the army was leaving behind at Beauport.[7]

On September 14th, then, the general situation was this.

The Governor and the remains of the French field army were
retreating up the St Lawrence towards Jacques Cartier. Bougainville with his unengaged detachment was at Pointe-aux-
Trembles, covering the rear. The British army was entrenching
itself on and near the battlefield and preparing to construct
batteries and besiege Quebec in form. And within the city a
weak garrison of mixed composition and very doubtful morale
was contemplating an almost empty larder. Its low spirits
must have been further depressed by the death of Montcalm.
He had died at four o'clock that morning, and was buried in a
bomb-crater in the chapel of the Ursulines.[8]

On the 17th Lévis arrived at Jacques Cartier and put himself
at the head of the disorganized army. He considered that the
retreat had been an error, and with Vaudreuil's concurrence
decided to march the army back to Quebec. His plan, he says,
was 'to do and risk everything in the world to prevent the
taking of Quebec, and, if the worst came to the worst, to move
all the people out and destroy the city, so the enemy will not
be able to spend the winter there'. The British, he calculated,
were not numerous enough to rope the city off completely and
prevent communication with it.[9] But shortage of food prevented him from moving until the 18th, and he arrived too
late.

On the 15th the Chevalier de Ramezay had summoned the
senior officers of the Quebec garrison to a council of war. Its
proceedings have been preserved.[10] They make the point that,
weak as the fortifications are, the city might hold out for a
time if properly provisioned; but investigation had showed
that food stocks were so low that, with the ration reduced to
'half or even a quarter' of normal, there were only fifteen or
sixteen thousand rations left 'to feed more than six thousand
mouths', of which only 2,200 were those of combatants. De
Ramezay asked every officer to give his views in writing. Fourteen did so; and thirteen advised capitulation – chiefly on the
grounds of food shortage. The single exception was a bold
gunner captain, one de Fiedmont, who voted to 'reduce the
ration again and persevere in defending the place to the last
extremity'.

Confronted with this situation, and with Vaudreuil's instructions before him, it is not surprising that de Ramezay moved
towards surrender. But he moved fairly deliberately. By September 17th, however, the British were beginning to construct
batteries to breach the fortifications on the weak land side of
the town; they had actually brought up the cliff road, according to Knox, sixty guns and fifty-eight howitzers and mortars.
Perhaps still more daunting, their ships of the line moved up
this day, as Admiral Saunders said, 'in a Disposition to attack
the lower Town, as soon as General Townshend was ready to
do so by the upper'. It seems quite likely that it was those
'eight great ships' with their rows of black grinning guns that
finally convinced de Ramezay. At any rate, it was just past mid-
day when the ships moved up; and at three o'clock that afternoon, according to his own account, he hoisted the white flag
and sent Joannès, the town major of Quebec, to the British
camp to propose a capitulation.[11]

By this time Vaudreuil was trying to communicate with de
Ramezay to urge him to hold out until Lévis could relieve the
city. Just what happened is a trifle uncertain (letters which the
Governor sent to de Ramezay were lost by the horseman who
was carrying them!) but Vaudreuil says that there was contact
with the commandant through Bougainville, and through a detachment of the French cavalry which had occupied the 'horn-
work' at the head of the St Charles bridge. On the night of the
17th/18th de la Rochebeaucourt, the cavalry commander, rode
round the British and reached Quebec with a force of his men
carrying on their saddles 'a hundred and some pouches of
biscuit'. De Ramezay told him it was too late. The British had
accepted the terms of the proposed capitulation (except a provision permitting the garrison to march to join Lévis' army)
and he had sent Joannès back to them with full powers to make
a final agreement. He added, however, that if any article was
refused he would break off the negotiation, provided only
Vaudreuil would send him four or five hundred men next
day.[12]

No such hitch took place. 'The thing was far too advanced
to be able to withdraw', de Ramezay wrote to Vaudreuil.[13]

One is left with the impression that he did not particularly want to withdraw and have the shooting begin again. The militia and sailors who made up the greater part of the garrison were deserting, and he was under strong pressure from the inhabitants to surrender.[14] The capitulation of Quebec was signed in the British camp on the morning of the 18th. The garrison was allowed the honours of war, and was to 'be embarked as conveniently as possible, to be sent to the first port in France'. The inhabitants' property was to be respected and protected, the 'free exercise of the Roman religion' was guaranteed, and special safeguards were accorded to the clergy and particularly the Bishop of Quebec.[15]

Both chief signatories of this document apologized for it to their superiors. De Ramezay, as we have seen, represented himself as bound in honour by his agreements with the British to proceed with it, and again called attention to the very small amount of food remaining in Quebec.[16] Townshend on his side evidently felt that he might be criticized for the leniency of the terms. He listed in his dispatch the circumstances which had made it desirable to get possession of the city as soon as possible: 'the enemy assembling in our rear, the inclemency of the season which would scarcely admit of our bringing a gun up the precipice, the critical situation of our fleet from the Aequinoctial gales . . . , add to this the entering the town in a defensible state, against any attack which might otherwise be attempted against it in the winter'. Nobody in England seems to have complained; but poor de Ramezay was much abused, not least by Vaudreuil, who wrote to him that he could send the news of his capitulation to France himself.[17] Considering that de Ramezay's crime was that he had carried out Vaudreuil's original written instructions of September 13th to the letter, this seems a little hard.

The British took possession of the fortress on the evening of the 18th. First to enter were fifty men of the Royal Artillery with a field piece 'with the British colours hoisted on its carriage'; they were followed by the Louisbourg Grenadiers, who mounted guard on the gates. To Colonel Williamson of the Artillery went the honour of hoisting the Union Jack on the walls of Quebec. Simultaneously Captain Palliser of the navy landed in the Lower Town with a body of seamen.[18]

At this moment the French army, its morale and organization at least in some degree restored by the efforts of Lévis, was approaching the city. On hearing from de la Rochebeaucourt of de Ramezay's intention to surrender, Lévis had ordered Bougainville forward with all speed; and his detachment was only half a league from Quebec when the bitter news arrived that the British were in the city. Their hopes shattered, the French fell back. On Lévis' advice Vaudreuil built a fort at the mouth of the Jacques Cartier River, and that stream became the 'frontier' of the French territory. The Governor, leaving the command of the army to Lévis, arrived at Montreal on October 1st and addressed himself to composing his apologia for the year's reverses.[19]

The British made rapid arrangements for the security of their conquest during the winter. Monckton, on the surgeons' advice, left for New York; Townshend returned to England; and it fell to Murray, the junior brigadier, to remain at Quebec as Governor and military commander. Virtually the whole army stayed, except that the Louisbourg Grenadiers were sent back to their own regiments, only a hundred Rangers were retained, and Williamson with one company of artillery and the siege guns went off to Boston. Saunders did not dare leave large ships in the river over winter, but he arranged to leave a couple of sloops at Quebec, and at Halifax he stationed a strong detachment under Lord Colville with orders to re-enter the St Lawrence as early in the spring as possible. Having provisioned the city, the Admiral dropped down the river on October 18th. The last ships departed on the 26th, and Murray and his regiments were left to their own resources.[20]

It had been a disastrous campaign for the French; and yet all was not irretrievably lost. The country's capital and chief fortress had fallen to the enemy; nevertheless, Vaudreuil's instructions from the Court had been carried out. A large and important part of the colony, including the town of Montreal, remained in French hands. A considerable French military force was still in being. The Governor and the leaders of the army had gained for the Court the time it had asked for. It remained to be seen what it would do with it.

The departure of the British fleet permitted the French to take the risk of slipping a number of their own ships past Quebec, and although some were wrecked in the attempt others got away successfully late in November. By them Lévis was able to send to the Court his proposals for the next year's campaign. The story of that campaign is an essential epilogue to this book; but it must be very briefly told.

If the King wished to support Canada, said Lévis, he must send a squadron that would arrive in the St Lawrence in the month of May before the British, carrying a landing force of six or seven thousand troops in addition to 4,000 recruits for the emaciated regular battalions in Canada. A train of artillery was also essential, and warlike stores of every sort to replace those lost with Quebec. An armament of this sort could recover Quebec, for the place could not stand ten days' siege; and, this once accomplished, the landing-force could return to France with the squadron. Failing such help, mere want of everything would compel the colony to surrender.[21]

Versailles was no more disposed to undertake an effort of this sort in 1760 than it had been in 1759, and the crushing British naval victory at Quiberon Bay on November 20th had rendered the relief of the colony less practicable than ever. The Court sent, belatedly, a little squadron carrying food, munitions, and 400 recruits. And even these inadequate 'succours' never reached Quebec; for this year the British Navy was in the St Lawrence first. The squadron took refuge in the Restigouche, where it was destroyed in July.[22] But Lévis and Vaudreuil worked with as much energy as though they felt certain of the most formidable reinforcements in the spring; and New France's last forlorn campaign was a gallant adventure worthy of the generations of valiant men who had so long sustained the colony against great odds.

It was also a skilful military performance. Lévis undoubtedly knew that he was almost certain to be assailed in the summer from three different directions — up the St

Lawrence from Quebec and the sea, down the river from Lake
Ontario, and by way of Lake Champlain. He clearly resolved to
concentrate his forces for a blow at Quebec in the early spring,
before the British could begin their advances by other lines
and before the season would allow Muray to fortify the Buttes
à Neveu, the high ground outside the walls which offered a
natural emplacement for the batteries of a besieger. Taking
what we would call today a 'calculated risk', he gathered for
this enterprise the whole of his eight battalions of regulars –
it will be remembered that Montcalm had had but five at
Quebec – and virtually the whole of his disposable militia
force, almost all of which he incorporated in the regular battalions of the *troupes de terre* and the colonial regulars. Spar-
ing only a small detachment under Bougainville for Lake
Champlain, he set off in April for his blow at Murray. Vaudreuil,
committing the army fully to Lévis, remained at Montreal.
The force collected for the expedition amounted to nearly
7,000 men – according to a careful return in Lévis' journal,
3,889 regulars and 3,021 militiamen, including officers.[23] He
may have picked up some reinforcements before arriving
before Quebec.

Thus Lévis had a larger regular force, and a considerably
larger army generally, than Montcalm had commanded in the
September battle. Murray, on the other hand, was worse off
than Wolfe had been. Apart from the units that had been withdrawn, and the battle casualties that had been suffered, his
army had been decimated by scurvy during the cold winter it
had spent in Quebec living on salt provisions. Hundreds of men
had died, and larger numbers were unfit for duty. Murray's
return gives the actual strength of his force in the battle he was
now about to fight as 3,866 officers and men.[24]

Lévis struck before the ice was out of the St Lawrence, landing at Pointe-aux-Trembles on April 24th. He had hoped to cut
off Murray's advanced posts at Lorette and Ste Foy, but the
British general, warned in time, made a sortie on April 27th
and withdrew them. Then, on the 28th, he boldly marched out
of Quebec with his little army. He says in his journal that he
had resolved 'to give the Enemy battle, before they could

Establish themselves'; how closely the words parallel Montcalm's just before his fatal attack! However, since the army took entrenching tools with it, he may initially have had in mind the possibility of digging in on the Buttes à Neveu and denying this commanding ground to the French. He had a formidable force of field artillery – no less than twenty-two guns – on which he placed much reliance.

The British line formed, then, on the Buttes à Neveu – on generally the same ground as that on which Montcalm had formed on September 13th. This rise was an admirable position for a defensive battle; and with his numerous guns disposed in the intervals between his battalions Murray could expect to inflict a severe reverse on Lévis if the latter had the temerity to attack him. But Murray, like Montcalm, was too impatient. He went forward to reconnoitre the enemy and, he says, 'preceiv'd their Van busy throwing up Redoubts while their Main body was yet on their march'. This, he thought, was the 'Luckey Minute'; and throwing away the advantages of his position he ordered his troops forward 'to attack them before they could have time to Form'. But conditions were not favourable to a quick blow. There was still much snow about, and this and the mud hampered the advance of the manhandled guns. The French main body formed successfully, though it was a near thing (according to Bourlamaque, Lévis, fearing they were not going to manage it, ordered a retirement on the left which might have had serious results). The British light troops gained a momentary advantage over the French advanced guard, but this was lost when Lévis' superior main force came into action. The French concentrated their attack upon the British flanks. After bitter fighting the left flank crumpled and the line broke. The British army retired precipitately into Quebec, losing all but two of its guns. Murray claimed, doubtless truly, that he was the last man to enter the gates. In an early return of casualties he stated his loss as 1,104 officers and men, of whom 259 were killed; the final total may have been a little higher. Lévis recorded his own as 833, including 193 killed. This engagement, usually called the Battle of Ste Foy, had been a bloodier fight than Wolfe's.[25]

Lévis now proceeded to besiege Quebec. Had powerful help arrived from France at this moment, as he hoped, the city must have fallen. But what happened was quite different. Murray took stringent measures to restore the discipline and morale of his beaten army, and made an active defence. And the French were short of everything required for a siege. In particular, they had few heavy guns (the largest, says Lévis, being a single 24-pounder) and those few were bad. Their batteries opened fire on May 11th, directed mainly at what they knew for a weak spot, the right face of the Glacière bastion. The very next day Murray's journal recorded alarming damage here. Yet the British fire from the ramparts was far superior to what the besiegers could bring to bear; while the effect of their own continued firing was so damaging to the French guns, and the French were so short of powder, that on the 12th Lévis was forced to limit firing to twenty rounds per gun per day.[26] This is not the way to take fortresses; but Lévis' eye was on the river. A squadron flying the lily banner would solve all his problems.

The spring's first ship came up the St Lawrence on the 9th, even before his batteries opened; and she was not French, but British – the familiar *Lowestoft*, which had worn Holmes' 'blew flag' on the day of the September victory. The garrison shouted themselves hoarse in salute to her colours and defiance of the French. But Lévis still hoped and persisted doggedly. On the evening of May 15th, however, the blow fell. Two more vessels arrived, and they proved to be British: the ship of the line *Vanguard* and the frigate *Diana*. Next day the three British ships attacked and destroyed the French frigates supporting the besieging army. Lévis' position was now quite hopeless. That night he raised the siege and retreated, abandoning his heavy guns and some of the field pieces taken from the British on April 28th.[27]

This was really the end. British sea-power had dealt its final, fatal blow to New France. The rest of the year's operations was merely a leisurely march towards a foregone conclusion. Gradually Amherst's ponderous war machine constricted and crushed the French resistance. Murray moved up the St Lawrence from Quebec, Brigadier William Haviland captured Isle-aux-Noix and pushed on up the Richelieu line, the Commander-in-Chief himself ran down the St Lawrence rapids from Lake Ontario. All three converged on Montreal. There on September 7th Vaudreuil and Lévis, with (so Lévis says) scarcely more than 2,000 troops left, confronted 17,000 under Amherst. There was no choice but capitulation.

The British were complete masters of the situation, and the terms were harder than those Townshend and Saunders had conceded at Quebec. Amherst, recalling the long record of atrocities committed by the Indian allies of the French, refused the honours of war. At the victorious end of his long road, he could well have afforded to be more generous to the thin rem-nant of an army that had fought so valiantly. Lévis protested violently to Vaudreuil; but the Governor, with the people of the colony to think of, as he said, ordered him to submit. The general gave himself one bitter satisfaction. He ordered the troops to burn their colours, to spare themselves 'the hard condition of handing them over to the enemy'.[28]

On September 9th the British army took possession of the city of Montreal. What was left of the eight brave French bat-talions, some 2,100 officers and men, laid down their weapons on the Place d'Armes; and Canada passed into British hands. Almost exactly a year after Wolfe's death on the Plains of Abraham, the crown had been placed on his already famous victory.

# Generalship at Quebec, 1759

The last word will never be said on the remarkable happenings at Quebec in 1759. But before taking leave of them here we should at least try to arrive at some estimate of them, in human and military terms. 'The verdict of history' on the two generals who are commemorated by the famous monument in the Governor's Garden above Dufferin Terrace has so far been curiously mixed. It can do no great harm to add one more voice to the confusion of tongues.

Of the Marquis de Montcalm we have already said much. He was a gallant and attractive figure, still remembered as something of a national hero in modern France. But was he a really great commander? The answer surely must be no.

His difficulties were great, and for a long time he struggled against them successfully. He had to contend with the disadvantage of divided command, and this was the worse because his personal relations with Vaudreuil were so thoroughly bad. Yet it is hard to avoid concluding, we have suggested, that Montcalm was in part responsible for the badness of those relations; and we have seen that the evidence indicates that Vaudreuil's interference was less serious in 1759, and had rather less influence on the operations that year, than has usually been admitted.

Montcalm was certainly an officer of considerable competence, though we need not agree with Bougainville that he had 'made a campaign worthy of M. de Turenne'.[1] Some have thought him too much disposed to the defensive. But under the conditions existing at Quebec the defensive was the intelligent course, the one dictated by his means and his circumstances. The battle that finally took place shows that he was right to be, in Wolfe's phrase, 'doubtful of the behaviour of his army'. The soundness of Montcalm's general policy is attested by the fashion in which it frustrated Wolfe for so long. The British General's letters bear ample witness to the difficulties it imposed upon him. The fortification of the Beauport shore was assuredly a highly effective measure; though it was apparently Lévis who was responsible for extending the defences as far as the Montmorency, and the course of the operations suggests that without this extension the Beauport lines would have been much more vulnerable. One is tempted to rank Montcalm far above Wolfe on the strategic level of command – though that is not saying a great deal; but he was guilty of a serious and finally a fatal miscalculation. The supply arrangements he adopted made the French field army and the city of Quebec dependent from day to day on a line of communication from the west which could easily be severed, and whose severance would immediately destroy his whole defensive system by forcing him out to fight in the open. Here the French fell victims to an assumption which seems to have been almost an article of belief with them before the campaign – the assumption that the British fleet would never be able to pass Quebec and operate above the city.

In one quality Montcalm was notably deficient. He lacked the invaluable ability to penetrate his antagonist's intentions. (It is only fair to add that Wolfe's planning had an illogical and unpredictable quality that made it a very difficult intelligence problem.) A few days before Wolfe's attack at Montmorency on July 31st Montcalm told Lévis he was convinced that no such enterprise would take place. And after the British evacuated their Montmorency camp Montcalm absolutely failed to fathom what they were about. At a time when they were preparing to land, first between St Augustin and Pointe-aux-Trembles, and subsequently at the Foulon, everything goes to show that Montcalm still thought the Beauport shore the

most likely point of attack, with the area from Jacques Cartier
to Deschambault the next possibility. And his failure to note
the importance and vulnerability of the Anse au Foulon, where
there was a track by which cannon could be brought up to the
Plains of Abraham, and to take more effective steps to protect
it, reflects seriously on his military capacity.

Of Montcalm's final tactical error on September 13th we
have spoken. By attacking prematurely, at a time when Bougainville was marching to his assistance, he threw away his
best hope of victory. The same quick impulsiveness and ner-
vous impatience which made it impossible for him to bear with
the pompous ways of Vaudreuil doubtless drove him on to this
unsound and fatal decision. The French débâcle would probably have taken place anyway, but Montcalm's action made it
more certain. To be a great general requires a calmer mind and
a surer judgement than this.

It should be added that Montcalm got very poor support
from Bougainville, his former aide-de-camp – a brilliant man
but inexperienced as an officer. Bougainville botched the task
of guarding the area above Quebec. He failed to ensure that the
posts nearest to the city were duly watchful; he failed to provide adequate communications from those posts to the Beauport camp and to his own headquarters; he failed to see to it
that the posts were warned of the cancellation of the movement of the provision boats on the fatal night of September
12th/13th; finally, he failed to observe what was happening
that night and to march to counter Wolfe's action, with the
consequence that Wolfe landed without difficulty and Bougainville himself was too late to cooperate with his chief on the
Plains of Abraham at the critical moment the following morning. His inefficiency had much to do with the French disaster.
It is proper to remark, however, that among all the extant
letters from Vaudreuil and Montcalm to Bougainville there is
not one that directs his attention to the Foulon area; whereas
there are several that urge him to watch the sector above Cap
Rouge. It is interesting that a marginal note to the *Journal
tenu à l'armée*, probably written by Vaudreuil, makes the point
in connexion with the latter's council of war on the evening

of September 13th (which decided not to risk another fight) that Bougainville's rank now made him commander of the army under Vaudreuil: 'This young Colonel's good fortune and even his talents had made people jealous of him.' This was doubtless true, but it is also conceivable that some of the officers in the council did not relish the idea of fighting a hazardous action under so green a commander.

Turning to the other side, what is to be said of Wolfe? Is one to agree with Beckles Willson that 'this singular youth was to war what the younger Pitt was to politics or John Keats to letters'? Or are we to accept the opinion stated by Field-Marshal Lord Wolseley and developed by Professor E. R. Adair, that Wolfe was never anything more than 'a good regimental officer'? Or is it possible that the truth lies somewhere between these extremes?

What are the qualities of a great captain? He is, surely, the officer who, faced with a strategic problem, analyses it with sure judgement and notes its essential features, the elements of strength and weakness in the enemy's situation and his own; who then produces a clear-cut plan of operations designed to exploit those elements to the best advantage; and who, finally, puts his plan into efficient execution, pushing it through to victory with an energy and a resolution that overcome all obstacles.

Judged by this formula, Wolfe cannot be ranked among the great commanders. His performance as a strategist before Quebec during July and August 1759 was sadly ineffective. ('Strategy' is a big word to use for operations in so small a theatre and employing such relatively tiny forces; yet there is no other that really meets the case.) The letters to Monckton utilized in this book, most of which were unknown either to his admirers or his critics in the past, document his ineffectualness in this phase. The succession of plans made, cast aside and then revived with variations is a remarkable record of vacillation. As we have seen, the final plan, the one that succeeded, can be called his eighth of the campaign. The high point of instability was reached on July 20th, when Wolfe developed a new plan, for a landing above the town, in the morning, issued detailed orders with a view to acting on it the same night, and then cancelled it early in the afternoon. It is not surprising that the events of that day struck James Gibson as extraordinary; nor should Murray be abused for writing later, 'his orders through out the campaign shews little stability, stratagem, or fixt resolution';[2] after all, this is no more than the truth. For his immediate subordinates, who unlike the great mass of the army knew what was going on, the experience of serving under him was exasperating and frustrating in the last degree.

Grappling with his strategic problem, week after week as the summer ran away, and utterly failing to solve it, Wolfe presents a painful spectacle. The most pathetic of all military characters is the general who cannot make up his mind. Wolfe was in fact a Hamlet-figure.

> . . . the native hue of resolution
> Is sicklied o'er with the pale cast of thought;
> And enterprises of great pith and moment,
> With this regard, their currents turn awry,
> And lose the name of action.

About his decision at the end of July, to attack at Montmorency, there is almost an air of desperation. The idea of seizing the detached redoubt in the hope that Montcalm would come out of his works and enable him to fight a defensive battle was eccentric, not so much a plan as a substitute for one, and the brigadiers very naturally did not like it. Then, when on the afternoon of the 31st he found that his calculations had been at fault and the redoubt was not tenable, he was betrayed into a spur-of-the-moment decision that had little to commend it: to attempt a risky frontal attack at the wrong end of the French position. Even if he had succeeded in establishing his army on the heights here, the great mass of the French force was between him and the St Charles and well placed to withdraw safely across that river and dispute Wolfe's further progress from its prepared positions on the far bank. It is not surprising that Montcalm found it hard to believe that he was really going to attack in this sector.

It remains to discuss the issues between Wolfe and his brigadiers as they arose following his request to them in August to consult together on the best method of attacking the enemy. We have already suggested that the plan the brigadiers recommended, of abandoning the Montmorency camp and concentrating the army for a blow above Quebec, was sounder than any expedient Wolfe himself had so far produced; simply because it enabled the British force to act as a whole, and because it exploited the fundamental weakness of the French position – their dependence on food supplies from the west. By cutting Montcalm's essential line of communication the new plan would – and did – force him to come out of his defences and fight. It should be emphasized (for it has not always been understood) that in its most essential features the brigadiers' plan was accepted, and followed, by Wolfe, and that his adoption of it had the happiest results for the British cause. The brigadiers put the campaign 'back on the rails'.

But beyond a certain point, we noted, Wolfe took leave of the brigadiers' recommendation. They had advised a landing at some place above Cap Rouge. After issuing orders for such a landing, between St Augustin and Pointe-aux-Trembles, he changed his mind, and apparently without consulting anyone decided to strike the blow at the Anse au Foulon. Leaving aside, for the moment, the certainly not irrelevant fact that Wolfe's plan succeeded, and produced a famous victory, let us compare it on its merits with the brigadiers' scheme for a landing higher up the river.

The latter had the important advantage of being less hazardous. The proposed landing area was much farther from the French main force than the Foulon, and much less formidable by nature, the shore being a great deal lower. A successful landing at the Foulon would depend entirely upon surprise; if surprise were not achieved, the enterprise would have to be abandoned. But in the region between St Augustin and Pointe-aux-Trembles a landing in the face of opposition was a practicable military operation. And the opposition in the first instance was unlikely to be extremely formidable. In the worst case, it would consist of Bougainville's force; and a descent here would have given Wolfe an excellent chance of beating Bougainville before Montcalm could march the sixteen or more long miles from Beauport to reinforce him.

At the same time, in strategic terms the upper area was more favourable to the British than the lower one. It fulfilled the basic object of placing the British army between the French and their supplies, and thereby forcing Montcalm to fight. And it offered the French less possibility of successful withdrawal after a lost battle. At the Plains of Abraham they could, and did, withdraw across a river obstacle, the St Charles, and subsequently, covered by the same obstacle, retire westwards by the inland road through Charlesbourg and the Lorettes. These possibilities were not open to them above St Augustin. About four miles east of Pointe-aux-Trembles the inland road joined that along the river; west of that point there was no inland route, and if the British had cut the river road here the French would have been hopelessly trapped, except for such parties as might get away through the woods.[3] It must be said, however, that there is no evidence that Wolfe's brigadiers were acquainted with these facts about the roads.

When Wolfe turned away from the Pointe-aux-Trembles area and decided to land at the Foulon, then, he was abandoning a sound plan in favour of one that was not so sound. Nevertheless, there were some advantages to the Foulon scheme. We have seen that Wolfe was quite right when he wrote to Monckton, 'I have fix'd upon that spot, where we can act w$^h$. most force.' The Foulon plan brought two additional British battalions to the battlefield, no mean reinforcement. Moreover, as it turned out, it enabled Wolfe to strike his adversaries where they were not expecting him. This is something every general strives to do; for surprise is a great battle-winner. The question arises, did Wolfe know that the Foulon was so badly guarded? If he had information that serious opposition was not to be expected there, it places his enterprise in a much more favourable light. If he merely took a long chance on catching Vergor's men napping, his decision is less entitled to respect. But we

have already said that we know nothing about the information
– if any – that prompted Wolfe to take the risk. There is
nothing to support the stories of treachery on the part of some
Frenchman or Frenchmen. It is possible that Wolfe did get
solid information about conditions at the Foulon post from a
deserter. It is equally possible that he had no information, and
simply acted on his own observation that there was a practicable path at that point, and that it seemed to be guarded
only by a relatively small party.

Wolfe has been censured for placing his army in a critical
position, because of the inadequacy of the Foulon path as a
line of withdrawal in case of defeat. Actually, that path, as we
have seen, was a better communication than has commonly
been supposed; with some improvement, it served for the
movement of more than a hundred pieces of artillery within
five days of the battle. And the superior military quality of
Wolfe's army gave him virtual assurance of victory once the
French were brought to battle in the open field. His letters
show that he relied on this with confidence, and the events of
September 13th show that his confidence was well founded.
The risk he ran in giving battle on the Plains was an eminently
legitimate one.

It has often been pointed out, however, that the success
actually achieved was due to a whole sequence of what seem to
have been lucky chances, which Wolfe could scarcely have
counted upon however good his intelligence. The French plan
to send the provision boats down the river, and the warning to
their posts to pass them through; the decision not to send the
boats, and the neglect to inform the posts of the cancellation;
the arrival of the deserters who gave the information about the
intended French movements which enabled the quick-witted
Scot to represent the British boats as French; Bougainville's
failure to observe and follow the British movement; and the
careless guard kept by Vergor's detachment – surely the luck
of the British army was working overtime that night.

It is obvious that a little less good fortune at one of these
points could have wrecked the whole enterprise. But it is not
true that Wolfe, by adopting so daring a plan, was risking his

whole army. Bigot related a story which is at least interesting.[4]
British officers, he says, told him that Wolfe did not expect to
succeed, but comforted himself with the reflection that if
things went wrong at the Foulon he would sacrifice only his
advanced guard of 200 men. In the event of the French post
being alert and firing, the whole force would have re-embarked
and a week later the fleet would have sailed for England – and
Wolfe, we must suspect, sailing out of the St Lawrence defeated, would also have sailed out of the pages of history. This
account is not specifically confirmed by any British record, but
Barré's story of Wolfe's order to him suspending the landing
gives some colour to it, and Townshend wrote to Murray in
1774, in connexion with that story, 'The General's view was
to support the experiment, if he found it practicable.'[5] It
seems quite likely that Bigot's tale is true.

Viewed strategically, then, Wolfe's Foulon plan – in spite of
its result – was not really a good one. 'Something,' he had
written after Rochefort, 'must be allowed to chance and fortune.' But fortune should not be tempted unnecessarily. There
was, as we have seen, a better alternative available – the landing higher up the river, as recommended by the brigadiers;
such a landing would have gained the desired strategic end
more satisfactorily and with much less risk. The fact that Wolfe
succeeded should not blind us to the weakness of his conception, for he owed his triumph largely to luck, and a plan which
requires so much luck to succeed is not a good plan.

Fifteen years after the dramatic events before Quebec, Townshend and Murray exchanged letters about them. Murray was
planning to write a narrative of the American campaigns –
an intention which apparently he did not carry out, or if he
did the narrative has not survived. Townshend, the firebrand
of 1759, had now grown older, more prudent and more
tolerant; he advised Murray to reconsider his plan to attack
Wolfe on the basis of the Barré story ('the Public', he wrote,
'admire M[r]. Wolfe, for many eminent qualities, and revere
his memory'). He confessed, in effect, to being a little bored
now with the Quebec expedition, saying that if an account of it

lay on his table alongside one dealing with the operations at Tanjore in India (1773), he would pick up the latter first. But Murray had lost none of his dislike for Wolfe. He wrote back in sarcastic disgust:[6]

> It does not appear to me that it ever was M^r Wolfes intention to bring the Enemy to a general Action; His rejection of landing above the Town, by means of the Redans [radeaux?], before our Ships passed the place; His refusing to Execute M^r. Pallisiers plan of assaulting [the Lower Town of] Quebeck, His absurd, visionary, attack of the Enemy's Lines at Beauport; and at last his desertion of the Sensible, well conserted, Enterprise to land at the point Au Tramble, where without opposition, with his whole Army, and Artillery, he might have taken Post, and Entrenched himself betwixt the Enemy and their Provisions, with the almost impossible, tho successfull attempt, thanks to Providence at the Foulon, and many, many &c^as. are evident proofs to me that my Conjecture is well founded.
>
> God forbid My Lord I should interrupt your Amusements: Tanjour you may quietly Enjoy, while I am knocking my obstinate Scotch head, against the Admiration, and Reverence of the English Mob for M^r Wolfes memory.

Murray was very unfair to Wolfe – as Townshend at once told him – in arguing that he did not intend to bring on a general action. If Wolfe's letters and reports mean anything at all, this was always his chief object. But Murray's detailed criticisms of his strategy, and particularly the remark on the abandonment of the Pointe-aux-Trembles plan, have a great deal of force.

In justice to Wolfe, however, comment cannot stop here. When we pass from strategic planning to tactics – the actual business of directing the battle – Wolfe presents a different aspect. The plan for the approach and landing at the Foulon, whoever made it, was an admirable one, and it was most admirably executed. And Wolfe's handling of the preliminaries and the battle itself was flawless. It is true that we cannot lightly dismiss the story of the order said to have been suppressed by Barré; it may be that even at this late hour the Hamlet in Wolfe was asserting himself. It is true also that his enemy's mistakes greatly helped him. But from the moment he was established ashore to the time when he suffered his mortal wound he maintained a firm and effective grip on the operations. He was as decisive as he had been indecisive during the long weeks of futile vacillation. The movements of the little army were smooth and rapid; there was no waste motion. Two hours after the first landing he had occupied his chosen ground; six hours after it he had won his battle and was dying.

It is not given to every general to be both strategist and tactician. It may be recalled that Lord Montgomery, while admitting at least by implication that his antagonist Rommel was a skilful tactician, asserted roundly that he was 'no strategist'; while Rommel, we now know, wrote in his comments set down after the Normandy campaign that though it would be difficult to accuse Montgomery of ever having made a serious strategic mistake, he was less distinguished as a tactician! As a strategist Wolfe was hopeless: he was the sort of officer who should never be given a large independent command, and in this respect he would probably never have got any better. But as a battlefield commander, so far as one can judge from his short career, he deserves to rank high. He was a man of striking personal gallantry, who seems almost to have enjoyed being under fire; and largely because of this he had great prestige and reputation among the officers and men who served under him. In action he seems to have been capable of prompt and sound decisions. All this went to make him an effective controller of the battle.

It may be said that Wolfe's performance at Montmorency on July 31st belies this. His decisions to attack there – both the original decision to take the redoubt, and the later one to risk a full-scale frontal attack – proved unsound; but these were examples of his fumbling as a planner. The one definite tactical decision he made that day was the resolution to withdraw, and that was a sound decision and made in good time. And the withdrawal was well conducted.

It does not follow that he was no more than a 'good regimental officer'. It takes more than a good regimental officer to direct a large force in action with energy, authority and effect, as Wolfe did on September 13th. It would be truer to say that

Wolfe's military talents were merely those of a good tactician. To use the jargon of the Second World War, he had a definite 'ceiling'. One suspects that, in modern military terms, he had it in him to be an excellent corps commander, but no more. In an appointment where he could lead, inspire and direct on the battlefield, carrying out tasks prescribed for him by a higher commander, he would have been an enormously valuable officer – the sort of right arm that Sir Brian Horrocks was to Lord Montgomery in Africa and north-west Europe.

Montcalm and Wolfe, though in many ways dissimilar, had much in common. Both were exceptionally gallant fighting soldiers. Both had defects of temperament and personality which affected their dealings with other men in a manner damaging to their military usefulness. Both had some military talent. And the abilities of both have been grossly exaggerated by partial and sentimental historians, writing under the spell of the romantic circumstances in which the two generals fought and died in that extraordinary campaign on the St Lawrence 200 years ago.

# APPENDIX

# *Wolfe's Correspondence with the Brigadiers, August 1759*

## WOLFE'S MEMORANDUM TO THE BRIGADIERS

(NC, Townshend Papers, I)
(Apparently in Wolfe's handwriting)

That the Publick service may not suffer by the General's indisposition, he begs the Brigadiers will be so good to meet, & consult together for the publick utility & advantage; & to consider of the best method of attacking the Enemy.

If the french Army is attacked & defeated, the General concludes the Town wou'd immediately surrender, because he does not find they have any provisions in the Place.

The General is of opinion that the Army shoud be attacked in preference to the Place, because of the difficulties of penetrating from the lower to the upper Town; in which attempt neither the Guns of the Shipping, or of our own Batteries coud be of much use.

There appears to be 3 methods of attacking their army

1st. —in dry Weather a large Detachment may march in a day & a night so as to arrive at Beauport (fording the Montmorency 8 or 9 miles up) before day in the morning – it is likely they wou'd be discovered upon their march on both sides the River – If such a Detacht. penetrates on their entrenchments & the rest of the Troops are ready, the consequence is plain.

2<sup>d</sup>.    If the Troops encamped here pass'd the Ford n<sup>r</sup>. the fall-
ing Water, & in the night march on directly towards the
Point of Beauport — the light Infantry have a good chance
to get up the woody Hill, trying different places; & moving quick to the right, wou'd soon discover a proper
place for the rest: the upper redoubt must be attack'd,
& kept by a Company of Grenad<sup>r</sup>. — Brig<sup>r</sup>. Monkton must
be ready off the Point of Beauport to land when our People
have got up the Hill — for which Signals may be appointed.

3<sup>dy</sup>.    All the chosen Troops of the Army attack at the Beauport at Low Water — a Division across the Ford an hour
before, the other attack. —

NB    for the first — it is enough if the Water begins to fall a
little before day light or about it.
For the other two, it wou'd be best to have it low water —
about half an hour before day —
The General thinks the Country shou'd be ruined &
destroyed, as much as can be done consistent w<sup>h</sup>. a more
Capital Operation.

N    There are Guides in the Army for the Detach<sup>t</sup> in Question.


## THE BRIGADIERS' REPLY

(Chatham Manuscripts, PRO, Bundle 50)
(Transcript in PAC)
(Partial facsimile in Mahon's *Life of Murray*)

Point Levi August y<sup>e</sup> 29<sup>th</sup>. 1759

Having met this day, in consequence of General Wolfes
desire, to consult together for the publick utility, and advantage, and to consider of the best method of attacking the
Enemy; We read his Majesty's private Instructions which the
General was pleas'd to communicate to us, and consider'd
some propositions of his with respect to our future Operations,
and think it our duty to offer our Opinion as follows.

The natural Strength of the Enemys Situation between the

river S$^t$. Charles, and the Montmorenci, now improved by all the art of their Engeneers makes the defeat of their army if attack'd there very doubtfull; The advantage their easy communication along the Shore gives them over our attack by the ford of the Montmoranci, and from boats unprotected by the fire of our Ships is evident from late Experience: And it appears to us that, that part of the Army which is proposed to march through the Woods nine miles up the Montmorenci to surprize their Camp is exposed to certain discovery, and to the disadvantage of a continual Wood fight. But allowing we could get footing on the Beauport side the Marquis de Montcalm will still have it in his power to dispute the passage of the River S$^t$ Charles 'till the place is sufficiently supply'd with Provisions from the Ships, and Magazines above from which it appears they draw their Subsistance.

We therefore are of Opinion that the most probable method of striking an effectual blow, is to bring the Troops to the South Shore, and to direct the Operations above the Town: When we establish ourselves on the North Shore, the French General must fight us on our own Terms; We shall be betwixt him and his provisions, and betwixt him and their Army opposing General Amherst:

If he gives us battle, and we defeat him, Quebec and probably all Canada will be ours, which is an advantage far beyond any we can expect by an attack on the Beauport Side; and should the Enemy pass over the River S$^t$. Charles with Force sufficient to oppose this enterprize we may still with more ease, and probability of Success execute the Generals third proposition (which is in our opinion the most Eligible of those he made) or attempt any thing else on the Bauport Shore necessarely weakend by the Detatchments made to oppose us above the Town.

With respect to the expediency of making an immediate attack, or the postponing it more effectually to prevent the Harvest, and otherwise distroy the Colony, or with a View to facilitate the Operations of General Amhersts Army now advancing into the heart of the Country, we cannot presume to advise, although we are fully convinced that the progress of his troops hath, and must still depend upon the detention of the greatest part of the Enemys Force on this Side, for the defence of their Capital.

We can not conclude without assuring the General, that whatever he determines to do, he will find us most hearty, & Zealous in the execution of his Orders.

Rob^t. Monckton.    Geo: Townshend.    Ja: Murray

(NC, Townshend Papers, XII) (fair copy)
Plan of operations in consequence of the preceeding Answer.

It is proposed to remove the Ordnance and Troops from the Montmorency in three days, beginning with the heavy Artillery tomorrow night, the stores to be carried to the Waterside directly to gain time.

The Troops to be transported to the Isle of Orleans, some Corps may go from hence tomorrow night that they may assist in putting the Works at the point of Orleans in a good state of defence. The sick to be transported the day after tomorrow by which time provision must be made for them in the Hospitals. Six Hundred Men of the Marines and Hardy's Corps for the defence of Orleans – Six Hundred for Point Levy – and a thousand for the Batteries.

The Army to encamp on the other side of the Itchemin. As many Transports as will contain two Months provisions to get up the first opportunity. The boats of the Fleet will disembark 2,500 Men, the remainder of the Troops or any part of them to be put on board the Ships which are to be stationed so as to be ready to land the Men as immediately as possible to sustain the 1^st. Corps that disembarks from the Boats. There can be no difficulty to effectuate a landing in the night without the least loss, it may be done any where for an extent of four Leagues, viz^t. from the heights of S^t. John to Carouge River, two attempts may be made, either of which succeeding is sufficient, allowing the Transports cannot get up in a few days the Enterprize need not for that reason be delay'd a moment, we have a sufficient number of Carts to make a Depot at the Camp of the Itchmen, and we have a further resource from our Boats, which at all times we know without interruption can pass and repass the Town.

Another method of effecting a landing on the North Shore.

Two thousand Men to embark at the point of Levy in the Boats at low Water the middle of the night, by break of day they will have pass'd the Town have arriv'd & disembark'd at a proper place for the purpose half a League above the River Caprouge. The same night the Troops to move up to the Camp of the Itchmen already mention'd, previous to this it will be right to fill the Ships already above the Town with as many Troops as they will contain, that may be done from Goram's post in three nights without giving the smallest jealousy, by the boats already above the town, but for this purpose the Ships now above must fall down to a proper station. The Ships already above the Town will contain for the requisite time two thousand Men consequently four thousand Men may in one tide be landed without the least jealousy given to the Enemy and the remainder may be brought over with any number of Artillery the next from the Itchmen Camp.

# WOLFE'S DISPATCH TO PITT

---

This famous dispatch has seldom been printed in full; in 1759 the two paragraphs beginning with the words 'At my first coming into the Country' were suppressed, and Doughty, Willson, etc, did not observe this, though the document is complete in Kimball. The text now given is that published in the *Annual Register*, 1759, which in matters of spelling, punctuation and capitalization is easier for a modern reader than the manuscript in the Public Record Office (CO 5/51, transcript in PAC). But passages omitted from the *Annual Register* version, or differing seriously from that in CO 5/51, are printed as in the latter.

Head quarters at Montmorenci, in the river St. Laurence, Sept. 2. 1759.

SIR,

I wish I could, upon this occasion, have the honour of transmitting to you a more favourable account of the progress of his majesty's arms; but the obstacles we have met with, in the operations of the campaign, are much greater than we had reason to expect, or could foresee; not so much from the number of the enemy, (though superior to us) as from the natural strength of the country, which the Marquis de Montcalm seems wisely to depend upon.

When I learned that succours of all kinds had been thrown into Quebec; that five battalions of regular troops, compleated from the best inhabitants of the country, some of the troops of the colony, and every Canadian that was able to bear arms, besides several nations of savages, had taken the field in a very

advantageous situation; I could not flatter myself that I should
be able to reduce the place. I sought however an occasion to
attack their army, knowing well, that with these troops I was
able to fight, and that a victory might disperse them.

We found them encamped along the shore of Beauport, from
the river St. Charles to the falls of Montmorenci, and intrenched
in every accessible part. The 27th of June we landed upon the isle
of Orleans; but receiving a message from the admiral, that there
was reason to think that the enemy had artillery, and a force
upon the point of Levi, I detached Brigadier Monckton with four
battalions to drive them from thence. He passed the river the
29th at night, and marched the next day to the point; he obliged
the enemy's irregulars to retire, and possessed himself of that
post: the advanced parties upon this occasion had two or three
skirmishes with the Canadians and Indians, with little loss on
either side.

Colonel Carleton marched with a detachment to the western-
most point of the isle of Orleans, from whence our operations
were likely to begin.

It was absolutely necessary to possess these two points, and
fortify them, because, from either one or the other, the enemy
might make it impossible for any ship to lie in the bason of
Quebec, or even within two miles of it.

Batteries of cannon and mortars were erected with great dispatch on the point of Levi, to bombard the town and magazines,
and to injure the works and batteries: the enemy perceiving
these works in some forwardness, passed the river with 1600 men
to attack and destroy them. Unluckily they fell into confusion,
fired upon one another, and went back again; by which we lost
an opportunity of defeating this large detachment. The effect of
this artillery had been so great, (though across the river) that the
upper town is considerably damaged, and the lower town entirely
destroyed.

The works for the security of our hospitals and stores on the
isle of Orleans, being finished, on the 9th of July at night, we
passed the N. channel, and incamped near the enemy's left, the
river Montmorenci between us. The next morning Capt. Dank's
company of rangers, posted in a wood to cover some workmen,
were attacked and defeated by a body of Indians, and had so
many killed and wounded, as to be almost disabled for the rest of
the campaign: the enemy also suffered in this affair, and were
in their turn driven off by the nearest troops.

The ground, to the eastward of the falls, seemed to be (as it really is) higher than that on the enemy's side, and to command it in a manner which might be made useful to us. There is besides a ford below the falls, which may be passed for some hours in the latter part of the ebb and beginning of the flood tide; and I had hopes, that possibly means might be found of passing the river above, so as to fight M. Montcalm, upon terms of less disadvantage than directly attacking his intrenchments. In reconnoitring the river Montmorenci, we found it fordable at a place about three miles up; but the opposite bank was intrenched, and so steep and woody, that it was to no purpose to attempt a passage there. The escort was twice attacked by the Indians, who were as often repulsed; but in these rencounters we had forty (officers and men) killed and wounded.

The 18th of July, two men of war, two armed sloops, and two transports, with some troops on board, passed by the town without any loss, and got into the upper river. This enabled me to reconnoitre the country above, where I found the same attention on the enemy's side, and great difficulties on ours, arising from the nature of the ground, and the obstacles to our communication with the fleet. But what I feared most, was, that if we should land between the town and the river Cape Rouge, the body first landed could not be reinforced before they were attacked by the enemy's whole army.

Notwithstanding these difficulties, I thought once of attempting it at St. Michael's, about three miles above the town; but perceiving that the enemy were jealous of the design, were preparing against it, and had actually brought artillery and a mortar, (which, being so near to Quebec, they could increase as they pleased) to play upon the shipping: and as it must have been many hours before we could attack them, (even supposing a favourable night for the boats to pass by the town unhurt) it seemed so hazardous that I thought it best to desist.

However, to divide the enemy's force, and to draw their attention as high up the river as possible, and to procure some intelligence, I sent a detachment under the command of Colonel Carleton to land at the Point de Trempe, to attack whatever he might find there, bring off some prisoners, and all the useful papers he could get. I had been informed that a number of the inhabitants of Quebec had retired to that place, and that probably we should find a magazine of provisions there.

The colonel was fired upon by a body of Indians the moment he

landed, but they were soon dispersed and driven into the woods:
he searched for magazines, but to no purpose, brought off some
prisoners, and returned with little loss.

After this business, I came back to Montmorenci, where I
found that Brigadier Townshend had, by a superior fire, prevented
the French from erecting a battery on the bank of the river, from
whence they intended to cannonade our camp. I was resolved to
take the first opportunity which presented itself, of attacking the
enemy, though posted to great advantage, and every where prepared to receive us.

As the men of war cannot (for want of a sufficient depth of
water) come near enough to the enemy's intrenchments, to
annoy them in the least, the admiral had prepared two transports
(drawing but little water) which upon occasion could be run
a-ground, to favour a descent. With the help of these vessels,
which I understood would be carried by the tide close in shore, I
proposed to make myself master of a detached redoubt near to
the water's edge, and whose situation appeared to be out of
musket shot of the intrenchment upon the hill: if the enemy
supported this detached place, it would necessarily bring on an
engagement, what we most wished for; and if not, I should have
it in my power to examine their situation, so as to be able to
determine where we could best attack them.

Preparations were accordingly made for an engagement. The
31st of July in the forenoon, the boats of the fleet were filled
with grenadiers, and a part of General Monckton's brigade from
the point of Levi: the two brigades under the brigadiers
Townshend and Murray, were ordered to be in readiness to pass
the ford, when it should be thought necessary. To facilitate the
passage of this corps, the admiral had placed the Centurion in
the channel, so that she might check the fire of the lower battery
which commanded the ford: this ship was of great use, as her fire
was very judiciously directed. A great quantity of artillery was
placed upon the eminence, so as to batter and enfilade the left
of their intrenchments.

From the vessel which run aground nearest in, I observed that
the redoubt was too much commanded to be kept without very
great loss; and the more, as the two armed ships could not be
brought near enough to cover both with their artillery and
musketry, which I at first conceived they might. But as the enemy
seemed in some confusion, and we were prepared for an action, I
thought it a proper time to make an attempt upon their intrench-

ments. Orders were sent to the brigadiers general to be ready with the corps under their command. Brigadier Monckton to land, and the brigadiers Townshend and Murray to pass the ford.

At a proper time of the tide, the signal was made, but in rowing towards the shore, many of the boats grounded upon a ledge, that runs off a considerable distance. This accident put us into some disorder, lost a great deal of time, and obliged me to send an officer to stop Brigadier Townshend's march, whom I then observed to be in motion. While the seamen were getting the boats off, the enemy fired a number of shells and shot, but did no considerable damage. As soon as this disorder could be set a little to rights, and the boats were ranged in a proper manner, some of the officers of the navy went in with me to find a better place to land: we took one flat bottomed boat with us to make the experiment, and as soon as we had found a fit part of the shore, the troops were ordered to disembark, thinking it not yet too late for the attempt.

The thirteen companies of grenadiers, and 200 of the second royal American battalion, got first on shore. The grenadiers were ordered to form themselves into four distinct bodies, and to begin the attack, supported by Brigadier Monckton's corps as soon as the troops had passed the ford, and were at hand to assist. But whether from the noise and hurry at landing, or from some other cause, the grenadiers, instead of forming themselves as they were directed, ran on impetuously towards the enemy's intrenchments in the utmost disorder and confusion, without waiting for the corps which were to sustain them, and join in the attack. Brigadier Monckton was not landed, and Brigadier Townshend was at a considerable distance, tho' upon his march to join us, in very great order. The grenadiers were checked by the enemy's first fire, and obliged to shelter themselves in or about the redoubt, which the French abandoned upon their approach. In this situation they continued for some time, unable to form under so hot a fire, and having many gallant officers wounded, who (careless of their persons) had been solely intent upon their duty. I saw the absolute necessity of calling them off, that they might form themselves under Brigadier Monckton's corps, which was now landed, and drawn up on the beach, in extreme good order.

By this new accident, and this second delay, it was near night, a sudden storm came on, and the tide began to make; so that I thought it most adviseable, not to persevere in so difficult an attack, lest (in case of a repulse) the retreat of Brigadier Town-shend's corps might be hazardous and uncertain.

Our artillery had a great effect upon the enemy's left, where Brigadiers Townshend and Murray were to have attacked: and it is probable, that if those accidents I have spoken of had not happened, we should have penetrated there, whilst our left and center (more remote from our artillery) must have bore all the violence of the musquetry.

The French did not attempt to interrupt our march. Some of their savages came down to murder such wounded as could not be brought off, and to scalp the dead, as their custom is.

The place, where the attack was intended, has these advantages over all others hereabout. Our artillery could be brought into use. The greatest part, or even the whole of the troops, might act at once; and the retreat (in case of a repulse) was secure, at least for a certain time of the tide. Neither one nor other of these advantages can any where else be found. The Enemy were indeed posted upon a commanding Eminence. The beach upon which the troops were drawn up, was of deep mud, with holes, and cut by several gullies. The hill to be ascended, very steep, and not every where practicable. The enemy numerous in their intrenchments, and their fire hot. If the attack had succeeded, our loss must certainly have been great, and theirs inconsiderable, from the shelter which the neighbouring woods afforded them. The river of St. Charles still remained to be passed, before the town was invested. All these circumstances I considered; but the desire to act in conformity to the King's intentions, induced me to make this trial, persuaded that a victorious army finds no difficulties.

The Enemy have been fortifying ever since with Care, so as to make a second Attempt still more dangerous.

Immediately after this check, I sent Brigadier Murray above the town with 1200 men, directing him to assist Rear Admiral Holmes in the destruction of the French ships, (if they could be got at) in order to open a communication with General Amherst. The brigadier was to seek every favourable opportunity of fighting some of the enemy's detachments, provided he could do it upon tolerable terms, and to use all the means in his power to provoke them to attack him. He made two different attempts to land upon the north shore, without success; but in a third was more fortunate. He landed unexpectedly at De Chambaud, and burnt a magazine there, in which were some provisions, some ammunition, and all the spare stores, cloathing, arms, and baggage, of their army. Finding that their Ships were not to be got at, & little Prospect of bringing the Enemy to a Battle, He reported his Situation to me & I order'd him to join the Army.

The prisoners he took, informed him of the surrender of the fort of Niagara; and we discovered, by intercepted letters, that the enemy had abandoned Carillon and Crown Point, were retired to the isle Aux Noix; and that General Amherst was making preparations to pass the lake Champlain, to fall upon M. Bourlemaque's corps, which consists of three battalions of foot, and as many Canadians as make the whole amount to 3000 Men.

The admiral's dispatches and mine would have gone eight or ten days sooner, if I had not been prevented from writing by a fever. I found myself so ill, and am still so weak, that I begged the general officers to consult together for the public utility. They were all of opinion, that, (as more ships and provisions have now got above the town) they should try, by conveying up a corps of 4 or 5000 men, (which is nearly the whole strength of the army, after the points of Levi and Orleans are left in a proper state of defence) to draw the enemy from their present situation, and bring them to an action. I have acquiesced in their proposal, and we are preparing to put it into execution.

The admiral and I have examined the town, with a view to a general assault: but, after consulting with the chief engineer, who is well acquainted with the interior parts of it, and, after viewing it with the utmost attention, we found, that though the batteries of the lower town might be easily silenced by the men of war, yet the business of an assault would be little advanced by that, since the few passages that lead from the lower to the upper town, are carefully intrenched; and the upper batteries cannot be affected by the ships, which must receive considerable damage from them, and from the mortars. The admiral would readily join in this, or in any other measure for the public service; but I could not propose to him an undertaking of so dangerous a nature, and promising so little success.

At my first coming into the Country, I used all the means in my Power, to engage the Canadians to lay down their Arms, by offer of such Protection & Security for themselves, their Property & Religion, as was consistent with the Known Mildness of His Majesty's Government. I found that good Treatment had not the desired Effect, so that of late, I have changed my Measures & laid waste the Country, partly to engage the Marquis de Montcalm to try the Event of a Battle to prevent the Ravage, And partly in Return for many Insults offer'd to our People by the Canadians, As well as the frequent Inhumanity's exercised upon our own Frontiers – It was necessary also to have some Prisoners as Hostages for their good Behaviour to our People in their hands, whom I had reason to think they did not use very well. Major Dalling surprized the Guard of a Village & brought in about 380 Prisoners, which I keep, not proposing any Exchange till the end of the Campaign.

In case of a Disappointment, I intended to fortify Coudres & leave 3000 men for the Defence of it; But it was too late in the Season, to collect Materials sufficient for covering so large a Body.

To the uncommon strength of the country, the enemy have added, (for the defence of the river) a great number of floating batteries and boats. By the vigilance of these, and the Indians round our different posts, it has been impossible to execute any thing by surprize. We have had almost daily skirmishes with these savages, in which they are generally defeated, but not without loss on our side.

By the list of disabled officers (many of whom are of rank) you may perceive, Sir, that the army is much weakened. By the nature of the river, the most formidable part of this armament is deprived of the power of acting, yet we have almost the whole force of Canada to oppose. In this situation, there is such a choice of difficulties, that I own myself at a loss how to determine. The affairs of Great Britain, I know, require the most vigorous measures; but then the courage of a handful of brave men, should be exerted only, where there is some hope of a favourable event. However, you may be assured, Sir, that the small part of the campaign which remains shall be employed (as far as I am able) for the honour of his majesty, and the interest of the nation, in which I am sure of being well seconded by the admiral, and by the generals. Happy if our efforts here can contribute to the success of his majesty's arms in any other parts of America. I have the honour to be, with the greatest respect, Sir, your most obedient, and most humble servant,

Jam: Wolfe.

# ABBREVIATIONS AND SELECT BIBLIOGRAPHY

---

B    Lettres Envoyées, Archives des Colonies, Paris (transcripts, PAC).

Bell   Capt Thomas Bell's Journal, NC.

C 11 A  Correspondance Générale, Canada, Archives des Colonies, Paris (transcripts and microfilms, PAC).

Casgrain H.-R. Casgrain, ed, *Collection des Manuscrits du Maréchal de Lévis* (12 vols, Montreal and Quebec, 1889–95). The manuscripts are now in PAC. Casgrain's edition is broadly accurate, though the transcription is not meticulous and there are occasional serious misreadings. In general, invaluable.

DJ   Rear-Admiral Philip Durell's Journal. PRO, Admiralty 50/7 (transcript, PAC).

Doughty A. G. Doughty with G. W. Parmelee, *The Siege of Quebec and the Battle of the Plains of Abraham* (6 vols, Quebec, 1901). A curious production, half history, half collection of documents, containing some irrelevancies and inconsequentialities; the documents are absolutely indispensable to the student of the time, but the narrative is less important.

F 3   Collection Moreau de St-Méry, Archives des Colonies, Paris (transcripts, PAC).

JS   Journal du Siège de Québec (NC, calendar, 223–66).

JT   'Extrait d'un Journal tenu à l'armée que commandoit feu M$^r$. de Montcalm Lieutenant general' (C 11 A, vol 104–11). Anonymous, very informative.

Kimball　　Gertrude S. Kimball, ed, *Correspondence of William Pitt . . . with Colonial Governors and Military and Naval Commanders in America* (2 vols, New York, 1906). Accurate text of fundamental documents; enclosures not printed, notes of limited value.

Knox　　Capt John Knox, *An Historical Journal of the Campaigns in North America*. First published 1769. All references are to the useful edition by A. G. Doughty (3 vols, Toronto, Champlain Society, 1914–16).

*Logs*　　William Wood, ed, *The Logs of the Conquest of Canada* (Toronto, Champlain Society, 1909). Selections from the masters' logs of ships of the Royal Navy, 1758–60.

MJ　　Montcalm's Journal, in Lévis Papers, PAC. Published in Casgrain, VII.

Malartic　　Lt-Gen le Comte de Maurés de Malartic, *Journal des Campagnes au Canada de 1755 à 1760* (Paris, 1890).

NC　　Northcliffe Collection, PAC Monckton Papers, Townshend Papers, and some other items.

PAC　　Public Archives of Canada.

PRO　　Public Record Office, London.

RAPQ　　*Rapport de l'Archiviste de la Province de Québec.*

Vaudreuil　　Vaudreuil dispatch to the Minister of Marine, Oct
Report　　5th, 1759, F 3, 15. Numerous appendices.

WJ　　General Wolfe's Journal. The version followed is that in the McGill University Museum (photostat in PAC).

Willson　　Beckles Willson, *The Life and Letters of James Wolfe* (London, 1909). A useful collection of documents, but often textually inaccurate.

Wright　　Robert Wright, *The Life of Major-General James Wolfe* (London, 1864). The first biography of Wolfe, and still far from the worst.

# REFERENCES

---

## INTRODUCTION
### Two Hundred Years of History

1. *Annual Register*, 1759, 43.
2. William Wood, *The Fight for Canada* ('Definitive edition', London, 1905; Boston, 1906), and *Unique Quebec* (in *The Centenary Volume of the Literary and Historical Society of Quebec*, Quebec, 1924).
3. W. T. Waugh, *James Wolfe, Man and Soldier* (Montreal, 1928). E. R. Adair, 'The Military Reputation of Major-General James Wolfe', Canadian Historical Association *Report*, 1936.
4. Bougainville to his brother, Nov 7th, 1756, PAC, Bougainville transcripts, MG 18, K 10, I.
5. 'Fresh Light on the Quebec Campaign – From the Missing Journal of General Wolfe', *Nineteenth Century and After*, March 1910.
6. Julian S. Corbett, *England in the Seven Years' War* (2 vols, London, 1907), I, 398. PRO, CO 5/213 (transcript, PAC).

## CHAPTER ONE
### Dramatis Personae

1. Julian S. Corbett, *England in the Seven Years' War* (2 vols, London, 1907). L. H. Gipson, *The Great War for the Empire: The Victorious Years, 1758–1760* (NY, 1949). Kimball.
2. Nov 5th, 1757: Willson. Wolfe's letters to Rickson were published in *Tait's Edinburgh Magazine*, December 1849. PAC has photocopy of that of Dec 1st, 1758.
3. PRO, WO 34, vol 46b (part 2) (transcript, PAC).

4. Willson, 423–33. Embarkation return accompanying Wolfe to Pitt, June 6th, 1759, PRO, CO 5/51 (transcript, PAC). Lt-Col M. E. S. Laws, *Battery Records of the Royal Artillery* (Woolwich, 1952), 24–5. Wolfe to Maj Walter Wolfe, May 19th, 1759, Willson, 427.

5. Adair. Wolfe to Sackville, July 30th, 1758, Willson, 387–90. Maj-Gen J. F. C. Fuller, *The Decisive Battles of the Western World* (3 vols, London, 1957), II, 265.

6. To Pitt, Dec 24th, 1758, Willson, 407.

7. *Logs*, 95–6. Wm Laird Clowes, *The Royal Navy, A History*, III (London, 1898), 205–6, 218.

8. Pitt to Durell, Dec 29th, 1758, Kimball, I, 444–5. DJ, April 7th–May 21st, 1759. Bell, May 3rd–5th, 1759.

9. Guy Frégault, *Le Grand Marquis: Pierre de Rigaud de Vaudreuil et la Louisiane* (Montreal, 1952), 90.

10. Guy Frégault, *François Bigot, Administrateur français* (2 vols, Ottawa, 1948), II, 395.

11. *Ibid*, II, 186–7.

12. Montcalm to Maréchal de Belle-Isle, April 12th, 1759, C 11 A, 104–1.

13. F 3, vol 15.

14. MJ, July 29th, 1758. Cf Frégault, *Le Grand Marquis*, 97–8.

15. Vaudreuil to the Minister of Marine ('Vaudreuil Report'), Oct 5th, 1759; same to same, May 28th, 1759, both F 3, vol 15. 'Précis du plan des opérations Generales de la Campagne de 1759', April 1st, 1759, C 11 A, 104–1.

16. To Le Normand, April 12th, 1759, C 11 A, 104–1.

17. Guy Frégault, *La Guerre de la conquête* (Montreal, 1955), 173–4.

18. Thomas Chapais, *Le Marquis de Montcalm* (Quebec, 1911).

19. The system is well described in Capt Maurice Sautai, *Montcalm au combat de Carillon* (Paris, 1909).

20. March 14th, 1756: Casgrain, III, 39–43.

21. Wood, *Fight for Canada*, 68. Frégault, *La Guerre de la conquête*, 186–8. Vaudreuil to the Minister, Sept 16th, 1757, F 3, vol 15.

22. Correspondence in F 3, vol 15. Supplément. Cf Chapais, *Montcalm*, 394 ff.

23. PAC, Lévis Papers. The printed Casgrain version omits the word 'né' in the last sentence quoted.

24. May 16th, 1759: Chapais, 541–2.

25. Vaudreuil to the Minister, Aug 4th, 1758, F 3, vol 15.

26. Parkman, *Montcalm and Wolfe* (ed 1910), III, 12–13. Bougainville's memoranda, C 11 A, 103–2; published in RAPO, 1923–24,

pp 8–70. List of them, Casgrain, IV, 74–8. Chapais, *Montcalm*, 512–13.

27. Bougainville to Montcalm, Mar 18th, 1758 [1759], Casgrain, III, 103–11.

28. C 11 A, 103–2.

29. Microfilm, PAC. Chapais misdates the document. There is only one date, Dec 28th, 1758, on the paper, and it is not clear whether it belongs to the paper itself or the minute; probably the former, but it seems likely the minute was written the same day. It is worth noting that F.-X. Garneau assumed that the decision was the King's.

30. Feb 3rd[?], 1759: B, 109.

31. Feb 3rd[10th?], 1759, *ibid*, printed in Casgrain, III, 161–4.

32. Feb 3rd, 1759: B, 109.

33. Minister to Vaudreuil, nd, *ibid*, Bougainville to Montcalm, Mar 18th, 1758 [1759], Casgrain, III, 104–5.

34. Feb [3rd?], 1759: B, 109.

## CHAPTER TWO

### The Fortress

1. For documentation, see C. P. Stacey, 'A Note on the Citadel of Quebec', *Canadian Historical Review*, Dec 1948.

2. Capt John Montresor, 'The Present Situation of the Town of Quebec', Doughty, IV, 332–3.

3. Frontenac to the Minister, Oct 25th, 1693; Frontenac and Champigny to same, Nov 4th, 1693: C 11 A, 12–2.

4. [Levasseur], 'Memoire concernant les ouvrages . . .', 1700, Dépôt des Fortifications des Colonies, Carton 7 (transcript, PAC), Levasseur to the Minister, Nov 6th, 1702, C 11 A, 20. Vaudreuil and Bégon to the Minister, Nov 12th, 1712, *ibid*, 33. Beaucours, 'Explication des Fortiffications de Quebec', Nov 8th, 1712, Dépôt des Fortifications, Carton 7. De Léry to the Council, Oct 20th, 1720, C 11 A, 42, and his 'Memoire', Aug 10th, 1745, *ibid*, 84–2. Stacey, 'Note on the Citadel of Quebec'.

5. De Léry to the Minister, Oct 26th, 1744, C 11 A, 82. Beauharnois and Hocquart to the Minister, Oct 19th, 1745 and Oct 10th, 1746, *ibid*, 83 and 85. De Léry to the Minister, Oct 10th, 1749, *ibid*, 94–1.

6. 'Situation du Canada en hommes, moyens, positions' and 'Ce que La France ne peut se dispenser de faire pour le Canada',

C 11 A, 103–2; printed in RAPQ, 1923–24, 8–10, 11–14. MJ, Oct 10th, 1757. Montcalm to Le Normand, Apr 12th, 1759, C 11 A, 104–1.

7. Oct 26th, 1758: C 11 A, 103–2.

8. *Journal des Campagnes du Chevalier de Lévis* (Casgrain, I), 273. De Léry to the Minister, Oct 8th, 1749, above, n 5; cf his 'Plan de la Ville de Quebec', Oct 20th, 1752, PAC. Unsigned 'Report of the State of the Fortifications of this Place', Quebec, Oct 20th, 1759, PAC, NC, Monckton, XXXII.

9. Montresor, Doughty, IV, 333. 'Report of the State', above, n 8. 'Précis du plan des opérations Generales de la Campagne de 1759', Apr 1st, 1759, C 11 A, 104–1.

10. *Traité de Fortification divisé en huit livres*, 421. 'Journal de Foligné', Doughty, IV, 164. S. M. Pargellis, ed, *Military Affairs in North America, 1748–1765* (NY, 1936), 439. 'Report of the State', n 8.

11. Levasseur to the Minister, Nov 6th, 1702, C 11 A, 20. Cf his 'Plan de Quebec', Oct 1702, Dépôt des Fortifications des Colonies, Carton No 7, copy in PAC.

12. C. P. Stacey, ed, *Introduction to the Study of Military History for Canadian Students* (5th ed, Ottawa, 1956), 47–56.

13. Gerald S. Graham, ed, *The Walker Expedition to Quebec, 1711* (Navy Records Society, 1953).

14. Oct 20th, 1752. Dépôt des Fortifications des Colonies, Carton 8.

15. Memoir Oct 26th, 1757, with covering letter Oct 28th, 1758, C 11 A, 103–2, microfilm in PAC.

16. Appendix to Vaudreuil Report. Translation, *The Northcliffe Collection* (calendar) (Ottawa, 1926), 209–13.

17. 'Que peut faire de son côté la France pour la défense de Québec . . .', C 11 A, 103–2.

## CHAPTER THREE

### May and June: Contact

1. C 11 A, 104–1.

2. MJ, May 21st–28th, 1759. Gridley to Monckton, Sept 23rd, 1759, NC, Monckton, XXXII.

3. MJ, June 1st. Vaudreuil Report. J. T. Bernier to ———, Oct 15th, 1759, Archives de la Guerre, Paris, vol 3540 (transcript, PAC); cf MJ, June 8th.

4. MJ, May 26th. Casgrain, V, 331. Vaudreuil and Bigot to the Minister, Oct 22nd, 1759, C 11 A, 104–1.
5. MJ, June 4th–7th. Casgrain, V, 327–8.
6. Casgrain, V, 16–17.
7. Vaudreuil Report; Bigot to the Minister, Oct 15th, 1759, F 3, 15.
8. Malartic, 243. Montcalm to Lévis, July 1st, 1759, Casgrain, VI, 166–9. Casgrain, V, 16–17.
9. Original of Mackellar's report in NC, Townshend, VI; published in Knox, III, 151–60. For one version of the legend, see *Montreal Star*, Nov 7th, 1953, p 6.
10. Willson, 427–9.
11. PRO, WO 34, vol 46 b (transcript, PAC).
12. NC, Monckton, XXIV and XXV (Calendar, *The Northcliffe Collection*, Ottawa, 1926, 182–202).
13. DJ, May 28th–29th.
14. MJ, June 7th. 'Relation du siège de Québec', *The Northcliffe Collection*, 215.
15. DJ, June 3rd–16th. *Logs*, 92, 263. Cook's *Directions for sailing from the Harbour of Louisbourgh to Quebec* . . . (1760?) are preserved in the Hydrographic Department of the Admiralty (microfilm in PAC).
16. MJ, June 16th–17th. Montcalm to Bourlamaque, June 18th, Casgrain, V, 329–30. JS. *Logs*, 209, 264. DJ, June 21st.
17. DJ, June 21st. *Logs*, 209–10, 264.
18. *Logs*, 227, 255–6, 303. DJ, June 25th.
19. Knox, I, 372–7. *Logs*, 281–2.
20. Knox, I, 378–9. Bell, June 27th. MJ, June 24th–27th and 28th.
21. MJ, June 8th and 28th. JT. *Logs*, 210, 266, 282. Knox, I, 381–3. See Chapais, *Montcalm*, 577–9.
22. WJ, June 29th. Knox, I, 386. MJ, June 30th.
23. MJ, June 30th–July 1st.
24. Bell, June 29th.
25. *Ibid*, July 2nd, WJ, July 2nd.
26. To Townshend, Nov 5th, 1774, Amherst Papers, Packet 15 (photostat, PAC).
27. Vaudreuil Report.
28. DJ, June 27th–Aug 4th.

## CHAPTER FOUR

### July: Montmorency

1. Bell, July 9th.
2. Unless otherwise particularized, the letters from Wolfe to Monckton referred to in this chapter are in the Monckton Papers, vol XXII (NC).
3. Casgrain, VI, 179–81.
4. July 9th.
5. Appendix to Vaudreuil Report.
6. Vaudreuil Report.
7. MJ, June 21st.
8. JT. Journal of Father Récher, ed Father H. Provost, La Société historique de Québec, 1959.
9. JS.
10. JT.
11. *Ibid*, Cf MJ, July 13th.
12. Casgrain, IV, 95.
13. William Wood, *In the Heart of Old Canada* (Toronto, 1913), 171.
14. July 12th.
15. *Plan of Quebec with the Positions of the Brittish and French Army's* . . . (King's Library, CXIX-27, British Museum; copy, PAC).
16. JS. JT. Knox, II, 22.
17. JT, re July 8th, and marginal note.
18. WJ.
19. Capt Schomberg to Admiral Forbes, Doughty, V, 59. *Logs*, 212–13, 317. HMS *Sutherland*, master's log, July 17th, PAC. MG 13, A 4, 11 (transcript).
20. Saunders to Townshend, July 20th, Doughty, V, 194. 'Proceedings up the River St Laurence', July 20th–21st, *ibid*, 250.
21. JT. 'Journal of the Particular Transactions', Doughty, V, 173. Bell, July 21st.
22. MJ, July 28th. JS. *Logs*, 309.
23. WJ, July 31st.
24. Aug 30th, *Gentleman's Magazine*, June 1801.
25. 'Extract of a Letter from an Officer in Major Gen¹ Wolfe's Army', Aug 10th, 1759, in Pargellis, *Military Affairs in North America*, 433–5.

26. JS. Jean-Claude Panet, *Siège de Québec en 1759* (journal), Literary and Historical Society of Quebec, 1875.
27. Capt A. Schomberg to Admiral Forbes, Sept 5th, 1759, Doughty, V, 59–60. 'Journal of Major Moncrief', *ibid*, 43.
28. NC, Townshend, V (calendar, 423).
29. See Lewis S. Winstock, 'Hot Stuff', *Journal of the Society for Army Historical Research*, Spring 1955. For the British side of the Montmorency battle, Knox, I, 449–56; *Logs*, 211, 309–10; WJ, July 31st; Wolfe to Saunders, Aug 30th, 1759, above, note 24, and to Pitt, Sept 2nd, 1759, Kimball, II, 149–59 (original, PRO, CO 5/51; transcript, PAC).
30. Montcalm to Lévis, July 25th, 1759, Casgrain, VI, 198–9. For the French side of the battle, Malartic, 260–2; *Journal des Campagnes du Chevalier de Lévis* (Casgrain, I), 184–8; Lévis to Belle-Isle, Aug 2nd, 1759, Casgrain, II, 227–33; MJ, July 31st; Montcalm to Bourlamaque, Aug 1st, 1759, Casgrain, V, 338–41; JT.
31. Vaudreuil to Bourlamaque, Aug 6th, 1759, Bourlamaque Papers, PAC. (The version of this letter printed by Parkman in inverted commas in *Montcalm and Wolfe* [ed 1910, III, 75] is not a quotation at all, but an extremely free paraphrase.) Montcalm to Bourlamaque, Aug 1st, above, note 30.

## CHAPTER FIVE

*August: 'Skirmishing, Cruelty and Devastation'*

1. NC, Monckton, XXII.
2. WJ, Aug 3rd. Wolfe to [Monckton], Aug 4th, 1759, NC, Monckton, XXII. Knox, II, 14. Wolfe to Pitt, Sept 2nd, 1759.
3. JT. MJ, Aug 6th.
4. 'Journal of Major Moncrief', Doughty, V, 45–6, but see Townshend, *ibid*, 267. Master's log, HMS *Sutherland*, Aug 9th–10th (transcript, PAC). MJ, Aug 8th. Murray to Wolfe, Aug 9th, 1759, Chatham MSS, PRO, Bundle 50 (transcript, PAC).
5. Fragment of Murray's report, Knox, III, 163–4. 'Journal of Major Moncrief', Doughty, V. Bougainville's account, RAPQ, 1923–4, 388.
6. MJ, Aug 18th–20th.
7. Doughty, VI, 68–9. 'Journal of Major Moncrief', *ibid*, V, 44. Knox, II, 34.
8. MJ, Aug 9th–10th. Montcalm to Bourlamaque, Aug 9th, 1759, Casgrain, V, 343. JS, Aug 10th–15th.

9. NC, Monckton, XXII.

10. Wolfe to Amherst, Dec 29th, 1758, PRO, WO 34/46b; quoted in Rex Whitworth, *Field Marshal Lord Ligonier* (London, 1958) 278–9. Lt-Col C. V. F. Townshend, *The Military Life of Field-Marshal George First Marquess Townshend* (London, 1901), 143–4.

11. PRO, Chatham MSS, Bundle 98, vol 7 (transcript, PAC).

12. Peter Cunningham, ed, *The Letters of Horace Walpole* (9 vols, Edinburgh, 1906), III, 257–8.

13. Doughty, V, 241–5.

14. *Ibid*, 61–9.

15. NC, Monckton, XXII. Several of the caricatures, less Townshend's captions, are in Waugh.

16. Willson, 389.

17. Proclamation of June 27th, annexed to Vaudreuil Report. Loose English translation, Willson, 439–40. JS. Version of second proclamation in Panet gives the deadline as Aug 1st.

18. NC, Monckton, XXII.

19. To Lévis, July 25th, 1759, Casgrain, VI, 197.

20. Knox, II, 23, 38. 'Placart' in Bell. Gorham's report, Aug 19th, 1759, NC, Monckton, XXI.

21. Wolfe to Monckton, Aug 15th, 1759, NC, Monckton, XXII. Knox, II, 41. Townshend, Doughty, V, 260. 'Relation du siège de Québec', NC, calendar, 221.

22. DJ, Sept 3rd. Knox, II, 55. Doughty, VI, 68–9. Scott's report, Sept 19th, 1759, NC, Monckton, XXI.

23. *Boston News-Letter*, Dec 6th, 1759, quoted in Frégault, *La Guerre de la conquête*, 341–2. Cf 'A Journal of the Expedition up the River St Lawrence', *New York Mercury*, Dec 31st, 1759, Literary and Historical Society of Quebec, nd.

24. Vaudreuil to de Portneuf, Aug 20th, 1759, NC, Monckton, XXVII.

25. *General Orders in Wolfe's Army* . . . (Literary and Historical Society of Quebec, Fourth Series, Quebec, 1875), 29.

26. Fraser's journal, *ibid*, Second Series, Quebec, 1868.

27. Doughty, V, 194–5 (Sept 6th, 1759).

28. *Ibid*, 258; VI, 68.

29. *Ibid*, VI, 68–9.

30. Journal de Foligné, *ibid*, IV, 199. JT. JS. *Logs*, 311–13.

## CHAPTER SIX

### The British Change Direction

1. Doughty, V, 194–5.
2. Transcript in PAC.
3. Notes, NC, Townshend, vol V; printed in full in Northcliffe Collection calendar, 422. Townshend's journal, evidently based on these notes, Doughty, V, 261–3.
4. PAC. *Report*, 1939, 36–7.
5. *Gentleman's Magazine*, June 1801. In Wright, 548–52. Incomplete in both Doughty and Willson.
6. Adair.
7. Townshend, Doughty, V, 263.
8. Knox, II, 70–1. 'Moncrief', Doughty, V, 47. JT. Cf MJ, Sept 3rd, and Montcalm to Lévis, Sept 3rd, 1759, Casgrain, VI, 222–3.
9. Knox, II, 73. 'Moncrief', Doughty, V, 47–8, and Townshend, *ibid*, 264–5. *Logs*, 221, 320.
10. Knox, II, 76–80. Townshend, Doughty, V, 265–6. *Logs*, 268.
11. See Maj-Gen Whitworth Porter, *History of the Corps of Royal Engineers*, I (London, 1889), 190. Internal evidence supports this interpretation.
12. Doughty, IV, 295.
13. 'Moncrief', Doughty, V, 48; Murray to Townshend, Oct 5th, 1759, NC, Townshend, vol XII; Knox, II, 80–1; Townshend's journal, Doughty, V, 266.
14. *Logs*, 241 (*Lowestoft*).
15. Knox, II, 82.
16. Maj-Gen R. H. Mahon, *Life of General the Hon James Murray* (London, 1921), 140.
17. Wright, 563–5.
18. Doughty, V, 267. On Stobo, *ibid*, VI, 44.
19. Montcalm to Bourlamaque, June 11th, 1759, Casgrain, V, 327–8.
20. Mahon, Chap. VIII.
21. Knox, II, 84–5; 'Moncrief', Doughty, V, 48–9; Townshend, *ibid*, 266–7; Remigny to Bougainville, Aug 11th, 1759, *ibid*, IV, 121; Captain's log of *Sutherland, Journal of the Society for Army Historical Research*, XXI, 184–5 (1942).
22. Wright, 568–70.
23. Knox, II, 86–9.
24. PAC, NC, Townshend, vol XII; text, Northcliffe Collection calendar, 425.

25. *Ibid*, vol I (originals signed by Wolfe). Text in calendar, 412, 415.

26. Knox, II, 92–3; cf NC calendar, 167.

27. Bourlamaque Papers, PAC.

28. Montcalm to Bourlamaque, Sept 8th, 1759, *ibid*; Montcalm to Lévis, Sept 3rd, 1759, Casgrain, VI, 222–3. MJ, Sept 4th.

29. Vaudreuil Report.

30. Mgr H. Têtu, 'M. Jean-Félix Récher, Curé de Québec, et son Journal, 1757–1760', *Bulletin des recherches historiques*, IX, April–June 1903.

31. Chapais, *Montcalm*, 572–5. MJ, Sept 13th. Johnstone, *A Dialogue in Hades* (Literary and Historical Society of Quebec, 1868).

32. The question is fully discussed, with documentation, in the present writer's article 'The Anse au Foulon, 1759: Montcalm and Vaudreuil', *Canadian Historical Review*, March 1959.

33. Doughty, IV, 84, 116–17, 93.

34. Annexes to Vaudreuil Report. Wood's two references are in his *Unique Quebec* and in *The Passing of New France* (Toronto, 1920), 128.

35. Doughty, IV, 94.

36. *Ibid*, V, 51.

37. *Ibid*, IV, 112–13. Casgrain, VIII, 102–6.

38. Vaudreuil Report. Vaudreuil to Bougainville, Sept 6th, 1759, Doughty, IV, 99–101.

39. *Logs*, 321, 241–2.

40. JT. Vaudreuil Report. Wolfe to Burton, Sept 10th, 1759, Wright, 568–70.

41. Wolfe to Burton, Sept 10th, 1759.

42. To Lévis, Sept 8th, 1759, Casgrain, VI, 223–4. To Bourlamaque, Casgrain, V, 347–9. The final paragraph of the letter of Sept 2nd, 1759, as here printed is evidently part of another letter, probably written in August.

43. Casgrain, V, 349.

# CHAPTER SEVEN

## *The 13th of September: Approach*

1. Doughty, IV, 126.

2. JT.

3. NC, Townshend, III. *Logs*, 314, 287.

4. *Logs*, 242, 300, 321. Tide table, Mahon, 136. 'Journal of the Particular Transactions', Doughty, V, 187. Astronomical information from Dominion Observatory, Ottawa.

5. Holmes and Saunders letters, Doughty, IV, 296 and VI, 121.

6. Doughty, V, 187.

7. John Playfair, 'Biographical Account of the late John Robison . . .', *Transactions of the Royal Society of Edinburgh*, VII, 1815. William Wallace Currie to James Currie, Feb 10th, 1804, in W. W. Currie, ed, *Memoirs of the Life, Writings, and Correspondence of James Currie* . . . (2 vols, London, 1831), II, 248.

8. Beckles Willson, 'General Wolfe and Gray's "Elegy" ', *Nineteenth Century and After*, April 1913.

9. Vaudreuil Report. *Logs*, 232. Doughty, V, 187.

10. NC, Townshend, V. Bigot to the Minister, Oct 15th, 1759, F 3, 15. JT. Vergor's account, *Canadian Historical Review*, December 1966.

11. Information from Dr F. FitzOsborne. La Pause, 'Itinéraire de ma route', RAPQ, 1933–4, 95–7.

12. NC, Townshend, I; calendar, 412.

13. Doughty, V, 102.

14. *Ibid*, 50.

15. Frégault, *La Guerre de la conquête*, 250.

16. Literary and Historical Society of Quebec, 1873.

17. RAPQ, 1933–4, 170.

18. In Amherst Papers, Packet 28 (transcript, PAC): Henry Caldwell to Murray, Nov 1st, 1772.

19. Doughty, IV, 296.

20. Annexed to Vaudreuil Report.

21. Doughty, IV, 126–7.

22. MJ, Sept 13th.

23. Malartic to Bourlamaque, Sept 28th, 1759, Bourlamaque Papers, *Variarum*, 213–15 (PAC).

## CHAPTER EIGHT

### The 13th of September: Battle

1. 'March to the Field of Battle' on *Plan of Quebec with the Positions of the Brittish and French Army's* . . ., King's Library, CXIX–27, British Museum. Knox, II, 97. 'Moncrief'. Doughty, V, 51.

2. Knox, II, 97, n.

3. Doughty, II, 289–309.

4. Mackellar's *Plan of the Town of Quebec* . . . (the great plan of the whole campaign, original in PAC). *Plan of Quebec with the Positions of the Brittish and French Army's* . . . Knox, II, 98. 'Moncrief', Doughty, V, 52.

5. To Lévis, July 1st, 1759, Casgrain, VI, 166–9.

6. Malartic, 284. *Journal abrégé d'un aide-de-camp*, Doughty, V, 296. *Plan of the Town of Quebec. Plan of Quebec with the Positions* . . . On uniforms, *Etat Militaire de France, pour l'année 1759* . . ., 228; cf Dr Lienhart et René Humbert, *Les uniformes de l'Armée française depuis 1690 jusqu'à nos jours* (5 vols, Leipzig, 1897–1906), III.

7. Malartic to Bourlamaque, Sept 28th, 1759, Bourlamaque Papers, *Variarum*, PAC.

8. PRO, CO 5/51 (transcript, PAC).

9. Sept 28th, 1759, note 7 above.

10. Wolfe to Monckton, Aug 6th, 1759, NC, Monckton, XXII.

11. To Lévis, July 1st, 1759, note 5 above.

12. De Kerallain, *La Jeunesse de Bougainville*.

13. Doughty, III, 96–7.

14. RAPQ, 1923–4, 387–9.

15. Casgrain, V, 357.

16. Doughty, III, 107.

17. Literary and Historical Society of Quebec, 1868 (translation). On de Ramezay's absence [Joannès?], 'Memoire sur la Reddition de la Place de Québec', Archives de la Guerre, vol 3540.

18. Literary and Historical Society of Quebec, 1868.

19. Partial transcript in French included in Johnstone's *Memoires* (transcript, PAC).

20. C 11 A, 104–2.

21. Doughty, IV, 204.

22. Casgrain, X, 115–17.

23. Malartic, 284. MJ, Sept 13th. Townshend's notes, NC calendar, 424–5. *Journal abrégé d'un aide-de-camp*, Doughty, V, 297.

24. MJ, Sept 13th (Lévis Papers). Casgrain's transcriber made a serious error here, reading the phrase in the MS. 'l'Espece de troupes que nous avons' as 'le peu de troupes que nous avons'.

25. Knox, II, 99.

26. Letter to Bourlamaque.

27. NC, Townshend, III.

28. *Plan of the Town of Quebec* . . ., PAC.

29. The best French first-hand accounts are those of Montbeillard (MJ, Sept 13th), Malartic (*Journal des campagnes*, 284–6, and letter to Bourlamaque, Sept 28th, 1759, note 7 above), and Montreuil (letter to Lévis, Sept 15th, 1759, Casgrain, X, 115–17). On the British side, Townshend's dispatch (CO 5/51) (Kimball, II, 164–9), his notes (NC calendar, 422–5), Knox, Mackellar ('Moncrief') and Fraser are valuable.

30. Willson, 280 (Nov 8th, 1755).

31. *The London Chronicle for 1788*, Aug 16th–19th, Doughty, VI, 147. Cf Wright, 583–4.

32. R. H. Hubbard, ed, *The National Gallery of Canada Catalogue of Paintings and Sculpture*, I (Ottawa and Toronto, 1957), 133.

33. To the Principal Officers of the Ordnance, Sept 20th, 1759, Knox, III, 339–40.

34. *Extracts from a Manuscript Journal . . . kept by Colonel Malcolm Fraser . . .* (Literary and Historical Society of Quebec, 1868), 21–3.

35. Return annexed to Townshend's dispatch, CO 5/51. Vandreuil Report.

36. Vaudreuil Report.

37. *A Journal of the Expedition up the River St Lawrence* (Literary and Historical Society of Quebec, nd, from *New York Mercury*, Dec 31st, 1759).

## CHAPTER NINE

### The Fall of Canada

1. Vaudreuil Report.

2. Facsimile, NC calendar, undated.

3. Minutes annexed to Vaudreuil Report. Bigot to the Minister, Oct 15th, 1759, F 3, 15.

4. Malartic to Bourlamaque, Sept 28th, 1759 (second letter of this date), Bourlamaque Papers, *Variarum*, 211. MJ, Casgrain, VII, 576. *Journal des Campagnes du Chevalier de Lévis* (Casgrain, I), 211.

5. Mahon, 136.

6. Vaudreuil to de Ramezay, 6 PM, Sept 13th, 1759, annex to Vaudreuil Report.

7. Bigot to the Minister, Oct 15th, 1759, F 3, 15.

8. Journal de Foligné, Doughty, IV, 207. Cf Parkman, *Montcalm and Wolfe*, III, Appendix 'J'.

9. Casgrain, I, 211–13.

10. Dépôt des Fortifications des Colonies, Carton 8, Pièce no 430. Printed in Knox, III, 174–8.

11. Saunders, Doughty, VI, 121; *Logs*, 316; de Ramezay to Vaudreuil, Sept 18th, 1759, annex to Vaudreuil Report.

12. Vaudreuil Report, and Rochebeaucourt to Vaudreuil, Sept 18th, 1759, annexed. Mémoire de Joannès, Doughty, IV, 227–9.

13. De Ramezay to Vaudreuil, Sept 18th, 1759, annexed to Vaudreuil Report.

14. De Ramezay to [Vaudreuil?], Sept 17th, 1759, NC calendar, 441. Knox, III, 172–4.

15. Knox, II, 126–32.

16. De Ramezay to Vaudreuil, Sept 18th, 1759, above, note 13.

17. Sept 19th, 1759, annexed to Vaudreuil Report.

18. Knox, II, 124–5. Williamson to Officers of Ordnance, Sept 20th, 1759, *ibid*, III, 339–40. Saunders, Doughty, VI, 120.

19. Lévis to the Minister, Nov 10th, 1759, F 3, 15. Vaudreuil Report.

20. Monckton to Pitt, Oct 8th, 1759, Kimball, II, 177–82. Saunders to Pitt, Sept 20th or 21st, 1759, *ibid*, 170–2. Knox, II, 238. Murray's Journal, Oct 26th, 1759 (photostat, PAC).

21. Lévis to the Minister, Nov 10th, 1759, F 3, 15.

22. Belle-Isle to Lévis, Feb 9th, 1760, Casgrain, III, 207–9. Various documents in B 112–1. *Logs*, 333–4. See Frégault, *La Guerre de la conquête*, 367–72.

23. Lévis' Journal, April 1760, Casgrain, I; strength return, *ibid*, 257.

24. Dispatch to Pitt, May 25th, 1760, CO 5/64. Cf Knox, II, 397.

25. Murray's Journal, Apri 28th, 1760. Lévis' Journal, Casgrain, I, 263–9. Lévis to Vaudreuil, Apr 28th, 1760, Casgrain, II, 292–4. Bourlamaque to Bougainville, May 3rd, 1760, Kerallain, *Jeunesse de Bougainville*, 166–7. Knox, II, 390–8. British engineers' *Plan of the Battle fought the 28th of April 1760 ...*, PAC.

26. Casgrain, I, 278–9.

27. *Ibid*, 281–2; see also Lévis' letters to Vaudreuil, May 13th, 15th and 18th, Casgrain, II, 304–12. Murray's Journal, May 15th–17th, 1760. *Logs*, 330–2. Knox, II, 415, 419, 425–35.

28. Lévis Journal, Casgrain, I, 305–15. Knox, II, 559–89.

## POSTSCRIPT

### *Generalship at Quebec, 1759*

1. RAPQ, 1923–4, 389.
2. To Townshend, Oct 5th, 1759, NC, Monckton, XII (calendar, 407).
3. The 'Murray' map of 1763 (PAC).
4. Bigot to the Minister, Oct 15th, 1759, F 3, 15. Much the same story is in JT.
5. Amherst Papers, Packet 15 (transcripts, PAC): Townshend to Murray, Oct 29th, 1774.
6. *Ibid*, Murray to Townshend, Nov 5th, 1774.

# Index

Amherst, Maj-Gen Jeffrey, 1–2, 4–5, 84; campaign (1759), 87; (1760), 168–9

Barré, Isaac, 6, 121; story re Foulon landing, 135, 178; wounded, 155
Beaucours (Beaucourt), Josué du Boisberthelot de, 30
Bell, Capt Thomas, 53, 59, 74, 98
Berryer, Minister of Marine, 11, 22
Bigot, François, 10, 11, 109–10, 159; story re Wolfe's plans, 178
Bombardment, see Quebec
Botwood, Edward, 79, 81
Bougainville, Col Louis-Antoine de, mission to France, 20–25, 41; biography, 20; on Quebec fortifications, 31, 37; in command above Quebec, 85, 120; responsibility for disaster, 123, 172–3; Vaudreuil letter to, 138; night of Sept. 12th/13th, 145–6; Battle of the Plains, 156–8
Bourlamaque, Brigadier, 43–4, 87, 122
Braddock, Maj-Gen James, 13, 39, 64
Bradstreet, Lt-Col John, 2
Burton, Lt-Col Ralph, 76, 88, 106, 112, 121, 123, 153

Cadet, Joseph, 10, 11, 25, 109–10, 123
Carillon, see Ticonderoga
Carleton, Guy, 6, 8; expedition to Pointe-aux-Trembles, 73; 'abominable' behaviour to Wolfe, 89; 106, 121, 124; wounded, 155
Chads, Capt James, 125, 129
Citadel, Quebec, 29
Cook, James, 7, 35, 43, 51, 76, 77
Coudres, Ile aux, proposed French battery, 37; capture of midshipmen, 50; Wolfe's proposal to fortify, 194

Delaune, Capt William, 6, 125, 131
Deschambault, British raid on, 85; 118, 157
Dieskau, Baron, 14
Dumas, Jean-Daniel, 64–5, 72, 137, 156
Durell, Rear-Admiral Philip, 7, 8, 25; at Coudres, 48–51; moves up river, 60

Fire-ships, etc, 35, 38, 42, 51, 53, 75
Fontbonne, Lt-Col de, 155
Forbes, Brig-Gen John, 2
Foulon, Anse au, 109ff; description, 128–9; landing at, 130–5
Fraser, Malcolm, 95, 154, 156
Frontenac, Count, 29–30, 91

Gibson, James, 89–90, 174
Gordon, Capt William, 50–52, 59
Gorham, Joseph, 92–3
Gray's Elegy, 125–6

Haviland, Brig-Gen William, 169
Holderness, Lord, dispatch to, 108–9
Holmes, Rear-Admiral Charles, 60; goes above Quebec, 73, 106; 107, 124, 129; on Foulon landing, 136

Howe, Lt-Col William, 6, 125, 131

Johnson, Sir William, 86–7
Johnstone, Chevalier, 117, 139, 147–8

Knox, John, 52, 80, 94–5, 96, 134, 144, 150, 151, 153

Le Mercier, François, 11, 51, 72
Léry, Capt de, 49, 54
Léry, Gaspard Chaussegros de, 30–33, 35
Levasseur de Néré, Denis, 30, 33
Lévis, Chevalier de, 13, 16, 19, 22; on Montmorency fortifications, 37; in Montmorency action, 81–2; sent up St Lawrence, 87; in command after Montcalm's death, 161–4; proposals for 1760 campaign, 165; campaign against Quebec, 166–8; capitulation of Montreal, 168
Lévis, Point, French proposals for fortifying, 33, 37–8; British landing on, 54–7; Wolfe's batteries, 56, 63; French enterprise against, 63–5
Ligonier, Field-Marshal Lord, 4–5, 88
Louis XV, King, 21–2
Louisbourg, 1, 19, 31
Lowther, Katherine, 126

Mackellar, Major Patrick, report on Quebec, 45–7; 69, 107, 108, 110, 119, 127, 133
Malartic, Major, 82, 140, 143, 149–50
Militia, Canadian, proposed re-organization, 20–21; number on service, 1759, 44–5; in Montmorency action, 82; in Battle of the Plains, 149, 155
Monckton, Brig-Gen Robert, 6; lands at Point Lévis, 54;

Wolfe's letters to, 63, 68–72, 92; Wolfe apologizes to, 90; Battle of the Plains, 141–2, 155, 156; to New York, 164
Montbeillard, artillery officer, 117, 137, 147–50
Montcalm, Marquis de, on war in Canada, 14; biography, and comments on, 14–19; quarrel with Vaudreuil, 17–18; plans defence of Quebec, 35–8; measures of defence, 41–5; stands on defensive, 63; and Dumas' enterprise against Point Lévis, 64–5; in Mont-morency action, 81–2; failure to penetrate Wolfe's intentions, 115–16; and Foulon landing, 136–40; decision to attack, 148–9; death, 154, 161; last advice to Vaudreuil, 159; tactical error, 157; critique, 170–2, 181
Montgomery, Capt Alexander, 94
Montmorency, establishment of British camp at, 56, 57, 62; artillery, 69; Wolfe reconnoitres ford, 74; Wolfe's attack, July 31st, 77–83; evacuation, 105–6
Montreal, capitulation of, 169
Montresor, John, 32
Montreuil, 'major-général', 82, 118, 122, 139, 148
Murray, Brig-Gen James, 6; reconnaissance of St Michel, 57; at Montmorency, 57, 62; expedition up St Lawrence, 84–7; Battle of the Plains, 134, 142, 155, 158; in command at Quebec, 164; Battle of Ste Foy, 166–7; advance on Montreal, 168–9; criticism of Wolfe, 174; discusses campaign with Townshend, 178–9

Niagara, Fort, 2, 44, 86

Notre Dame des Victoires, church, 34, 67

Palliser, Hugh, 75, 164, 179
Phips, Sir William, 30, 34, 48
Pitt, William, war plan, 1–2; appointment of Wolfe, 5
Plains of Abraham, battle, 141ff.; artillery present, 142, 146–8
Pointe-aux-Trembles, Carleton at, 73; Murray at, 85; scheme for landing near, 107
Pompadour, Madame de, 24
Pontleroy, King's Engineer, 31, 36, 66
Portneuf, Father René, 94
Prideaux, Brig-Gen John, 2, 86

Quebec, description, 27–8; fortifications, 27–35, 45–7; bombardment, 65–8; British ships pass, 70, 97; proposed attack on Lower Town, 74–5; surrender, 163–4; siege of, 1760, 168–9
Quiberon Bay, battle of, 7, 165

Ramezay, Chevalier de, 146–7, 160–3
Récher, Father, 117
Regiments, etc.
  *British*
  Light Infantry, 6, 53, 71, 74, 105–7, 127, 129–35, 142
  Louisbourg Grenadiers, 5, 106, 141, 153, 163, 164
  Rangers, 5, 87, 92, 112, 164
  Royal Americans, 79, 106, 107, 142, 153, 155
  Royal Artillery, 5, 142, 163
  Royal Engineers, 45, 128
  15th, 142
  20th, 3
  28th (Bragg's), 105, 141, 153
  35th, 141, 158
  43rd, 52, 94, 141

  47th, 79, 81, 141
  48th (Webb's), 106, 141, 153, 158
  58th, 130, 141, 155
  67th, 2, 6
  78th (Fraser's Highlanders), 80–81, 141, 154, 155, 158
  *French*
  Béarn, 45, 82, 143
  Berry, 15
  Carignan-Salières, 13
  Guyenne, 116ff, 138, 139, 143
  Languedoc, 143
  La Reine, 127
  La Sarre, 143
  Royal-Roussillon, 127, 143
Rickson, William, 3, 4
Rochefort Expedition, 3
Royal Navy, Wolfe's comments on, 59–60, 66

St Charles River, bridges, 42, 43
St Michel, proposed landing at, 57–9, 70–74
Ste Foy, Battle of, 166–7
Saunders, Vice-Admiral Charles, 7; Wolfe consults, 56, 74; his policy before Quebec, 60–61; consultation with brigadiers, 102–3; on Foulon climb, 132; feint at Beauport, 137; ships threaten Quebec, 162; departure, 164
Scott, George, 93, 112
Sénezergues, Brigadier, 122, 155
Ships
  *Alcide*, 52
  *Centurion*, 8, 50–51, 53, 59, 77
  *Devonshire*, 50
  *Diana*, 70, 168
  *Goodwill*, 52
  *Hind*, 52
  *Hunter*, 97, 127
  *Lowestoft*, 97, 121, 124, 134, 154, 168
  *Neptune*, 1, 7, 52, 60

Ships – contd.
  Pembroke, 7, 50, 51, 59, 70, 76
  Porcupine, 7, 51, 59
  Princess Amelia, 7, 50, 52
  Richmond, 52, 70
  Royal William, 7
  Russell, 77
  Seahorse, 97, 124
  Shrewsbury, 75
  Somerset, 7
  Squirrel, 50, 51, 70, 72, 85, 97,
    124, 134
  Stirling Castle, 52, 60, 75, 102,
    124
  Sutherland, 8, 52, 70, 72, 74, 97,
    106, 121, 145
  Three Sisters, 77
  Vanguard, 168
Stobo, Robert, 109
Strength of Forces, British, 5–8; in
    Battle of the Plains, 144; in
    Battle of Ste Foy, 166; French,
    44; in Battle of the Plains, 144;
    in Lévis' expedition 1760, 166

Ticonderoga (Carillon), 2, 17, 19,
    44, 84
Tourmente, Cape, 35, 37–8, 50
Townshend, Brig-Gen George, 6;
    lands at Montmorency, 62;
    appointment to expedition, and
    difficulties with Wolfe, 88–90;
    comment on Wolfe, 96;
    in command after Wolfe's
    death, 156, 158; returns to
    England, 164; discussion with
    Murray, 1774, 178–9
Traverse Channel, 35, 43, 50

Vaudreuil, Marquis de, biography,
    8–10; comments on, 11–14;

ordered to defer to Montcalm,
    22–4; and Montmorency action,
    82; and Foulon landing, 117–20,
    138–9; Battle of the Plains,
    142, 155; action after it,
    159–60; and surrender of
    Quebec, 162–3; campaign of
    1760, 165–6; capitulation of
    Montreal, 169
Vaudreuil, Rigaud de, 16
Vauquelin, Jean, 60
Vergor, Louis du Pont du
    Chambon de, 120, 127, 133–4,
    138, 176

Walker, Rear-Admiral Sir
    Hovenden, 34
Walpole, Horace, 7, 88, 132
Weapons, British superiority, 85,
    156
Williamson, Col George, 154, 163
Wolfe, Maj-Gen James, biography,
    1–4; appointment to Quebec
    command, 1, 4–5; intelligence
    and first plans, 47–9; arrival
    before Quebec, 52; health, 4,
    56, 96, 152; further plans, 62;
    difficulties with brigadiers,
    88–91; policy of terror, 91–6;
    consults the brigadiers, 98–105;
    dispatch to Pitt, 104, 187–94;
    letters to his mother, and to
    Saunders, 104; decision to land
    at Anse au Foulon, 107–11;
    exchange with brigadiers,
    112–15; and Gray's Elegy,
    125–6; Battle of the Plains, 141,
    149; death, 151–4; critique,
    173–81
Wolfe, Major Walter, letter to, 47,
    54

*British Battles Series*

WATERLOO (illus)
John Naylor                                        30p

'Was it won by Wellington and Blucher, or
lost by Napoleon and Ney? ... a clear vivid
account ... includes two first-rate chapters on
the men who fought the battle and on the
arms they fought with' — TIME AND TIDE

'Successfully combines retrospective comment
with contemporary accounts of what it was
like to fight in the smoke and roar of that day
in June' — THE ECONOMIST

'Graphic descriptions present a moving story
of courage, devotion and endurance'
— BRITISH ARMY REVIEW

# British Battles Series

**TRAFALGAR** (illus)
Oliver Warner                                    30p

'A stirring picture of the battle in which Nelson died destroying Napoleon's power at sea. Mr Warner brings to his scenes, before, after and during the battle, dozens of illuminating incidents' – NEW YORK TIMES

'Enables even the most non-naval readers to appreciate not only the actual battle itself but the brilliance of the strategy which led up to it' – THE TIMES

'A book one is proud to place on one's shelves' – SUNDAY TIMES

These and other PAN Books are obtainable from all booksellers and newsagents. If you have any difficulty please send purchase price plus 7p postage to PO Box 11, Falmouth, Cornwall.
While every effort is made to keep prices low, it is sometimes necessary to increase prices at short notice. PAN Books reserve the right to show new retail prices on covers which may differ from those advertised in the text or elsewhere.